With Joseph in the University of Adversity: The Mizraim Principles

With Joseph in the University of Adversity: The Mizraim Principles

Thirty-two timeless and effective lessons for practical living, from the hardships of the life of Joseph the Hebrew.

Jerry L. Parks, Th.D

iUniverse, Inc.
New York Lincoln Shanghai

With Joseph in the University of Adversity
The Mizraim Principles

iUniverse, Inc.

For information address:
iUniverse, Inc.
2021 Pine Lake Road, Suite 100
Lincoln, NE 68512
www.iuniverse.com

ISBN: 0-595-29651-3

Printed in the United States of America

Author Information

Dr. Parks earned B.S., M.A., & Ed.S degrees in education, and his Th.D in Biblical Theology from Trinity Seminary, Newburgh, IN.

Jerry is a Nationally Board Certified Teacher, and currently teaches the *GodStudy* Adult Bible Fellowship at Southland Christian Church, Lexington, KY—one of the ten largest churches in America.

Abbreviations

Scripture quotations, unless otherwise noted, are taken from *The Message*. Copyright © 1993, 1994, 1995, 1996, 2000, 2001, 2002. Used by permission of NavPress Publishing Group.

Other translations used are noted as follows:

KJV: The King James Version (Authorized)

NKJV: The New King James Version New King James Version. Copyright © 1982 by Thomas Nelson, Inc. All rights reserved. Used by permission.

NASB: Scripture taken from the NEW AMERICAN STANDARD BIBLE®, Copyright © 1960,1962,1963,1968,1971,1972,1973,1975,1977,1995 by The Lockman Foundation. Used by permission.

NLT: Scripture quotations marked NLT are taken from the Holy Bible, New Living Translation, copyright © 1996. Used by permission of Tyndale House Publishers, Inc., Wheaton, Illinois 60189. All rights reserved.

GNT: Scripture taken from the Good News Translation—Second Edition, Copyright © 1992 by American Bible Society. Used by Permission.

Contents

Chapter 1—**Parenting:**
       "The Principle of Effective Parenting" .1
As a parent, you stand in the place of God in raising your children and are
responsible to learn from Him how to do it right.

Chapter 2—**Jealousy:**
       "The Principle of Taming the Green-Eyed Monster" 15
Unchecked jealousy will grow into a destructive force that can divide
families, multiply sorrow, and lead to even greater sins.

Chapter 3—**God Isn't Finished with Me Yet:**
       "The Principle of Understanding
       God's Refinement Process" 20
God will do whatever it takes to conform you into the image of His Son,
and often His method depends on what He has to work with.

Chapter 4—**Influence:**
       "The Principle of Personal Influence" .31
In one way or another, you make a lasting influence on someone's life with
every action that you do and every word that you speak. That influence
reaches further than you know.

Chapter 5—**Personal Choice:**
       "The Principle of Effective Decision-Making" 39
Every decision has consequences that affect not only you, but also others.
Decide carefully.

Chapter 6—**The Danger of Complacent Success:**
       "The Principle of the Little Foxes" 45
You are most susceptible to misfortune when you rest in the small successes
of life and drift from dependence upon God.

Chapter 7—**Godly Contentment:**
   "The Principle of Blooming Where You're Planted" 52
God has a purpose in where He has placed you. Be satisfied and productive there, and do what you can to prepare for where He may take you.

Chapter 8—**I Am Third:**
   "The Principle of Others First" 60
You will accomplish more with others in two weeks trying to meet their needs than you will in two years trying to have them meet yours.

Chapter 9—**Using your Gifts:**
   "The Principle of God's Multicolored Garden" 65
God has equipped you to serve Him as He has equipped no one else, and you will be responsible for what He has given you.

Chapter 10—**Carpe Diem:**
   "The Principle of Personal Responsibility" 72
God's sovereignty controls all His plans-including His sovereign decision requiring you to do everything you can to fulfill those plans.

Chapter 11—**Survival in the Pit:**
   "The Principle of Sacrificial Praise" .79
Your most valuable praise to God is to glorify Him for His goodness in allowing you to hurt as you have never hurt before.

Chapter 12—**Turning Lemons into Lemonade:**
   "The Principle of Unexpected Opportunity" 86
God often wraps His greatest opportunities in the cloak of hardship and presents them to you when you least expect them.

Chapter 13—**The World is Watching Me:**
   "The Principle of Glorifying God" 93
The world will conclude more about God through observing your life than through any other observation it can make.

Chapter 14—**Telling it Like it is:**
   "The Principle of Integrity" 100
The measure of your personal integrity is determined by how honest you are according to God's standard-not the world's.

Chapter 15—**Being Too Heavenly-Minded:**
"The Principle of Practical Living" .106
You will turn off more people to God by being too holy in irrelevant issues than by just about anything else you can do.

Chapter 16—**Chickens Always Come Home to Roost:**
"The Principle of Sowing" 115
You will harvest what you plant. The time factor alone is the variable.

Chapter 17—**Continually Trusting God:**
"The Principle of Daily Bread" 123
Recognizing the provision and opportunity God gives you today reveals more about your trust in God than all your assumptions about what tomorrow may bring.

Chapter 18—**Safe Forever:**
"The Principle of Salvation's Security" 129
An all-knowing God considered every provision necessary to get you home and promised you would not get lost along the way.

Chapter 19—**When Delay Can Become Disaster:**
"The Principle of Procrastination" .136
Delay gives trouble an opportunity tomorrow that is closed to a task completed today.

Chapter 20—**Weeds in My Garden:**
"The Principle of the Long Arm of Sin" 143
The costly effects of Adam's disobedience have invaded every realm of the world we live in, and both man and nature are forced to pay the price.

Chapter 21—**God, Standing in the Shadows:**
"The Principle of Discerning God's Mysterious Ways" 149
God is never surprised, defeated, or limited in His ability to perform His will, though His ways often defy explanation.

Chapter 22—**Vows:**
"The Principle of Rash Promises" .156
A promise without consideration can result in a disaster without a remedy.

Chapter 23—**Love That Draws us Near:**
       "The Principle of Fellowship" 160
The greatest benefit of God's redemption plan is our privilege in sharing
our love with Him and with each other.

Chapter 24—**Delay Is Not Denial:**
       "The Principle of Patient Expectation" 171
God's most difficult lesson to learn is that when He asks you to wait, He is
not delaying-He is perfecting!

Chapter 25—**My Boss Is a Jewish Carpenter:**
       "The Principle of Work Ethic" 177
Your faithfulness to God can be measured by your faithfulness to the job
that God has entrusted to you, and He is your Supreme Supervisor.

Chapter 26—**Preparation, Anticipation and Tact:**
       "The Principle of Critical Persuasion" 183
The manner in which you choose your words, and the timing with which
you use them, are the greatest tools God has given you to shape what the
world offers in the mold of your need.

Chapter 27—**Provisions of God:**
       "The Principle of Recognizing God's Blessings" 189
Though God owes you nothing, through Christ, He has poured out His
blessings upon you in ways you may not even realize.

Chapter 28—**Planning for the Future:**
       "The Principle of Wise Use of Money" 196
It is not important how much money God has entrusted to you, but what your
attitude toward it is, and how faithfully you put to work the money you have.

Chapter 29—**Earned Respect and Honor:**
       "The Principle of Effective Leadership" 203
Leadership is a position of responsibility to be evaluated by a Higher
Authority in light of how the shepherd cared for his sheep.

Chapter 30—**'What If…?':**
       "The Principle of Unfounded Worry" 211
The degree to which you worry is directly proportional to the measure with
which you distrust the God holding your future.

Chapter 31—**Forgiving Others:**
        "The Principle of Unconditional Forgiveness" 216
Forgiveness opens for others, doors through which you too must someday
pass.

Chapter 32—**Life in the Rearview Mirror:**
        "The Principle of God's Overruling Sovereignty" 221
When all accounts are settled, you will look back and see that God was the
Master Craftsman of your life, able to weave every triumph and tragedy
into your ultimate good.

Introduction

Mizraim. The land of Egypt.

Into this setting Joseph the Hebrew was thrust by his jealous brothers, sold as a slave only to learn and mature in God's *University of Adversity*, and become the second most powerful man in the world.

I have had the privilege of studying and teaching the Life of Joseph in Genesis 37-50 for over twenty years. No other character in all Scripture elicits within the hearts of men the encouragement and satisfaction that comes from watching one rise to power and glory from the ashes of life's 'required courses' of persecution and discouragement.

As a teacher of ancient cultures to middle-schoolers, I am always searching in history for role models that exemplify qualities we would want our children to emulate. I have found few if any that can serve better than Joseph the Hebrew—son of Jacob, grandson of Isaac, great-grandson of the patriarch Abraham. Through his remarkable life, principles for right living become classic illustrations of how to live a life of integrity in a secular world, and fellowship with a holy God.

With Joseph in the University of Adversity presents thirty-two timeless and effective keys to successful living, drawn from the pain and hardship Joseph faced in his life. The keys relate to everything from parenting to money-management, from personal relationships to prayer. Underlying each principle is the acknowledgement of a sovereign and holy God, as well as the requirement for personal responsibility.

This book is designed to be practical and useable. The principles are not profound. Nevertheless, they have been tried, tested, and proven effective for nearly three thousand years. They are just as relevant today as they were in the life of Joseph. Who will benefit most from *With Joseph in the University of Adversity*?

Parents—seeking sound biblical keys to teaching integrity and personal responsibility, and raising children with character and conscience in a troubled world.

Leaders—searching for dynamic models of how to influence and persuade those whom they serve—even through adverse circumstances.

Teachers—desiring to convey to students basic acceptable skills of proper conduct in a world gone wrong.

Students—in need of role-model exemplars to follow in a 'how to' survival manual for life.

Group and Individual Bible Studies, and Pastors—desiring to study the life of Joseph in an in-depth, systematized manner, while gleaning spiritual principles for life application.

You and I—hoping to be all we can be in our decision-making, workplace, prayer life, and the sorrows and hardships that we must all endure.

As you read *With Joseph in the University of Adversity*, remember that basic human nature is universally similar. What Joseph learned through his difficult circumstances in Egypt, you can learn today. The story of Joseph is a timeless story of what one man can overcome with God's help and determined perseverance. To God be the glory.

~ Chapter 1 ~

Parenting: "The Principle of Effective Parenting"

Israel loved Joseph more than any of his other sons because he was the child of his old age. And he made him an elaborately embroidered coat. (Genesis 37:3)

The Joseph story....

Jacob is one of the most famous characters in Scripture, yet he was cunning, a deceiver, and not a role model as a father. He cheated his brother out of the family blessing and tricked him out of the family birthright. Jacob had loved the beautiful Rachel, but was tricked into marrying her sister Leah. After seven years of hard labor, Jacob married Rachel. In total, Jacob had twelve sons by four wives, but Joseph was special to Jacob. Not only was Joseph born when Jacob was advanced in age, he was also different from his brothers. Joseph had the best characteristics of his mother, while his brothers seemed to have the worst from their father. Jacob was a poor disciplinarian. He played favorites among his boys, and it was in this environment that Joseph spent the first seventeen years of his life.

Principle Truth: As a parent, you stand in the place of God in raising your children and are responsible to learn from Him how to do it right.

Parenting is the most important job on earth. Children are the future. Children do not grow up instinctively knowing right from wrong. Children must be taught, and God has entrusted this responsibility to parents. Whether or not a parent is biological is not as important as whether parents genuinely love and care for the children entrusted to them. The parent stands in God's place in care, discipline, and instruction regarding right and wrong.

Like children, who must learn right from wrong, the best parenting skills do not come naturally. Parenting skills must also be learned. Parents make many mistakes along the way, and learning how and when to discipline is an important part of a parent's education. "Am I being too strict?" "Am I letting them off too easy?" These are among the innumerable questions every parent asks in raising and disciplining their children. Often, how we raise our children depends on how we were raised. Our childhood and even our own personality traits, often becomes the background for the way we shape the environment of our children.

> Your children will see what you are all about by what you live rather than what you say.
>
> —Wayne Dyer

Jacob was one of the most famous characters in Scripture, yet Jacob was no role model. In many ways, Jacob became the product of his environment. His mother favored him over his brother, and Jacob in turn would show favoritism as a parent. Jacob was cunning, deceiving, and often self-centered, and most of his sons grew up to be the same way. Jacob cheated his brother out of the family blessing and tricked him out of the family birthright. Jacob deceived his father Isaac and was in turn deceived by his own sons.

Jacob grew up in a permissive atmosphere and parented a dysfunctional family. He had twelve sons by four wives and was nearly a hundred years old when he tried to raise them. Bible hero he may have been, but Jacob often exhibited questionable character in growing up and was a less-than-stellar parent. Jacob was not only a permissive parent. Jacob was also a passive parent. As a father, he seemed to discipline as a reaction to improper conduct rather than as a lesson on moral right and wrong. For example, when his daughter was raped, Jacob's sons exacted revenge by slaughtering all the males in the city. *"Jacob said to Simeon and Levi, 'You have gotten me into trouble; now the Canaanites, the Perizzites, and everybody else in the land will hate me. I do not* have many men; if they all band together against me and attack me, our whole family will be destroyed'" (Genesis 34:30 GNT).

Because Jacob was a permissive, as well as passive parent, discipline in his home was not what it should have been, and his sons grew up is an unstructured environment. Children do not resent the structure that discipline represents. The rules, limits, and consequences of the structure discipline provides make children feel safe.

As a teacher, the finest classrooms I have observed were classrooms where teachers set and enforced limits for their students. Permissive classroom environments are seldom more than organized chaos, and intentional learning is seldom a product of confusion. Students taught in structured environments did not resent such discipline. On the contrary. Such students respected teachers who cared enough to create such a learning climate, and were generally the most productive. No doubt, Jacob's other sons wondered why their father did not love them enough to discipline them.

Jacob also failed to learn as a parent the lessons he should have learned as a son. In playing favorites with Joseph, Jacob enjoyed showering the son of his favorite wife Rachel with gifts and cared little of how this might affect his other children. Jacob did not remember the hurt he felt when his own father favored Esau over him. Resentment from such favoritism was inevitable, but the resentment felt by the brothers was directed towards Joseph rather than their father. Because Jacob did not remember the lessons from his past, his children would encounter hardships that might have been prevented otherwise.

Parenting is a huge responsibility. As we all know, parents shape nearly every aspect of their children's lives. Jacob's life had been shaped by the pain of parental favoritism. It was in this family environment that Joseph spent the first seventeen years of his life. But although the environment of childhood may be a reason for how children grow up, it is not an excuse for children who become troubled adults. Joseph grew up in a family that would truly be classified as dysfunctional, yet nothing negative is ever spoken of him in all Scripture. Unlike his father's, Joseph's character was above reproach, despite his growing up in an environment where so many things worked against him. The fact that Joseph grew up so well was *in spite* of his father Jacob rather than because of him. More often than not, our actions as well as the actions of our children, result from personal choice.

We may not be responsible for our heredity, or even the environment into which we were born. However, we are responsible for our personal choices. Joseph's later success was due to his *decisions*—not his heredity. Neither was this success due solely to his environment. In fact, it was in spite of it. We are not told much of Joseph's parenting skills. We know that he had two children, and we can be sure Joseph raised them well.

Today's world is fraught with many of the same distractions to effective parenting as was the world of Jacob and Joseph. Dealing with sibling rivalry, the need for proper discipline, role modeling, and prayer are required tools of proper parenting regardless of the era. What are some keys to effective parenting that will allow you to raise functional children in a dysfunctional world? While every family is unique, no family is perfect, and there are no universal solutions. Following scriptural and practical principles can provide the best opportunity for raising successful children.

Do not compare your children—Even in my middle school classroom, I learned early that the quickest road to alienating children is to compare a student to a brother or sister. Never compare your children with brothers, sisters, or the neighbors' kids. Comparison is the fastest road to inferiority. Jacob should have remembered the folly of playing favorites among children. After all, his mother Rebekah had favored him, while his father Isaac favored Esau, Jacob's brother. In part due to this, the brothers parted company as adults, and only later reconciled. Let your children know that he or she is equally loved, respected, and important *(Genesis 25:28)*.

Celebrate each child's gifts and talents—As a teacher, I promised myself early in my career that I would search out whatever was *good* in even the *average* child. I would nurture that good, and make it a strength for each child. Find a strength in your children, and praise it. Make sure your children understand that every person is a gift from God. Each individual can make a unique contribution to life better than a brother, a sister, or anyone else can. Do you know what your talent is? Do you recognize the special talents given your children? Ask yourself:

- What does my child do best?

- What does my child do without my prompting?

- What does my child do that is complimented by teachers and others?

- What does my child talk about, write about, or draw?

Encourage the gifts and talents in your children, but do not set excessive expectations, which may be difficult or impossible for them to reach. Do not expect them to be you. Give them an example to follow, not a mold to fit. Celebrate their small victories and reward honest effort. Surprise them occasionally. Make a memory. Let them enjoy their childhood and remember that the world will never care as much about them when that childhood ends as you do right now.

Talk over sibling conflicts—Do you have a family time of discussion each day? If not, create a time to sit down and talk over the good as well as the difficult aspects of every day. Simply allowing an intentional time for expressing feelings can be a long-term solution for short-term problems. Being a mediator and parental authority has a more lasting effect than simply trying to be a friend to your children. Create an atmosphere of safety and listening for your children. When they feel you are actually listening, the need to solve every problem becomes secondary. Caring enough to just discuss possible solutions, implications, and consequences will mean more to your children than trying to always find a 'right' answer.

Require personal responsibility—In today's society, children are quicker to learn their *rights* than they are their *responsibility*. Teach them early that some rights such as free speech carry with them the responsibility to use that right with care. Children are also notorious for making excuses. Learn to distinguish between reasons and excuse. An excuse is what we *lean* on when we *choose* to. A reason is what we *fall* on when we *have* to. Learn to recognize your children's bluffs, and call them on it. Also, recognize honest misunderstandings and mistakes. Sometimes children fail to follow instruction out of spite—a rebellious spirit. At other times, there are legitimate reasons, which must be dealt with differently. Overprotection promotes underdevelopment in your children's social and moral development. Do not make excuses for your children. Teach them the effectiveness of admitting a mistake and the value of a well-timed apology. Above all, be sure to listen to your children. Be interested in their world. Let them have an opinion, and show them that their opinion matters. Do not do everything for your children. Teach them to not just *be* responsible, but *feel* responsible for certain things. Instill and cultivate 'ownership' opportunities such as cleaning their room, caring for pets, utilizing homework time. Respect your children's property and honor the boundaries of privacy you allow them.

> From my tribe, I take nothing. I am the maker of my own fortune.
>
> —Tecumseh

Discipline your children in love—Accept your children without tolerating their wrong actions. Your children not only require discipline, most children want it. Discipline is love, not punishment. *"If you don't punish your children, you don't love them. If you do love them, you will correct them" (Proverbs 13:24).* Remember that an ounce of encouragement will go further than a pound of demand. Always be *consistent* in your discipline. Be firm; be flexible. Never promise what you cannot deliver. Never discipline your children in anger, haste, or self-righteousness, or with hateful words, but do not see discipline as something a good parent avoids. Just remember the tone of the correction may be remembered after the lesson is forgotten. Solomon says that proper discipline leads your children toward 'understanding' *(Proverbs 10:13)* and that godly discipline is not to be despised *(Proverbs 3:11-12)*. Discipline brings wisdom *(Proverbs 29:15; Ecclesiastes 7:5)*, promotes obedience *(Proverbs 19:18)*, and drives out 'foolishness' *(Proverbs 22:15)*. You must set limits for your children, and discipline them when they disobey. Old Eli was an important priest in Israel, yet he was a poor father. Like Jacob, he failed to discipline his sons *"...Eli knew they were acting improperly, but he did not stop them" (I Samuel 2:22-29; 3:13)*, and this led to family disaster. David was Israel's greatest king, but he could not discipline. When incest plagued his own house, David got angry, but failed to discipline *(I Samuel 13:21)*. Set limits on what your children may read and watch. Before you encourage your children to have an open mind, be sure you know what is going into it.

Try not to frustrate your children—What does it mean to frustrate your children? Frustration is discipline taken too far. *"Parents, don't come down too hard on your children or you'll crush their spirits" (Colossians 3:21)*. Discipline your children, but do not break their spirit. Give your children a chance to correct themselves before you have to correct them. Excessive discipline will drain your children's reserves and result in diminishing positive return. When you must discipline, however, correct—do not criticize. Correction and criticism are different. Correction *streamlines* your children's road to success by reducing the weights they must carry toward adulthood. Criticism *clutters* that path with discouragement and self-doubt. Correction prunes excesses, but criticism reduces the inventory. Criticism of and sarcasm about positive efforts from your children will paralyze their desire to try something new. This leads to defensiveness and withdrawal. Celebrate even the small successes of your children. Do not provoke them to anger or lying through harsh discipline that never allows them a way of repentance, correction, or improvement *(Ephesians 6:4)*. Do not keep reminding your children of past mistakes. Emphasize lessons learned without rehashing the experiences that taught them. A gentle and firm hand is usually sufficient. Knowing when, how, and the limit to discipline are all equally important.

Accept and forgive your children—Your children will disappoint you. They are not perfect. They will not always fulfill your hopes and desires. Accept that your children will eventually have to make and be responsible for their own choices, but let them clearly know you love them with an *unconditional love.* Love them for who they are—not what they do. Some of their choices will bring consequences that hurt and disappoint both you and your children. Once you have dealt with the consequences of a wrong action however, let it go. The Prodigal Son demanded his inheritance and squandered it on wine, women, and song. Eventually, he came to himself, and returned to his father. The father welcomed his wayward son with open arms and a great feast. Let your children know that you accept them because they are *yours*—not because of their *actions*, right or wrong. Learn to forgive them for the mistakes in life they will surely make *(Luke 15:17-24).*

Motivate your children—Your children will function much more efficiently if you motivate them to do right instead of making right actions a sterile requirement. The best motivation is in *demonstration.* When you brought your children into the world, you had no choice in being their role model. Athletes may decline this privilege, parents cannot. As someone has said, good parenting requires perspiration. Great parenting requires *inspiration.* Be a demonstration of inspiration in your children's lives. *Show* your children the importance and benefits of correct action, and proper behavior. Give them role models. Inspire their souls; do not just fill their heads. The most effective parenting results from lighting fires, not filling buckets.

Teach your children practical wisdom—Your children are not born with the tendency toward wisdom. On the contrary. Our children are born with a bent toward foolishness. *"Foolishness is bound up in the heart of a child; the rod of discipline will remove it far from him"* (Proverbs 22:15 NASB). Wisdom must be taught. If your children learn wisdom, you will be brought *joy (Proverbs 23:24).* More often than not, children will return to the foundational training principles in which they were raised. Of course, there are exceptions to this rule, but God has instructed us: *"Train up a child in the way he should go: and when he is old, he will not depart from it"* (Proverbs 22:6 KJV). Understanding this, teach your children wisdom. Wisdom is more precious than gold *(Proverbs 16:16).* Wisdom is greater than power *(Ecclesiastes 9:16).* There are many aspects of wisdom you may teach your children:

➤ *I will teach my children the wisdom of seeking & serving God first*—
The first lesson of all wisdom is seeking God first. Everything else is secondary. God honored Abraham because He knew that Abraham brought up his children in a godly home *(Genesis 18:18-19)*. Hannah was a godly mother who dedicated her son Samuel to the Lord. Not to teach your children the godly perspective on right and wrong is to leave them to what has become known as *situation ethics.* Many

> *Success is not a doorway, it's a staircase.*
>
> —Dottie Walters
>
> ❧

kids feel that right and wrong actions are determined by whether or not they get away with something. Not to be caught means that the action must be right. Situation ethics is honesty stemming from *circumstance,* rather than honesty stemming from *integrity.* God does not condone situation ethics or partial truths. God requires complete honesty. Do you want to leave your children without a moral compass in our world? Teach your children to seek God first, and learn of His ways through His Word, and He has promised to direct their steps *(Ecclesiastes 12:1; I Samuel 1:11; I Chronicles 28:9; Psalms 111:10; Proverbs 3:6; 15:33; Cp. Matthew 6:32-34).*

➤ *I will teach my children the wisdom of the Golden Rule*—Treat others as you want to be treated. This wisdom also teaches your children not to be selfish, rude, dishonest, or conceited. The Golden Rule is the finest general principle you can teach your children *(Luke 6:31).*

➤ *I will teach my children the wisdom of courtesy*—Children today do not know how to exhibit common courtesy, or even the value of a proper compliment. The benefits of courtesy have to be taught as a part of character education in schools today, and what was yesterday's standard of proper conduct is today's missing link in teaching children how to interact with their world. I know as a teacher how much more receptive I tend to be toward students who say *'thank you'* and *'please'*. I have watched the positive responses of other children when one child pays a sincere compliment. The world will be no different. Teach your children the lasting value of courtesy, a smile, and the importance of a well-timed compliment. *"Withhold not good from them to whom it is due, when it is in the power of thine hand to do it"* *(Proverbs 3:27 KJV).*

➤ *I will teach my children the wisdom of seeking the Golden Mean*—The Golden Mean is also known as the *Divine Proportion*. The *Divine Proportion* is credited to Plato and teaches that we should not seek for great riches, which might lead to greed, or accept poverty, which might lead to stealing. Instead, we should strive for the middle road: that is, having what we need *(Proverbs 30:8)*. Sometimes moderation in all things is the best advice.

➤ *I will teach my children the wisdom of parental respect*—Wisdom does not make this a request, but a command *(Exodus 20:12; Matthew 15:6)*. God says this is the right thing to do *(Ephesians 6:1)*. As a parent, you must also set a good example for them to follow *(Proverbs 10:1; 13:1; 15:20)*. Your children will learn more from the light of your life than from the lessons of your lecture. Do not just teach your children character—show them what it looks like. Character and integrity are not inherited, but can be transferred. King David may have failed to discipline his son Amnon's sexual promiscuity was because David was guilty of the same weakness. Nevertheless, his having committed this sin was no reason for David to permit his son to make the same mistake. Your life may not be perfect, but your children can learn much from a carefully 'repaired' example *(I Samuel 11:4; 13:22)*.

➤ *I will teach my children respect for civil authority*—God created civil authority to protect us. Joseph respected the Pharaoh's right to enforce justice, even if that justice seemed unfair. Teach your children to obey even the laws they might see as unfair. Teach them to respect—not fear—civil authority. In doing this, you may save them a lifetime of heartache *(Romans 13:3; Cp. I Peter 2:13-15)*.

➤ *I will teach my children the wisdom of hard work, commitment and persistence*—Teach your children that winners seldom quit, and that quitters seldom win. Teach them to be *proactive*—not merely *reactive* to situations life presents them. Encourage them to do *what is right* and to do *their best* in life. These are the finest two lessons on work ethic you can teach them *(Galatians 6:9)*.

➤ *I will teach my children the wisdom of proper use of money*—Wise use of money will have an effect on the rest of your children's lives. Give your children an allowance, jobs to do, and responsibility with money.

Teach your children to tithe to God, support the needy, and save for a rainy day *(Proverbs 1:5; 30:25)*.

➤ *I will teach my children the wisdom of self-control*—Solomon teaches us that without self-control, your children are as defenseless as a city without walls *(Proverbs 25:28; 16:32)*. Teach your children to control the temptations of youth and especially the words that come out of their mouths. To laugh at their use of improper language is to encourage its use. Impress upon your children that the world will judge them first by their words and only later by their actions. Do not let your children learn by experience that the people may not care about the second if they have already been offended by the first *(Proverbs 10:19; 14:3; 15:2; 17:28)*.

➤ *I will teach my children the wisdom of understanding that experience is not always the best teacher*—Teach your children to learn from the mistakes of others. They will make enough mistakes in life without having to repeat yours and mine. Learning by experience can be painful. Sometimes experience gives the test first and teaches the lesson later.

➤ *I will teach my children the wisdom of a valuable reputation*—A good reputation is more valuable than riches *(Proverbs 20:1)*. Teach your children that their reputation is the most valuable asset they own. Someone has said that while the damage to a reputation can usually be repaired, the world will always take note of where the crack was. Teach your children to choose their friends carefully and that the

> Glass, china, and reputation are easily cracked, and never mended well.
>
> —Benjamin Franklin
>
> ✥

friends they choose plus the decisions they make result in the reputation they will have. Set boundaries within the freedom you allow your children in the choice of friends. Often, what their friends are, your children become *(Proverbs 13:20; I Timothy 5:22)*.

➤ *I will teach my children the wisdom of a good education*—Wisdom is applying knowledge. To be wise, your children must first have the knowledge the world requires *(Proverbs 15:14; 18:15; 23:12)*.

➤ *I will teach my children the wisdom of thinking before acting*—Every action has a consequence. Teach your children the wisdom of *personal accountability* and to consider what results may occur from decisions they will make. Jesus told the story of the virgins who went out to meet the bridegroom without proper preparation for the journey, and He called them 'foolish'. Thinking ahead is first rule of wise decision-making, and you cannot teach this principle too often *(Matthew 25:1-13)*.

➤ *I will teach my children the wisdom of trying, even if they fail*—Zig Ziglar, the popular motivational speaker, notes that failure is an act, not a person. Teach your children to make honest efforts, and that failure is merely an opportunity for improvement, not an analysis of their character. Stress that it is better to try and to fail than not to try at all.

➤ *I will teach my children the wisdom of goal setting*—The Apostle Paul never lost sight of his goal in life—to fulfill the mission for which he was called. Teach your children to establish goals throughout their lives. By definition, someone who does not know where he or she is going is lost *(Philippians 3:13-14)*.

Ruined Child (One Serving)

The ingredients herein have been tested and approved by the experience of many years. Product is harmless to plants and animals. Effective in small to moderate doses. If no results are seen in the first few months, continue as necessary.

Directions for Use:

For use beginning in early childhood. Mix thoroughly with situational ethics. May be flavored with excuse-making as needed. Continue through teenage years. **DO NOT USE SPARINGLY.**

Active Ingredients:

Double-strength Permissiveness...31%
Highly diluted Discipline...8%
Concentrate of Criticism...13%
Undistilled essence of Overprotection 26%
Triple-measure of Excessive Expectation...14%
Tincture of artificially flavored Improper Language..................................7%
Dehydrate of Character...<u>1%</u>
Total.. 100%

CAUTION:

Do not expose to Biblically based teaching!
Do not hug, forgive, or encourage UNDER ANY CIRCUMSTANCES!
Store in an open-minded container.

Power Points:

➤ How would you feel if you feel if you were one of Joseph's other brothers? Would you feel jealous, disfavored, and insulted?

➤ Remember, your sins are sometimes passed on to your children—"*The nation which does not remember the past is condemned to repeat the past.*" The words of George Santayana could well be applied to the life of Jacob. How soon he had forgotten the problems favoritism has caused within his own family.

➤ Parenting is the most important job on earth. Children must be taught right from wrong, and God has entrusted this responsibility to parents. As a parent or guardian, you stand in God's place in care, discipline, and instruction.

➤ Teach your children to be better than you are. Do not allow them to blame their environment alone for their mistakes. Teach them that life is what you make it.

➤ Remember, children are a gift from God. Most failures stem from *'would not'* rather than *'could not'*. Do what you can to raise godly children, and, when they are beyond disciplining, trust God that, as with Joseph, He can ultimately work good in a child's life even apart from parental intervention *(Jeremiah 31:29; Ezekiel 14:18)*.

Reflection Section:

Parental Inventory

❑ My child's gift or talent would be _____

❑ If my child had $100 to spend, he or she would spend it on _____

❑ My child's three closest friends are _____

- ❏ The one possession of my child that they would miss most if gone would be _____

- ❏ One major goal my child has is _____

- ❏ The thing that motivates my child best would be _____

- ❏ To my child, the most important thing in life is _____

- ❏ My child thinks cursing is _____

- ❏ If they spent a week with my child, someone else would describe my child's character in ten words or less as _____

- ❏ My child thinks the Bible is _____

My Personal Growth Journal—

- ❏ I will establish a quiet time to discuss the day's problems and events with my child, and actually listen to what he or she has to say.

- ❏ I will establish a *homework* and *telephone-use* time for my child and enforce it.

- ❏ I will study one Proverb a day with my child for the next thirty days.

- ❏ I will discuss with my child the difference between a *reason* and an *excuse*.

- ❏ I will discuss with my child the difference between a *right* and a *responsibility*.

- ❏ I will stress to my child the importance of saying '*please*' and '*thank you*'.

- ❏ I will teach my child the value of *money* through practical use of an allowance.

- ❏ I will stress to my child the lasting value of a good *reputation*.

- ❏ I will model for my child—*character* and *integrity*.

~ Chapter 2 ~

Jealousy: "The Principle of Taming the Green-Eyed Monster"

Joseph had a dream. When he told it to his brothers, they hated him even more. His brothers said, "So! You're going to rule us? You're going to boss us around?" And they hated him more than ever because of his dreams and the way he talked. They spotted him off in the distance. By the time he got to them they had cooked up a plot to kill him. (Gen. 37:5; 8; 18)

The Joseph story....

Jacob loved Joseph more than he loved any of his other sons. He created an environment of jealousy within the family, as Joseph's brothers watched Jacob display this favoritism without apology. First, Jacob favored Joseph with the coat of many colors. The coat was a symbol of the father's particular blessing and meant that Joseph would never have to do the hard labor reserved for his brothers. Second, the older brothers had to listen to Joseph tell of his dreams—dreams that sounded very much like predictions that, one day, the brothers would bow down to Joseph. Over time, Jacob's favoritism and Joseph's giftedness began to wear on Jacob's older sons. Tolerance for Joseph evolved into resentment and hate. One day, this hate would furnish the opportunity for an even greater sin. As Joseph was following his father's instruction to bring food to his brothers, jealousies boiled into hate, and hate into a murderous plot toward their younger brother. If they killed him, Joseph's brothers would be forever rid of the spoiled dreamer whose dreams predicted that they would one day serve him. Why not just cast Joseph out of their lives and tell Jacob that a wild animal had killed their brother? They could put the blood of an animal on Joseph's coat and convince their father, while not bringing the bloodguilt of Joseph's death upon their own consciences. Surely, a foolproof plan.

Principle Truth: Unchecked jealousy will grow into a destructive force that can divide families, multiply sorrow, and lead to even greater sins.

Jealousy has often been called the green-eyed monster. Why it is green is anybody's guess. Why it is called a monster is not a mystery. Jealousy is seldom a static condition. Jealousy evolves. Left unchecked, it can evolve into murder.

It has been said that jealousy is the full hand wanting more. Envy is the empty hand wanting some. However we distinguish them, jealousy and envy are monsters not just in themselves, but also for where they lead. They appear as such innocent vices. They are never smelled on our breath, yet they often get away with murder.

> As iron is eaten away by rust, so the envious are consumed by their own passion.
>
> —Antisthenes
>
> ৵৵

Sometimes we confuse jealousy and envy with wanting something very much. It's our nature to admire and want things. We all have particular things that strike our fancy. For example, I have a particular love for cars. Sports cars in particular. Whenever I see particular types of sports cars, I wish I could afford one like them. That is not jealousy or envy. Wanting things is natural. However, if I wanted one of those sports cars enough to steal one, or hurt someone to take theirs—that would be wrong. That would be desire out of hand.

Jealousy is an attitude. In God's eyes, jealousy is a sinful attitude. Jealousy's greatest evil is in what it can lead to. Because jealousy, like anger and hate, can lead to worse sins such as murder, Jesus instructed us that such sins were equally deserving of the same judgment *(Matthew 5:21-23)*. God hates a jealous heart.

God punishes jealousy. Miriam was the sister of Moses. Because God chose to speak through Moses, Miriam became jealous of her brother. God was displeased with Miriam's attitude and struck her with leprosy *(Numbers 12:1-10)*. For jealousy, Cain killed his brother Abel, and King Saul tried to murder David.

Scripture gives other examples of the perils of jealousy. For example, the Jews were jealous of the Apostle Paul's teachings to the Gentiles and tried to kill him *(Acts 13:45)*. The Jews also were also jealous of the effect the teachings of Jesus were having on the people, and we are told, "*...the chief priests had handed Him over because of envy*" *(Mark 15:10)*. For jealousy, the very people Jesus came to save were led to crucify their messiah. For Joseph's brothers, jealousy evolved into hate and the desire to kill a brother.

Because jealousy can be so destructive in what it leads to as well as what it is, jealousy is best dealt with early. Jealousy is fostered by comparison and grows through insecurity. Jealousy can destroy the one jealous of others, and, as in Joseph's case, even the one toward whom jealousy is directed.

Joseph's brothers hated Joseph because Jacob favored him. They were jealous of this favoritism. No doubt, they also resented that God had given Joseph a special gift. Joseph was able to interpret dreams. Because of favoritism from his father and his giftedness from God, the brothers no longer sought equality with Joseph in the father's eyes; they began to hate their brother. Jealousy festered into anger, and they wanted to kill him.

> *O! Beware, my lord, of jealousy; it is the green-eyed monster, which doth mock the meat it feeds on.*
>
> —Shakespeare

Envy and jealousy are not only wrong in themselves, but also wrong because of what they can lead to. Jealousy's effects are far-reaching. The jealousy of Joseph's brothers brought difficulty to Joseph in the short term, but much greater difficulty to his brothers and their father as time passed. For example, Joseph's brothers were forced to lie to Jacob and maintain that lie about Joseph's disappearance for twenty years. The jealous act of selling Joseph not only caused a guilty conscience for the brothers, but twenty years of grief for Jacob.

Today's world offers us many luxuries, opportunities for success, and fertile fields for envy and jealousy to take root. While we cannot—and should not—seek to eliminate our natural desire for the blessings and opportunities God has given us in our world, we should make every effort to be sure such desires do not sprout into jealousy toward others. Practical application of lessons learned from jealousy's destructive effects in Joseph's family are keys to prevention of the green-eyed monster's far-reaching tentacles.

❑   *I will not plant jealousy*—Jacob planted the seeds of jealousy in his children by openly favoring Joseph. Don't brag about successes or possessions that might cause jealousy to spring up in others. Jealousy leads to confusion, disorder, and evil *(James 3:16)*. In the case of Joseph's brothers, it nearly led to murder. Jealousy hurts not only others, but it hurts you *(Proverbs 14:30)* and hinders your spiritual growth *(I Peter 2:1-2)*. Dilute your successes with humility. Follow the example of Mary, when informed she was chosen to be the mother of Jesus: *"And why am I so blessed that the mother of my Lord visits me?" (Luke 1:43)* You inspire others as you help them see that their feelings are more important to you than your pride. Today, go to someone and sincerely compliment that person on something that means something to him or her.

❑   *I will not water jealousy*—Unchecked, jealousy can lead to murder. Jacob should have known this all too well from the jealousy he created in his own brother. "*Esau hated Jacob, because his father had given Jacob the blessing. He thought, 'The time to mourn my father's death is near; then I will kill Jacob'*" (Genesis 27:41 NASB). Psychologists tell us that one of the quickest ways to a feeling of inadequacy is to compare ourselves with others. Remember that there will always be people who are better than you are in some skills. There will always be people better looking and with better jobs. Don't blame them or God for this. Understand that you have your own gifts, talents, and blessings from God. Don't compare yourself with others you feel are more blessed than you are. Do not feed the green-eyed monster! Write down three things that you are jealous of in others, and ask God to make you see that true happiness does not come from the things of this world.

❑   *I will recognize jealousy as a sharp and painful thorn*—Jealousy is destructive to you, not just others. Jealousy is powerful (*Proverbs 27:4*). Its damage reaches deep into your inner being. "*...Jealousy is like a cancer*" (Proverbs 14:30). See jealousy as the hurtful thorn that grows with the rose of desire! Today, write down ten things that you are grateful to God for. Tell Him how much you appreciate the small blessings He's given you. Thank Him for simply allowing you to live another day. Cultivating thanksgiving will help you avoid the thorns of jealousy.

> *Jealousy is the tribute mediocrity offers up to genius.*
>
> ✍

❑   *I will defeat jealousy by sowing kindness*—When King Saul was jealous over God's decision that David would someday replace him as King of Israel, Saul sought to kill David. David feared for his life. He knew that jealousy unchecked would lead to his death. What did David do? David tried to serve and be a friend, and God honored David: "*Now Saul was afraid of David, for the LORD was with him*" (I Samuel 18:12 NASB). What was the result of David's response of kindness toward jealousy? Then Saul replied, "*I have sinned. Return, my son David, for I will not harm you again because my life was precious in your sight this day. Behold, I have played the fool and have committed a serious error*" (I Samuel 26:21). While this change of heart toward David did not come immediately, it came. Today, think of one person to whom it would be difficult for you to show kindness. Do him or her a favor. Good overcomes and disarms evil—not necessarily overnight, but eventually.

Power Points:

> ➤ Was Joseph in part responsible for the jealousy his brothers felt towards him?

> ➤ Who was more responsible for the jealousy in the family: Jacob? Joseph? The brothers themselves?

> ➤ What could Joseph have done to ease the feelings of jealousy shared by his older brothers?

> ➤ Why are jealousy and envy called *green*? How do the two differ?

Reflection Section:

❑ Do you have gifts or talents that might cause others to be jealous?

❑ Are you jealous of others who seem to be more blessed than you are?

❑ Realize that there will always be others more gifted in certain areas than you are, and celebrate such diversity.

❑ Know that you have your own special talents, and do not allow the green-eyed monster to evolve. Even if it does not create hurt for others, jealousy will bring nothing but grief to you.

My Personal Growth Journal—

❑ Today, write down ten things that you are grateful to God for. Tell Him how much you appreciate the small blessings He's given you.

❑ Write down three things that you are jealous of in others. Talk these things over with them. Kill the green-eyed monster.

~ Chapter 3 ~

God Isn't Finished with Me Yet: "The Principle of Understanding God's Refinement Process"

From that moment on, God blessed the home of the Egyptian—all because of Joseph. The blessing of God spread over everything he owned, at home and in the fields, and all Potiphar had to concern himself with was eating three meals a day. As time went on, his master's wife became infatuated with Joseph and one day said, "Sleep with me." (Gen. 39:5-7)

The Joseph story....

Joseph's brothers did not kill him. The cooler heads of the oldest sons prevailed. Instead, they stripped him of his special coat, and sold Joseph to Midianite traders and into Egyptian slavery. When the brothers returned home, Jacob and little Benjamin were convinced that a wild animal had killed Joseph. His bloodied coat lent credence to the story. Meanwhile, down in Egypt, a prison supervisor named Potiphar purchased Joseph, and the young man began his new life as a slave in the man's home. But Joseph was also given a measure of responsibility. In his new home, the young Hebrew was put in charge of Potiphar's house. Nevertheless, God had plans to refine Joseph's character. Joseph had no sooner become a trusted slave than he was immediately thrust into a furnace of affliction. Potiphar's wife began to seek sexual favors from Joseph. Despite living a godly life in every respect, Joseph was now made to face the powerful temptation of sexual sin.

Principle Truth: God will do whatever it takes to conform you into the image of His Son, and often His method depends on what He has to work with.

Ryan's pencil looked as if it had been chewed. Perhaps it had been. He was about to throw it away when another student in my classroom suggested he put it into the electric pencil sharpener. Couldn't hurt, he thought. After all, it was his only pencil. The grinding sound was as loud as it was unmistakable. "Sounds awful in there," commented Ryan. Finally, the grinding ceased, and Ryan pulled out the pencil. "Well, it sure got shorter, but it got ground into useable," said Ryan. Indeed. The pencil that had looked so hopelessly mangled was now ground to a fine point.

> It is only when the cold season comes that we know the pine and the cypress to be evergreens.
>
> —Chinese Proverb
> ✥

As Christians, we might be compelled to think that when trouble grinds our lives to a halt, it does so because of sin in our lives. While this may be the cause of some of our troubles, it does not follow that living a life as sin-free as possible exempts Christians from all trouble. After all, the fruitful trees get shaken! The tree bearing no fruit is left alone.

Trouble happens. Sometimes our troubles arise because of our own unwise decisions. Sometimes troubles are God's discipline—His grinding to sharpen us, His sandpaper to refine us. When that discipline has been achieved, we would do well to remember the lessons learned and throw that sandpaper away. God does not want us to dwell upon the hardships He allows in our lives. He wants us to forget the sandpaper of hard times, while never forgetting the lessons. However, God does not want us to be surprised when troubles happen. "*My dear friends, do not be surprised at the painful test you are suffering, as though something unusual were happening to you*" (I Peter 4:12 GNT).

> Obstacles are what you see when you take your eyes off the goal.
>
> —Joseph Cossman
> ✥

We so often think of discipline in a negative way. Sometimes, we see discipline as punishment. God's discipline is corrective, however, and the troubles He allows become the framework for spiritual growth and maturity. Just as the cage put around our tomato plant is to encourage stability and fruit-bearing, so God permits troubles in our lives to train us into becoming the very best we can be. The troubles God allows are not meant to punish and break us. They are meant to strengthen us.

The story was told many years ago about the *Long John Silver's* company's need to keep their codfish fresh while shipping it cross-country. After first attempting to freeze them, it was found that the fish lost their flavor. The second attempt at keeping the fish fresh was to ship them live, but the meat of the fish became soft, and again the fish lost their flavor. Finally, the fish were shipped alive along with their natural enemy the catfish, and the cod arrived as fresh and flavorful as the day they were shipped. Having to face that which made them struggle kept the fish strong and their best.

In the same way, God allows trouble in our lives to refine us. In the process of smoothing wood, course sandpaper is the initial tool. However, in wood-working, a good finish is rarely achieved through this sanding alone. The final process is no longer to smooth, but to refinish. In refinishing, the sandpaper used becomes increasingly fine, until the grain is raised, and the wood is refined to its final finish. In the same way, God allows many kinds of troubles to smooth our lives into the final finish of His intended perfection. As the refiner of precious gold ever increases the heat of the smelt to purify the treasure, so God refines us in the fire of trouble. When He sees His image in the melt, He knows we are perfected. We have become *"…conformed to the image of His Son…" (Romans 8:29 NLT).*

God teaches us in many ways through the troubles He allows in our lives. Sometimes He teaches us through our own mistakes. When Israel sinned under the wicked king Jeroboam, God allowed trouble that would eventually divide the nation. Nevertheless, God warned Rehoboam of Judah not to interfere, for *"…this thing is from me" (I Kings 12:24 KJV).* All troubles we experience in our lives must pass through the permission of God. God is in control and can even work troubles we bring upon ourselves for good. Sometimes God teaches us through the mistakes of others, as He did Joseph. However God uses the troubles in our lives, God wants to refine us. The way we deal with the troubles God allows is up to us. We can learn from them, or become resentful. The same abrasive that polishes a diamond will destroy glass. Whether God's work in our lives polishes us or grinds us depends on what we're made of. His goal is to train us, not frustrate us, to make us better—not bitter.

Joseph lived an exemplary life, yet his difficulties were many, not the least of which was being enticed to sin by Potiphar's wife. But Joseph learned to understand that his troubles were not because God didn't love him. God was testing Joseph. As in our world, testing usually precedes a time for advancement. Joseph's troubles were troubles that come with living in a sinful world and were used by God as sandpaper to refine Joseph into the excellent leader he was to become.

Troubles are not always directly due to our sins. While sin does indeed bring consequences, we must not assume that simply because we face difficulties at every turn in life, these are the result of being out of fellowship with God. In fact, it may be an indication of just the opposite. It may be that, like Joseph, we are serving God to the best of our ability, and God is allowing trouble to refine us for some greater good, as He did in the life of Joseph. It has been said: *"life's disappointments are often love's veiled appointments."* Learning to understand and deal with the troubles we face is also a refining process. Recognizing the nature of troubles helps us to grow into the spiritual maturity of learning that God is sovereign in all things—a lesson Joseph learned well through the troubles he endured.

> *God will not permit any troubles to come upon us unless He has a specific plan by which great blessing can come out of the difficulty.*
>
> *—Peter Marshall*

Are you experiencing troubles in your life at this moment? Remember that God controls even the troubles you are experiencing, and nothing can come to you without first passing through His permission. Someone has said that a path with no obstacles usually leads nowhere. Understand that, like Joseph, we must not resent every trouble that we endure.

❑ *This trouble may be my own fault*—Sometimes we get what we deserve. Often, we make wrong choices. We sometimes just do stupid things, for which we simply must pay the price. David lusted after Bathsheba. Problem was, Bathsheba was married to Uriah. David arranged to have Uriah killed in his plan to take Bathsheba for his own. But God knew and through Nathan the prophet told David: *"Now therefore, the sword shall never depart from your house, because you have despised Me and have taken the wife of Uriah the Hittite to be your wife. Thus says the LORD, 'Behold, I will raise up evil against you...'" (II Samuel 12:10-11 NASB).* David learned from his sin and poured out his heart to God *(Psalm 51).* Sometimes, we bring trouble on ourselves. Today, think about this trouble. Are you aware of anything you did that might have resulted in this consequence? If so, do your best to correct it immediately.

❑ *This trouble may not be my fault*—Troubles are promised you if you are a Christian. In fact, they are the proof that you are a Christian! *"Not that the troubles should come as any surprise to you. You've always known that we're in for this kind of thing. It's part of our calling" (I*

Thessalonians 3:3; Cp. John 16:33; II Timothy 3:12; I Peter 4:12-13). Therefore, do not assume this trouble is a punishment. Most of the troubles of daily life happen to us because Adam brought suffering and death into our world *(Job 14:1).* For example, did you ever wonder why babies—who commit no sins—still suffer and die? They die because Adam introduced sin into the world. Sometimes trouble really is not your fault. If your trouble is not from your sin, it might simply be a result of Adam's. If so, accept it and realize that pain, suffering and hardships happen to everyone.

❑ *This trouble may be God's education tool*—Job suffered more than any man in the Bible. Do you know why? We are never told. Even Job was never told! Through his troubles, however, Job learned much about God *(Job 1:7-22; 38-42).* Job trusted God without fully understanding God's ways. *"Though He slay me, yet will I trust Him"* *(Job 13:15, KJV).* Sometimes God doesn't explain why we go

> One of the secrets of life is to make stepping-stones out of stumbling blocks.
>
> —Jack Penn
>
> ❧

through the troubles we do. Nevertheless, troubles are often His sandpaper to refine us. *"For God is greater than man. Why do you contend with Him? For He does not give an accounting of any of His words"* *(Job 33:12-13 NKJV).* Job certainly spent much time in God's refining fire. God's refining is to make us better—not bitter. Someone has said that we will meet God in the fires before we'll meet Him in the sky. Is it possible God is allowing you to go through this difficulty so you can learn to know and trust Him better? Is He teaching you a lesson you will only learn later?

❑ *This trouble will bring me closer to God*—How will you respond to this trouble? Your heart is the key. Will it make you bitter or better? Remember, the same sun that hardens clay softens wax. It has been said that when trouble comes, some people are like a thermometer—as the heat rises, they reflect the change clearly. However, others are like a thermostat, they control the heat that trouble brings and trust God to bring them through it. What could God be telling you about the troubles in your life? Are you a *thermometer* or a *thermostat*?

- *God could be testing my faith*—God may be pruning you. Have you ever pruned the branches of a tree? Pruning helps a tree to grow straight and healthy. Pruning removes the excesses so that the tree can bear more fruit. Unpruned limbs become weak limbs. I do not like to prune my fruit trees. Somehow, cutting off the branches of my trees appears to me to be an unkind act. Nevertheless, pruning my tree will mean better fruit in the spring. The branches I do not prune now will sap the strength of my tree later. Someone has said the husbandman is never closer to the tree than when he's cutting it. Trouble that tests your faith is never bad. In fact, God calls it "precious" *(I Peter 1:5-9)*. Daniel's three Hebrew friends suffered for their faith in Babylon. The king put them in a fiery furnace. What could be worse than this? Certainly they had done nothing wrong. Yet tested they were. But don't miss this—they were not the only ones in that fire! *"But suddenly, as he was watching, Nebuchadnezzar jumped up in amazement and exclaimed to his advisers, 'Didn't we tie up three men and throw them into the furnace?' 'Yes,' they said, 'we did indeed, Your Majesty' 'Look!' Nebuchadnezzar shouted. 'I see four men, unbound, walking around in the fire. They aren't even hurt by the flames! And the fourth looks like a divine being!'"* (Daniel 3:24-25 GNT) God was with the three friends in the fire. The trouble was filtered through His permission. His eye was on the thermostat, and His hand was on the clock! Troubles that test our faith should be embraced, not resented. *"My friends, consider yourselves fortunate when all kinds of trials come your way, for you know that when your faith succeeds in facing such trials, the result is the ability to endure. Make sure that your endurance carries you all the way without failing, so that you may be perfect and complete, lacking nothing"* (James 1:2-4 GNT). God will allow us to suffer, but He is always with you through it. God often allows trouble to bring you closer to Him. *"Before I was afflicted I went astray, but now I keep Your word"* (Psalms 119:67 NASB).

- *God could be driving me to prayer*—How's your prayer life? Jonah was determined not to follow God's instruction to go to Nineveh. Jonah was set on having his own way. You know the story. God decided that if Jonah would not go to Nineveh by sail, he would be going 'by whale', and had the prophet swallowed by a great fish! Jonah changed his mind, and *"Then Jonah prayed to the*

LORD his God from the stomach of the fish..." (Jonah 2:1 NASB). It just might be that God is trying to encourage you to improve your prayer life.

- *God could be testing my obedience*—How much will you sacrifice to obey God? Abraham was asked to sacrifice his only son *(Genesis 22:1-18)*. God probably will not ask you to do this, but He may be allowing this trouble to help you discover what you would give up for Him. God even taught His own Son obedience by requiring Him to leave heaven and endure the troubles of this world in order to redeem us *(Hebrews 5:8)*. Joseph tested the obedience of his brothers to their sense of right and wrong when he placed the money they had paid for the grain back into their sacks *(Genesis 43:17-22)*. Are there things in your life that stand between you and God? Is God testing your obedience so that you might learn priorities?

- *God could be teaching me patience*—We all pray for patience. Patience seems to be something we feel safe in asking for. But patience means *endurance*, and endurance is seldom achieved without hard training. Are you in need of endurance training? Life is a marathon—not a sprint! Do not faint! *(Proverbs 24:10)* Troubles are one means God uses to improve our patience, so be careful what you pray for *(James 1:3,4,12)*.

❑ *This trouble is bringing glory to God*—Sometimes God allows suffering and hardship for His own glory and doesn't explain all the details to us. This may sound harsh, but God can do nothing wrong. He always has a purpose in bringing about a greater good.

> *Life is a quarry, out of which we must mold and chisel a complete character.*
>
> —Goethe

- Sometimes He works this way through physical hardships: *"And His disciples asked Him, 'Rabbi, who sinned, this man or his parents, that he would be born blind?' Jesus answered, 'It was neither that this man sinned, nor his parents; but it was so that the works of God might be displayed in him'" (John 9:2-3 NASB).*

- Sometimes He works through sickness: *"But when Jesus heard this, He said, "This sickness is not to end in death, but for the glory of God, so that the Son of God may be glorified by it"* (John 11:4 NASB)

- Sometimes He works through death: *"Now this He said, signifying by what kind of death he would glorify God"* (John 21:19).

❑ *This trouble will make me better*—Troubles are God's sandpaper. He uses them to smooth down our rough edges of pride and create a beautiful finish. God wants to refine you, as gold is refined in a hot fire *(Isaiah 48:10)*. He did this to Paul: *"Because of the extravagance of those revelations, and so I wouldn't get a big head, I was given the gift of a handicap to keep me in constant touch with my limitations. Satan's angel did his best to get me down; what he in fact did was push me to my knees. No danger then of walking around high and mighty!"* (II Corinthians 12:7 NASB). Even this trouble is a part of God's plan to shape you. Remember, it's that abrasive and painful grain of sand within the secure shell of the oyster that is eventually transformed into the pearl. This trouble is no accident: *"That's why we can be so sure that every detail in our lives of love for God is worked into something good. God knew what he was doing from the very beginning. He decided from the outset to shape the lives of those who love him along the same lines as the life of his Son"* (Romans 8:28-29). Ask yourself right now what 'rough edge' in your life God may be trying to smooth. Don't let this trouble come your way for nothing! What can you learn from this?

❑ *This trouble will make others better*—Troubles sensitize us to the difficult times of others. What can you learn about compassion for others from this difficulty? Right now, think of someone you can encourage through a time of trouble. Who do you know that is going through a difficult time you once endured? Call or visit them. Encourage them through what you endured.

❑ *This trouble may very well be a sign God loves me*—*"Because the Lord corrects everyone he loves, and punishes everyone he accepts as a child"* (Hebrews 12:6 GNT). God wants to make His children the best they can be. Take Job for example. We are never told that God revealed to Job that Satan had issued a challenge regarding Job's faithfulness. What Job thought might have been a *punishment* from God was actually God proving Job's *faithfulness*! When you see others who never seem to get the sandpaper treatment from God, maybe they aren't His children. A parent's role is to discipline his or her own child, not the neighbor's. God is not interested in refining the devil's children. C.S. Lewis once remarked that God whispers in our pleasure, speaks in our conscience, but shouts in our pain. Know that God's refining process is sometimes painful, but always an expression of His love! *"I am the one who corrects and disciplines everyone I love" (Revelation 3:19 NLT).*

❑   *This trouble will end*—Nothing lasts forever—not even this trouble you are going through right now. Remember that God's sandpaper will finish its job in due *time "Now no chastening seems to be joyful for the present, but painful; nevertheless, afterward it yields the peaceable fruit of righteousness to those who have been trained by it" (Hebrews 12:11 NKJ).* Remember, God loves you and will end it. He doesn't want to destroy you. When my mother was sick with cancer, a well-meaning friend remarked to me "God will never allow fruit to grow on branches too weak to bear it." Last spring, I recall looking out my back door as a limb on my peach tree laden with fruit broke completely off during particularly windy rainstorm. It was then I realized God sometimes *does* allow us to break in our self-reliance, so that we will trust Him completely. But He also knows the limits of our endurance. One of my favorite phrases in scripture is *"…and it came to pass"*. That's how we should see troubles. Troubles come to pass, not to stay. Even if this trouble doesn't seem to have a limit, it does. Troubles are small bumps along the way to something much better *(II Corinthians 4:17).* When all this ends, you will see God worked in the best of all possible ways *(Hebrews 12:11).* Someday, God will make you forget this trouble ever even happened! *"God will wipe every tear from their eyes" (Revelation 7:17 NASB).*

> Ye fearful saints, fresh courage take, the clouds ye so much dread—are big with mercy and shall break in blessings on thy head.
>
> His purposes will ripen fast, unfolding every hour. The bud may have a bitter taste—but sweet will be the flower.
>
> —William Cowper

Power Points:

➤ Why did God allow Joseph to experience such troubles? Was God unfair? Why? Why not?

➤ Do you think Potiphar was surprised by his wife's actions toward Joseph?

➤ How do the effects of Adam's disobedience in the garden parallel the effects of Christ's obedience on the cross?

➤ Do you think Joseph's troubles could have stemmed from his pride in his coat?

Reflection Section:

❑ Have you examined your life to see if there are sins which may be the source of difficulties you are experiencing? If so, deal with the sins. But know too, that the result of living within God's will is often His allowing trials to shape and shake you, that we may, like Joseph, be perfected into a finer life.

❑ Is there something in your life that, like Jonah, you may not be eager to do? What is it? Why do you hesitate?

❑ Is God refining you through some difficulty today? Examine your life to be sure your troubles are not merely the result of unwise decisions on your part. While God can still discipline through these, He expects us to correct our mistakes the best we can.

❑ Is God able to make good come from troubles in your life that *were* your fault?

❑ What opportunities might open up for you through what you're going through right now?

❑ How are you reacting to your troubles? Are you a *thermometer* or a *thermostat?*

❑ What is the difference between God's *discipline* and His *punishment?*

❑ Is the discipline you show your children more to *refine* them or *punish* them?

❑ Has God already begun to bless you after times of difficulty? What have you learned from those troubles?

❑ Do you glorify God by telling others of lessons learned through God's discipline? Are you still concentrating on the sandpaper (the trouble itself), which was only a *means* to this end?

❑ Complete this statement: "God chastens (disciplines) those He loves because _____ "

My Personal Growth Journal—

❑ List five troubles God has gotten you through in your life. How are you better because of them?

❑ Make up three questions you would ask Adam if you could. Why did you choose those three?

❑ Go back and read the first few chapters of Genesis, and list five things that happened to the world because Adam sinned.

~ Chapter 4 ~

Influence: "The Principle of Personal Influence"

From that moment on, God blessed the home of the Egyptian—all because of Joseph. The blessing of God spread over everything he owned, at home and in the fields. (Gen. 39:5)

The Joseph story....

How would Joseph respond to the trust placed in him by his master? Joseph was ever faithful in his service to Potiphar. Joseph cared for the matters of Potiphar's home to the best of his ability. He also served his God in the same way. Because of his work ethic and dedication to God, the Lord allowed Potiphar's house to prosper. Joseph's influence was felt in the house of the Pharaoh's chief steward. Later, in a remarkable chain of events, Joseph would cause all of Egypt to prosper in a time of famine. From the influence of Joseph's godly life, many would be blessed and saved. But how would Joseph handle the temptation to sin with his master's wife?

Principle Truth: In one way or another, you make a lasting influence on someone's life with every action that you do and word that you speak. That influence reaches further than you know.

Today, you will touch a life. Today, you may touch many lives. As a teacher, I understand the importance of influencing young lives. I also understand that influence is more than what we do and say. Influence is everything we are, and the effect of our personal influence reaches much further than we might imagine. Sometimes our influence is positive, and others are led to follow the good actions they see in us. Sometimes our actions are not such a positive influence, but our influence on others can often be profound.

Mrs. Beeler was my high school drama teacher. Although she never knew it, she had a dramatic effect on turning a shy young man into the teacher he is today. It wasn't Mrs. Beeler's words. She was not a particularly eloquent speaker. Neither was she the finest teacher I remember having. Mrs. Beeler influenced me most through the character she exhibited in the classroom every day I sat under her teaching. Mrs. Beeler never became famous before she died, but she lives on through the role-model influence she became in my life.

In 1858, a Sunday school teacher named William Kimball led a Boston shoe clerk to give his life to Christ. The clerk, Dwight L. Moody, became an evangelist in England, and in 1879 awakened the heart of Frederick B. Meyer a pastor in a small church. Mr. Meyer preached on a college campus in America and brought to Christ a young student named Wilbur Chapman. In work at a YMCA, Chapman employed a former baseball player, Billy Sunday, to do evangelistic work. Mr. Sunday held a revival in Charlotte, North Carolina, which so inspired the businesspersons of the community that they planned a second campaign in order to bring in a preacher named Mordecai Ham. In that revival, a young man yielded his life to Christ, His name was Billy Graham. That unknown Sunday School teacher in 1858 never knew his influence would set in motion a chain of events that would result in the conversion of the greatest evangelist of the century. Often, we have no idea of the ramifications one personal influence can bring.

> *Some people come into our lives and waken our understanding with their wisdom, move our souls with their joy, make our world a better place before they leave, and, because their footprints remain on our hearts, we are never the same.*
>
> ❧

When Joseph was sold into slavery as a young boy, he never dreamed of the influence he would have on Egypt and its people. Joseph served Potiphar, his Egyptian master, to the best of his ability, and his godly influence brought blessing to Potiphar's home. This positive influence, along with God's blessing on such conduct, opened the door to greater opportunity for Joseph's advancement. In the end, Joseph's influence led to his greatest interview—an audience with the Pharaoh—and his eventual exaltation to the second most powerful position in the world. Because of Joseph's positive influence wherever God placed him, Joseph would rise to a position that would make him the savior of two kingdoms.

Whom will you influence today? As with Joseph, your life will speak today to many people you may not even realize. Joseph understood that his influence was impressed upon others—not merely by his words and his conduct, but through his personal character. Understanding this, God would have you recognize how many ways persons you touch today might feel your influence.

❏ *My influence will bless even nonbelievers*—The house in Egypt that Joseph cared for was Egyptian. Egyptians did not accept Joseph's God. Nevertheless, God blessed the house solely because of Joseph. Paul tells us that the same happens today. In some mysterious way, God will bless those you encounter because of you! Your godliness actually blesses others in your home! *"For the unbelieving husband is sanctified through his wife, and the unbelieving wife is sanctified through her believing husband" (I Corinthians 7:14 NASB).* Do you realize Jesus calls you "salt" and "light"? *(Matthew 5:13-16)* Salt keeps things from decaying too quickly. Light brings sight to darkness. This sinful world is decaying in its morality, and darkening in its sinfulness. In the same way, the Apostle Paul and Silas convinced their jailer in Philippi that if he were to become a believer, his entire family would be influenced toward Christianity *(Acts 16:25-34)*. Your influence makes a difference—remember that. Joseph influenced all of Egypt by his life, his words, and his wisdom. Through these, Joseph brought glory to his God and praise from unbelievers.

❏ *My life is are being watched by others*—I am always careful as a teacher not to do or say anything that might affect how my students see me. They are watching me. The world is watching you. It's also listening. *"In all things show yourself to be an example of good deeds, with purity in doctrine, dignified, sound in speech which is beyond reproach, so that the opponent will be put to shame, having nothing bad to say about us" (Titus*

2:27-8 NASB; Cp. I Peter 2:11-12). The Egyptians—Egyptians who did not know Joseph's God—were watching Joseph's life. Through Joseph's influence, however, his chief steward, and even the Pharaoh himself, glorified Joseph's God *(Genesis 41:37; Cp. Genesis 43:23).* Are unbelievers bringing glory to God through *your* influence? Most of the time, the world holds Christians to a higher standard. Be careful today that you do not set a poor Christian example for a sinful world watching you. Not only is the sinful world keeping an eye on you, but so also are other Christians. Some of them may not be as strong in the

> *I shall pass through this world but once. If therefore, there can be any kindness I can show, or good I can do, let me not defer or neglect it, for I shall not pass this way again.*
>
> —Grellett

faith as you are. Be watchful today that you don't make your liberty in Christ a stumbling block to weaker believers *(I Corinthians 8:10-13).* What actions or words do you need to correct before this day is over? Is there something you planned to do that might be better left undone? *"You show the world the gospel, no matter where you go. All who watch will read your life—which gospel will you show?"*

❑ *My life is making an impression on my children*—Abraham did not tell the full truth to the Pharaoh about his wife Sara when he journeyed to Egypt. The Pharaoh noticed Sara's beauty and inquired as to her relationship with Abraham. Abraham said of his wife Sara, *"She's my sister"* *(Genesis 20:2).* A hundred years later, Abraham's son Isaac entered into the same temptation that his father had once faced and in the same way denied his wife, calling her his sister *(Genesis 26:7).* Did the son learn from the father? Had Abraham rehearsed this story to Isaac? If so, Isaac missed the lesson. Isaac followed his father's example. As a parent, God calls you to set a good example for your children to follow *(Proverbs 10:1; 13:1; 15:20).* King David may have failed to discipline his son Amnon's sexual promiscuity because David was guilty of the same weakness *(I Samuel 11:4; 13:22).* David is one of the godliest men in Scripture. Because of this, his sin with Bathsheba stands out like a lump of coal in a large snow bank. Perhaps David would not punish Amnon's sin because of his own guilt, but he was still responsible to correct his son's sin of which he too was guilty. Remember that your reputation is a part of your life your children are watching and listening to you more than you might imagine. What impressions are you creating in the minds of your children today? What do you need to transform into a positive impression? Are you neglecting to correct a mistake in your child's life because of the guilt you feel in making that mistake in yours?

❑ *My actions are being followed imitators*—Life is a race. Life is also like a highway with others always in front of and behind you. You are following some example of those you follow. Others are following yours. It has been said that people seldom improve when they have no other model but themselves to copy. Whether you want to or

> *Our deeds still travel with us from afar, and what we have been makes us what we are.*
>
> ✺

not, you are helping to shape lives of those who watch you. *"Clear the path for long-distance runners so no one will trip and fall, so no one will step in a hole and sprain an ankle" (Hebrews 12:13).* Whose life are you making better today? Who may be watching you as an example? Who will those people become because of you?

❑ *My influence will remain when I am gone*—Your influence doesn't stop when you die. The lives you touch also touch other lives, and the influence passes on. Because of the influence of one godly king, God spared Jerusalem *"…for David's sake…"* nearly three hundred years after the king's death *(II Kings 19:34; 20:5-6).* The influences of a first century carpenter, a tax collector, a physician, a tentmaker, and a handful of fishermen have changed the world and given us our New Testament. Are you investing in the life of someone who will outlive you? What are you investing in them? Will you be pleased when you stand before God someday, and He tells you of every influence you ever had? And never forget the millions of souls throughout the world that have been brought to Christ by the influence of a faithful Sunday School teacher. Think about it. You may never know how far your influence will reach.

Power Points:

➤ Do you think Joseph had any idea of the influence he was having in Egypt?

> ➤ Why did Joseph seem to have more influence in Egypt than he had back home?

Reflection section:

❑ We are put in this world to live for God and others. Many whom we will never know are watching our life, and we influence them for good or bad. Our influence does not stop there. Those whom we immediately influence will continue to influence others, and only heaven will reveal the extent of one godly life.

❑ Right now, know that your godly life is making a difference—even if you cannot see it yet! Know that the world is better because you are in it!

❑ What do you think is your greatest accomplishment in life up to now?
_____

❑ Live and work each day as though you were influencing more people than you might think, for you undoubtedly are. Like Joseph, influence often begins in the immediate household, and reaches far beyond.

❑ What are three things you want people to remember you for when you are gone? _____

❑ Who has been the greatest influence on your life? Were they great, or just ordinary like most of us? Do not feel that it is necessary to be great to influence greatly.

❑ Who are you influencing in your workplace?

❑ Can people also learn from *negative* influences in their lives? How?

❑ Who might hold you in particularly high esteem due to your influence on them? Is this fair?

❑ Finish this sentence: "If I have a few 'rough edges' that God needs to smooth, they would include _____"

My Personal Growth Journal—

❑ Call the three most influential people in your life, and tell them: "Thank you for making a difference in my life."

❑ List three things that you see happening in your world that you think are wrong in God's eyes. Decide how you can help effect a change in at least one of them.

❑ Ask five friends, *"What is a Christian?"* Listen to their responses. Anything they say a Christian *does* is not a definition of a Christian. Explain to them that salvation is by God's grace alone. Your influence may make a difference in their eternal life or death.

I'd Rather See a Sermon

I'd rather see a sermon than hear one any day.
I'd rather one should walk with me than merely show the way.
The eye's a better pupil and more willing than the ear.
Fine counsel is confusing, but examples always clear.
I soon can learn to do it, if you'll let me see it done.
I can see your hands in action, but your tongue too fast may run.
And the lectures you deliver may be very fine and true,
But I'd rather get my lesson by observing what you do.
For I may misunderstand you and the high advice you give,
But there's no misunderstanding how you act and how you live.

—*Unknown*

~ Chapter 5 ~

Personal Choice: "The Principle of Effective Decision-Making"

As time went on, his master's wife became infatuated with Joseph and one day said, "Sleep with me" He wouldn't do it. He said to his master's wife, "Look, with me here, my master doesn't give a second thought to anything that goes on here—he's put me in charge of everything he owns. He treats me as an equal. The only thing he hasn't turned over to me is you. You're his wife, after all! How could I violate his trust and sin against God?" (Gen. 39:7-9)

The Joseph story....

Joseph was human just like you and me. He had the passions and emotions of any seventeen-year-old boy. When Potiphar's wife tried to entice him to sleep with her, Joseph could have come up with many excuses to do so. He was far from home, he deserved a break, and everybody was doing it, weren't they? Why should he turn down her advances? After all, who would believe the denial of a slave if he spoke the truth anyway? Why not simply give in to natural desires—just this once? Surely, God would forgive him. Joseph made the decision not to sin against God. He refused to commit sexual sin with Potiphar's wife. He refused to betray Potiphar's trust. Joseph ran from the woman and never looked back. In the process, she caught him by his garment and told all who would listen that Joseph had raped her. Joseph would be falsely accused, but he could answer every charge with innocence. His decision not to violate the trust of his master or the God of his conscience was a decision of character. A small decision with truly great implications.

Principle Truth: *Every decision has consequences that affect not only you, but also others. Decide carefully.*

I often tell my students *"big doors swing on small hinges."* Sometimes small decisions can direct much larger consequences. A decision here or there in life can transform a life. Sometimes many lives.

We all make decisions every day. Some of our decisions involve nothing more than what we will eat, or what clothes we will wear. Some decisions are more important, such as family, relationships, and business. Which job we take, or whether or not something we do might be wrong, are vitally important decisions. Often, decisions we make involve not just ourselves, but others as well. For example, as parents, many decisions we make affect our children. Other decisions affect those we work for and with in our place of employment.

> The measure of a man's real character is what he would do if he knew he would never be found out.
>
> —Thomas Macaulay

Every decision involves a consequence. We hope the consequences of our decisions will be positive—not only on our own lives, but also the lives of others. Sometimes the consequences of our actions are not vital to our well-being. Sometimes the consequences of our actions affect lives forever. Whatever the consequences, we must bear the responsibility for our actions. Even small decisions can modify the future forever. Many times, we do not have sufficient time to think before we act. In such cases, it is best if we are prepared morally and spiritually in case we must fall upon the integrity into which our character has been molded.

Joseph began his life as a servant in Potiphar's house and faced the consequences of a personal decision that changed not only his life, but also the lives of Potiphar, Potiphar's wife, and eventually everyone in Egypt. His decision was based upon his principles and resulted in his refusal to sin against his God. Joseph knew the importance of wise decision-making skills and understood that consequences of his actions affected not only his present situation, but also his future. Joseph knew his actions affected not only himself, but also others.

> Common sense is the knack of seeing things as they are, and doing things as they ought to be done.
>
> —Harriet Beecher Stowe

Have you considered the importance of decisions you will be making today? While your decisions may not determine the fate of nations, they *will* result in consequences. Think before you act today. Small decisions can result in great consequences, and consequences may affect others. For example, a person who drinks and drives may think he affects only himself...until there is an accident. Sexual sins are private sins...until sexually transmitted diseases affect the child during a woman's pregnancy. A private moment by a public figure in an ill-advised place can destroy a career. Big doors do swing on small hinges. All too often, secret sins have public consequences.

Be as wise in your decision-making skills as preparation will allow you. Wise decisions are not guarantees of success, but poor ones certainly increase the odds of failure. Before you make a decision of consequence today, ask yourself the following questions which will lead you to wise decision-making:

❑ *How will God feel if I do this?*—Joseph was most concerned that his action would be a sin. A sin against God, but also, against himself. Before you act, be sure it is not a sin against God. We have all seen the WWJD bracelets. They are a constant reminder to think before you act, and ask yourself *'what would Jesus do?'* But how are you supposed to know this? You must study what God says in the Word. Paul tells us *to study the Word so that we won't be ashamed when we stand before its Author someday (II Timothy 3:16)*. Do you have the mind of Christ through diligent Bible study? *(Cp. I Corinthians 2:16)* Do you need to make a more concerted effort to study God's Word? We are instructed to walk as Christ walked *(I John 2:6)*. Would Christ do what you are considering, or go where you are planning?

❑ *How will I feel if I do this?*—Joseph never made a decision that violated his conscience, character, or integrity. If you do this, how will your conscience feel? Does this decision violate any aspect of your morality? If this decision were the headlines in tomorrow's newspaper, how would you feel? What is your intuition telling you? What is your gut feeling? The best rule of thumb: when in doubt, *don't*.

❑ *Is this even necessary?*—Sometimes just having the *opportunity* to do something doesn't mean it is necessary that we do it *(I Corinthians 6:12; 10:23)*. While it may be OK to do this, is it truly necessary to do it at all? Are you majoring on a minor concern and wanting to decide something you don't really need to decide on? Is this decision *that* important?

❑ *Is this the right time to make this decision?*—Joseph understood the urgency of storing grain before the famine came upon Egypt. Have you made proper preparation to make this decision? Have you gathered enough information to analyze the decision objectively?

❑   *Could there be a better alternative to this decision?*—Would waiting be detrimental to making this decision, or would it allow more time for a better decision? Decisions made in haste are seldom the best decisions.

> *In any moment of decision, the best thing you can do is the right thing, the next best thing is the wrong thing, and the worst thing you can do is nothing.*
>
> —Theodore Roosevelt

❑   *Am I the right person to make this decision?*—Are your skills suited to making this decision, or benefiting from what results from making it? Do the merits of this decision benefit, or deviate from, your goals in life? Would an objective observer tell you that doing this will truly achieve what you think it will?

❑   *Is my reason for doing this sound?*—In wanting to do this, ask yourself "why?" Is it going to bring glory to God? What is your motive in this action? Are you doing this selfishly, or for others? Are you being influenced by the proper people in making this decision? If you can't offer God the action to bring Him glory, you probably shouldn't do this. Be sure doing this is not merely a self-serving means to feed your own pride. *"Whether, then, you eat or drink or whatever you do, do all to the glory of God" (I Corinthians 10:31 NASB).*

❑   *Have I thought about the consequences of doing this?*—Joseph measured the consequences of his temptation and realized he would lose all trust Potiphar had for him. He counted the cost of what would happen. Have you thought about what may happen down the road in your life—and the lives of others—if you do this? *"For which one of you, when he wants to build a tower, does not first sit down and calculate the cost...?" (Luke 14:28 NASB)* Also, have you formulated a *"plan B"* in case this decision does not work out?

❑   *Will doing this hurt my witness to others?*—Joseph loved Potiphar. Certainly he hoped that someday Potiphar might come to know the Hebrew God. Joseph did not want to harm his own witness to his master. When others hear of what you're about to do, will they still respect you? Will they respect what you tell them about God? Will this decision affect what you want others to believe about you? Will this affect your relationship with other Christians? *"Among the weak in faith I become weak like one of them, in order to win them. So I become all things to all people, that I may save some of them by whatever means are possible"* (I Corinthians 9:22 GNT; Cp. I Corinthians 8:6-13; Romans 14:13).

❏ ***Will doing this cause others to sin?***—People are watching you. Many people that you don't even know respect you. To many, you are the example of what a Christian should be. Even if you are a mature Christian and know what you want to do is OK with God, think about others who are weaker in conscience than you are. If there is a chance your action could cause them to violate their conscience, you probably shouldn't do this. *"If an unbeliever invites you to a meal and you decide to go, eat what is set before you, without asking any questions because of your conscience. But if someone tells you, "This food was offered to idols," then do not eat that food, for the sake of the one who told you and for conscience' sake—that is, not your own conscience, but the other person's conscience"* (I Corinthians 10:27-29 GNT).

Power Points:

➤ How did Joseph know giving in to Potiphar's wife's advances would have been wrong?

➤ Did Potiphar realize what his wife was up to? Did he believe her? Had she done this before?

➤ What might Joseph's brothers have done in the same situation?

Reflection Section:

❏ Have you ever been in a situation such as Joseph's? How did you respond? Why?

❏ Have you ever handled a situation poorly? How would you handle it differently now?

❏ What did you *learn* from that poorly handled situation?

❑   Do you know your Bible well enough to understand what God thinks about certain right and wrong actions?

❑   What are the five most important decisions you ever made? Why did you choose these?

❑   How were you influenced in these decisions? How many of them did you *pray* about?

❑   Ask yourself how your responses in decision-making will affect the distant, as well as the immediate, future.

❑   Prepare yourself with strong convictions of right and wrong as Joseph did, just in case your decision-making requires an immediate response rather than proactive consideration.

❑   Do not second-guess yourself. If you have acted in the most proper manner you were able, do not let "what if…" drain your resources that might be better used later on.

❑   *"Large doors swing on small hinges."* How does this quote relate to decision-making?

❑   *"I am not a role-model, nor do I want to be. The responsibility is simply too great."* Do you agree or disagree with this statement?

❑   "The worst thing about improper sexual conduct is the risk of disease." Would your children agree or disagree with this statement?

My Personal Growth Journal—

❑   Write down the three tempting situations that it would be most difficult for you to run from. List the right and wrong ways you should handle those opportunities to sin if they happened. Be prepared to make a wise decision if they do!

~ Chapter 6 ~

The Danger of Complacent Success: "The Principle of the Little Foxes"

As time went on, his master's wife became infatuated with Joseph and one day said, "Sleep with me." (Genesis 39:7)

The Joseph story....

New life. New country. Joseph had settled into his new lifestyle in Egypt. Potiphar had entrusted everything in his house to Joseph, and God had blessed the household for Joseph's sake. Certainly, he wished for his home and family back in Canaan. What had become of his old father Jacob? What did he know of the truth regarding the sin Joseph's brothers had committed? Joseph missed Canaan. Nevertheless, at least for the time being, it seemed that God was working things out for Joseph's good. Nevertheless, even modest success brings with it the danger of complacency. It came to Joseph. It came by way of the deep valley of sexual temptation, resulting in charge of rape from Potiphar's wife. Though Joseph had remained sinless, because of the false accusations of an evil woman, this young man's life would never be the same.

Principle Truth: You are most susceptible to misfortune when you rest in the small successes of life and drift from dependence upon God.

The *Sports Illustrated* curse. A supposed curse of misfortune befalls any athlete whose face graces the cover of *Sports Illustrated*. For example, when former heavyweight boxing champion Mike Tyson was featured, he was upset in his next fight. Basketball teams often lose games they are supposed to win after they are featured on the cover of *Sports Illustrated*. It has been said that many athletes actually fear the supposed honor that comes with the success of being featured on this national publication.

Mike Tyson was the heavyweight champion of the boxing world in 1990. He was devastating in his string of decisive victories over quality opponents. *Sports Illustrated* featured Mike Tyson's bout against a heavily underdog boxer few had followed. The fighter's name was Buster Douglass. If there was an absolute certainty on the day of the fight, it was the certainty of victory for Mike Tyson, and Tyson told the world so. Twenty-four hours later, Buster Douglass had decisively defeated the world's greatest boxer. Later, someone wrote concerning Tyson: "The arrogance of 'absolute' often brings the embarrassment of 'impossibility.'" The *Sports Illustrated* curse had struck again.

> *When success turns a man's head, he's facing failure.*
>
> ✎✎

Kobe Bryant was the heir apparent to Michael Jordan as the most popular player in the NBA. At the age of twenty-four, he had become one of the wealthiest, most popular superstars in professional basketball. Numerous times he had appeared on the cover of *Sports Illustrated*. Then, in 2003—at the pinnacle of his career, came the charge of rape. His marriage, his career, his world were plunged into disarray.

While there is no accepted explanation for this phenomenon, it does illustrate the caution we would do well to observe when the little fox of complacent pride begins to nibble at the grapes of success that life may bring us. Pride is one of several "...*little foxes that spoil the vines*" (Song of Solomon of Solomon 2:15 KJV).

There is nothing wrong with success. It is when success makes us overly proud and complacent that the difficulty begins. Complacency is satisfaction resting on its laurels. The difficulty with success is that achievement is accompanied by pride. Like many athletes, we start to believe our success is due to our skills and talents alone. Like success, pride in itself is not wrong. Pride becomes wrong when it swells to proportions that elevate us instead of God. Through complacent pride, we become relaxed and self-sufficient. Eventually, self-sufficiency replaces our dependency on God, and our very success becomes our undoing. In the end, the same world system that exalted us brings down.

Sometimes God is the direct instrument of humbling the proud. Jim and Tammy Faye Bakker's *PTL Club* grew into one of the largest religious organizations in the world. Pride, complacency, and a sex scandal erupted in 1986, and Jim Bakker resigned in disgrace and was sent to prison. Within a few years, the *PTL* empire was no more. God hates pride and often allows troubles and difficulties to humble us.

> *Success is always temporary.*
>
> *When all is said and done, the only thing you have left is your character.*
>
> *—Vince Gill*

God wants us to be successful. Success is not always measured by monetary reward, however, and we must learn to appreciate the many ways God allows us to be successful. Sometimes success is merely the satisfaction of a job well done. Sometimes success is measured by the improvement in a quality of life—whether that life is ours—or the lives of others we have influenced. However, success can be deceiving. As a sly fox, success can cunningly lead us into complacency, and before we know it, we are prime targets—not only for others who would bring us down—but also for the foxes of life that seem to naturally gravitate to fruitful successes. We can and should take pride when God blesses us with measures of success. But beyond that, we should always remain on guard against the fox of elevated pride, which may follow. *"Whoever makes himself great will be humbled, and whoever humbles himself will be made great"* (Matthew 23:12 GNT).

Sometimes success just breeds difficulty in this world. Successful people often experience trouble for no apparent reason. It just might be that, like Joseph, an excess of pride is not the cause of difficulties. Trouble just came to Joseph because of his small degree of success. *"If you think you are standing firm you had better be careful that you do not fall"* (I Corinthians 10:12 GNT). Often the foxes of trouble seem to look for us for no reason at all. Even then, we must be on guard.

> *Luxury is the wolf at the door and its fangs are the vanities and conceits germinated by success. When an artist learns this, he knows where the danger is.*
>
> *—Tennessee Williams*

Joseph was now settled in Egypt. It seemed that God was working things for Joseph's good. Then came Potiphar's wife's charge of rape against Joseph. Joseph was not to blame for Potiphar's wife's false accusation, but it serves to illustrate that when things go *too* well, we would do well to guard against the world's foxes which can so easily turn our successes into failure.

❑ *Beware the fox of riches and prosperity*—Our world suffers from *affluenza*—the desire to be affluent, rich, and prosperous. Sometimes we misunderstand scripture and think that money is evil. God never says that. God says that the *love* of money is the root of all kinds of evil *(I Timothy 6:10)*. Money is evil only when it becomes the goal of our lust rather than the means of our sustenance. Wealth and prosperity are not wrong in themselves, but like the fox, they can be deceptive. God gives us sound advice about prosperity:

▪ *God is the one who decides who will be rich*—God, not chance, determines the riches and prosperity we have. *"All riches and wealth come from you. You rule everything by your strength and power; and you are able to make anyone great and strong" (I Chronicles 29:12 GNT).*

▪ *Don't seek to be rich*—How many times have you played the lottery hoping to win the millions of dollars? God tells us not to seek riches, for they will entrap us and lead us where we might not want to go. This does not make riches evil. Remember, it's not money, but the *love* of money that leads to evil. If God has made you wealthy and prosperous, give Him glory, and be content. If God has not made you rich, don't strive for it. Be content as you are. *"But those who want to get rich fall into temptation and are caught in the trap of many foolish and harmful desires, which pull them down to ruin and destruction" (I Timothy 6:9 NASB; Cp. Psalms 62:10; Proverbs 28:20).*

▪ *Riches will not satisfy you*—We think we would be happy if we could just have wealth. God says this is not true. *"...he is always working, never satisfied with the wealth he has" (Ecclesiastes 4:8 GNT).*

❑ *Beware the fox of sexual temptation*—Solomon was David's son and Israel's richest king. He was also the wisest man who ever lived. However, Solomon could not resist the temptations of foreign women. Like his father, Solomon too fell into sin at the peak of his success *(I Kings 11)*. Sexual temptation has been the undoing of many. Joseph understood this well. In the face of sexual temptation, Joseph ran away from it as fast as he could, and never waited for it to catch up. *"Flee also youthful lusts…" (II Timothy 2:22 KJV).* Put in the way of a hunter's maxim, it is better to shun the bait than to struggle in the snare. Joseph refused to sacrifice the pleasure of the immediate upon the altar of his future. Neither did Joseph call the adulterous advances of Potiphar's wife by another name in an attempt to justify it. Joseph called it what it was—*sin.* This fox will parade around in the cloak of acceptable names such as love, an affair, etc. This fox more than any other will tempt us at the edges of our strength, and plunge us into despair. James tells us to give in to this fox is spiritual suicide! *"But we are tempted when we are drawn away and trapped by our own evil desires. Then our evil desires conceive and give birth to sin; and sin, when it is full-grown, gives birth to death" (James 1:14-15 GNT).* Beware this sly fox! She will take you where you where you do not want to go! *"…she will take you down to the world of the dead; the road she walks is the road to death" (Proverbs 5:5 GNT; Cp. I Thessalonians 4:3-4).*

❑ *Beware the fox of desire*—Adam ruled over everything his eyes could see. He had everything he could possibly desire. Nevertheless, Satan tempted him with desire for just a little more. He promised secret wisdom *"God knows that the moment you eat from that tree, you'll see what's really going on. You'll be just like God, knowing everything…" (Genesis 3:5).* Adam surrendered to the deception and lost all his authority. The world does its best to deceive us, just as it did Adam and Eve. It shows us the paths that we think will lead to pleasure, power, and satisfaction. It dangles the gold and glitter of Hollywood in front of us and makes us think we won't be happy without it. The pleasures of the world reward us with diminishing returns. They tempt us with enticements first and seldom mention the consequences that can come after. The world puts its best face forward and saves the pain and heartache for later. Someone has said the world promises us cookies, but hands us an empty jar. The pleasures of the world are deceptive. Beware the fox of lust and desire! Don't follow the flashy signs it puts before you! Be satisfied with what God has given you. *"There is a way which seems straight before a man, but its end is the ways of death" (Proverbs 14:12 GNT).*

❑ *Beware the fox of pride*—God says He "resists the proud" *(James 4:6).* Often, the world's successes swell us with pride. Fame and power delude us. They cause us to confuse our priorities and misapply our praise. Instead of giving credit to God, we think the success is because of our talent and skill. *"First pride, then the*

> Egotism is the anesthetic that dulls the pride of stupidity.
> ❧

crash—the bigger the ego, the harder the fall" (Proverbs 16:18). *"Don't be so naive and self-confident. You're not exempt. You could fall flat on your face as easily as anyone else. Forget about self-confidence; it's useless. Cultivate God-confidence"* (I Corinthians 10:12). *"Pride lands you flat on your face; humility prepares you for honors"* (Proverbs 29:23). The fox of pride will lead you down the path of destruction *(Proverbs 16:18),* and Solomon says that, if pride and conceit are the attitude in which you live your life, your situation is pretty much hopeless *(Proverbs 26:12).* Always thank God for every blessing—right down to your daily food. Never presume on God's goodness to you. Give Him all the praise. In doing so, you will avoid any visit from the fox of pride *(cp. I John 2:16).*

Power Points:

➤ How would you explain the *Sports Illustrated* 'curse'?

➤ Why do you think God allowed the troubles Joseph endured to happen?

Reflection section:

❑ Which of the "little foxes" sneaks through your *'bewares'* most easily?

❑ What is the difference between being proud of an accomplishment and being proud *because* of one?

❑ Which of the "little foxes" would be the *hardest* and *easiest* for you to resist? Why?

❑ What are you having to go through because of one of the "little foxes"?

❑ How could you be *sure* you would not be affected in negative ways if you won the lottery?

❑ Learn to recognize and appreciate the small successes of each day. Thank God for them, and pray that they never make you complacent.

❑ Recognize the difference between *caution* and *fear* when successes occur, and be willing to share this principle with friends when the small victories in life come.

My Personal Growth Journal—

❑ Write down seven excuses Joseph could have offered if he had chosen to sin with Potiphar's wife.

~ Chapter 7 ~

Godly Contentment: "The Principle of Blooming Where You're Planted"

God was still with Joseph: He reached out in kindness to him; he put him on good terms with the head jailer. (Gen. 39:21)

The Joseph story....

Potiphar was informed of his wife's rape charge against Joseph. What would Potiphar do? Would he believe the slave to whom he had entrusted his home, or the wife to whom he had pledged allegiance? Because of Joseph's reputation, Potiphar did not kill Joseph for the charge of rape made against him. Potiphar did not appear to believe his wife's story that Joseph had made sexual advances toward her. Had she lied on other occasions? Did Potiphar have other reasons to be suspicious of his wife's fidelity? However he truly felt, Potiphar had to do something. He could not simply dismiss such a serious charge by his own wife against a mere slave. As a compromise, Potiphar sent Joseph to the Egyptian prison, where the young man would stay for many years. Surely, Joseph felt that being punished for something for which he was not guilty was most discouraging. In trying to do the right thing, he was made to suffer. In the deep and dark pit of discouragement, Joseph had no other choice but start his life over again. For the third time.

Principle Truth: God has a purpose in where He has placed you. Be satisfied and productive there, and do what you can to prepare for where He may take you.

We have all heard the expression: _"bloom where you're planted."_ It has also been said: _"be content wherever God has put you."_ This is often easier said than done. Let's face it; there are times when we would rather have a different lifestyle, a different job, maybe even a different life. Sometimes being content is frustrating, and we might even wish we were somebody else entirely.

I always wished I could be like Billy Graham. If God had just given me the audiences Billy Graham was given, maybe I too could become a great evangelist. But God put me in charge of shaping the lives of teenagers instead, and my work is no less important than Billy Graham's.

We've all wished that life could be fairer in the circumstances and situations it places us. However, over much of this, we have no control. God allows us to be where we are, and sometimes puts us in situations which He knows will refine us. Many times, where we are may not always be where we would choose to be. Joseph had gone from being Jacob's favored son to becoming a slave in Egypt. No sooner did Joseph advance to supervisor of his master's home than he was falsely accused of rape and put into an Egyptian prison. Nevertheless, God was still with Joseph, and the young boy realized he could only do his best wherever God put him. He must bloom where he was planted.

Contentment is not the same as satisfaction, however. Learning contentment does not always mean being satisfied with everything about where we are. How can we learn contentment? How can we truly _"bloom where we are planted"_?

> _Wealth consists not in having great possessions, but in having few wants._
>
> —_Epicurus_

Joseph learned contentment through faithful service. He kept busy in the charge of Potiphar's house and did not dwell on how far he was from home. Joseph also faithfully served the captain of the guard and helped make the jail a better environment for both himself and his fellow prisoners. Joseph also learned contentment through trusting God. Joseph understood that his God controlled even the circumstances that appeared to control him. Later, Joseph faithfully executed his office by utilizing good business-management skills throughout the famine. Joseph was content in his circumstances until He recognized God's hand in moving him from where he was.

But eventually God does move us. We should not be so content in our circumstances that we miss opportunities for betterment that God brings to us.

While Joseph was content through faithfully serving wherever he was, he also watched the movement of God's hand in giving him new opportunities,

Like Joseph, we must understand that wherever we are, and whatever may happen to us while we're there, God is still in control and allows us to be where we are for a reason. Joseph learned contentment through trusting God, and God eventually raised him to a high position in Egypt. We may think if God would just put us in a position of greatness as He did Joseph, we too would glorify Him. However, Joseph's greatness did not come without much difficulty that we might tend to overlook. That God elevated Joseph, however, does not mean He will always do the same for us. While it is true that if we are faithful over small things we prove we can be trusted with more (*Luke 16:10-12*), God does not always elevate us in this manner. God has promised us provision. He did not promise us prosperity. Our primary responsibility is doing what we can, to the best of our ability, wherever we are planted.

God may not always seem fair in the way He appoints tasks to us. Sometimes those we see as less qualified than ourselves are promoted ahead of us, and God sometimes appears to bring greatness to those we think are not as worthy as we are. But God does not always explain His reasoning to us. God tells us that He is sovereign in all His actions, and whatever He chooses to do will be right: *"But who are you, my friend, to talk back to God? A clay pot does not ask the man who made it, 'Why did you make me like this?' After all, the man who makes the pots has the right to use the clay as he wishes, and to make two pots from the same lump of clay, one for special occasions and the other for ordinary use"* (*Romans 9:20-21 GNT*).

In the same way, parents do not treat each of their children in exactly the same manner. Sometimes what's best for one child may not be best for another. Every child has different needs. A parent must recognize this, and what may appear unfair to some is actually the very best for the child. In the same way, God knows what's best for every one of His children. He only asks us to be content and bloom where He plants us, and be faithful over what He's given us.

Learning to bloom where we are planted involves understanding the true meaning of contentment. Contentment is not passive resignation. Contentment is not always based on the blessings of this world, but does require trusting God that like a loving Father, He will give us what's best for us.

❑   *Your contentment is not based upon money*—"Money may not buy happiness, but it certainly can finance the illusion!" Is this how you view financial success? Do you think you'd be happy with riches? Solomon was the wisest man who ever lived. God endowed him with both riches and wisdom. However, Solomon understood that true contentment did not depend on money, but on trust in God to provide his needs: "*...give me neither poverty nor riches! Give me just enough to satisfy my needs" (Proverbs 30:8 NLT)*. Of course, we all need enough money to survive. But *where is money on your priority list?* Would you trust God even if He took everything away from you? Joseph did.

❑   *Your contentment depends partly on others*—Joseph knew that part of his survival in the Egyptian prison would depend upon his relationship with the jailer. He knew that since God allowed him to be imprisoned through no fault of his own, God would care for him. But Joseph did his part too. He reached out to make peace and friendship in the situation where he was. He wanted contentment in his situation and realized he might have to make the first move. Joseph worked to offer kindness where God planted him. "*Work hard at living in peace with others" (I Peter 3:11 NLT)*. Make peace with others—even if you are dissatisfied with your current situation. This may require you to make the first move. Don't allow your disappointments to keep you from planting the seeds of kindness in the lives of others. As with Joseph, the very people to whom you show kindness may be the ones who help you out of your "prison."

❑   *Your contentment keeps you working*—Joseph started as nothing but a worker in the Egyptian jail. But he kept busy wherever God put him. We never see him sitting and waiting for God to deliver him. Joseph had faith in God, but Joseph put *feet* to his faith! Faith in God always results in *faithfulness* to God's service. We always find Joseph working so that God could work through him in bringing His plan to completion. Joseph sought out what he could do—for Potiphar, for the jailer, for the prisoners, for the

> *Every successful man I have heard of has done the best he could with conditions as he found them.*
>
> —Edgar Watson Howe
> ❧

Pharaoh. God expects you to be faithful in your service as you are trusting God. Joseph was faithful over everything he was given. He was faithful over his flocks, his dreams, his conscience, Potiphar, Potiphar's house and wife, the head jailer, the wine taster, the baker, his brothers, his father, his Pharaoh, and the people of Egypt. Joseph was faithful and served faithfully wherever he was. God uses you best when He finds you blooming where you're planted, whether that job is large or small. He knows how to use you as an important part of His larger plan *(I Corinthians 12:12-24)*. The first visitors to Bethlehem to visit the baby Jesus were not the kings who traveled hundreds of miles. The first visitors were the shepherds, who where doing exactly what they were called to do: *"...shepherds in that part of the country who were spending the night in the fields, taking care of their flocks" (Luke 2:8 GNT)*. Contentment keeps you working. Someone has said, "It's easier to steer a moving car." Likewise, God usually finds it easier to transplant us when we're already blooming! If you are unhappy in your present situation, remember Joseph in prison. If you feel your work is unimportant and never noticed, remember that the mighty oak tree begins as a small acorn. Your present job may not be your final job. *"Do not despise these small beginnings, for the LORD rejoices to see the work begin..." (Zechariah 4:10 NLT)*. Do your best, wherever you are, for as long as you are able, while keeping your eyes open for future opportunities. Be found faithful in doing what God has put you here to do *(Mathew 24:46)*. Trust God to move you in His time, and if you are found faithful in small things—as was Joseph—God will reward you greatly. *"Well done," he said; "you are a good servant! Since you were faithful in small matters, I will put you in charge of ten cities" (Luke 19:17 GNT)*.

❑   *Your contentment waits patiently*—Joseph was in the Egyptian jail for years, not months. Yet, Joseph knew how to wait patiently. He was just as faithful in trusting God in prison as he would be as governor. Joseph had learned the lesson of blooming where he was planted. It required many years for God to elevate Joseph from prisoner to vizier. God made Joseph wait while before God finished shaping Joseph into the man He wanted him to be. The patience Joseph learned 'perfected' him *(James 1:3-4)*. Waiting on God, Joseph patiently performed his duties wherever God allowed him to be. *"You should continue as you were when God called you" (I Corinthians 7:20 NLT)*. However, patiently waiting does not require you be perfectly satisfied. Being patient is accepting that God has a present and future plan for you, even if where you are isn't where you want to be. Like Joseph, you and I need to learn patience *(Hebrews 10:36)*. God did not promise learning patience would be easy. God did promised to strengthen you through the process *(Psalms 27:14; Isaiah 40:31)*, and for you not to not let the process weary you *(Galatians 6:9)*. Patience is trusting God today, not giving up on your hopes for tomorrow. Give God total dedication to your tasks today. Wait and watch for His hand to move you at the appropriate time.

❏ *Your contentment trusts God for everything*—When Joseph had done everything he could do, he trusted God for what he *couldn't* do. This type of trust is sometimes called *faith*. Faith is looking at things *future* with the same conviction you see things past, *realized*. Someone has said that faith is that which is *firmly anchored in trust and hope*. Trust and faith do not always understand what God is doing either. No doubt, Joseph wondered during many Egyptian evenings, what in the world God was doing. Joseph was guilty of no crime that should require him to go through what he was enduring. Did he think his situation was unfair? Joseph was just as human as you are. He had moments of doubt and discouragement just as you do. Joseph no doubt, became

> *Learn to be pleased with everything; with wealth, so far as it makes us beneficial to others; with poverty, for not having much to care for; and with obscurity, for being unenvied.*
>
> *—Plutarch*

just as weary as you are right now in trying to bloom where he was *planted (Gal. 6:9)*. Perhaps Joseph wondered if God would ever move in his life again. Sometimes your life seems to be going nowhere. You try to live for God, and it seems God doesn't even notice. However, as an old preacher once remarked: *"fret and worry only heats the engine; it never moves the wheels!"* As Joseph did, patiently trust what you cannot understand: *"Trust in the LORD with all your heart and do not lean on your own understanding. In all your ways acknowledge Him, and He will make your paths straight"* (Proverbs 3:5-6 NASB). Is God asking you to trust patiently right now as He perfects His plan for your life? Trusting God in faith is leaving Him with what's left when you've done everything you can. This is real contentment! *"Be satisfied with what you have. For God has said, 'I will never fail you. I will never forsake you'"* (Hebrews 13:5 NLT). *"For I can do everything with the help of Christ who gives me the strength I need"* (Philippians 4:11-13 NLT). As you trust God—blooming the best you are able wherever He's planted you—simply wait upon God *"...and having done all...stand"* (Ephesians 6:13 KJV).

Power Points:

➢   Why didn't Potiphar simply release Joseph? Why didn't he kill him?

➢   What would you have done if you had been Potiphar?

➢   What do you think ever became of Potiphar's wife?

➢   Why does God say money won't bring us happiness? Is He right?

➢   Was God unfair in making Joseph wait so long in the Egyptian prison?

Reflection Section:

❑   Are you unhappy in your job, your home situation, and your life in general? Are you there by choice? Are you there through circumstances that may or may not have been under your control? Is there something you can do to rectify your situation? If you've done all you can, wait and trust. Realize that God controls even your circumstances.

❑   As you look back over your life, are there things you are glad God *didn't* give you?

❑   Do you sometimes *honestly* feel God is 'out of control' regarding your life?

❑   Do you know someone where you work that is 'blooming where they're planted', but that might be able to advance with your help?

❑   Is God showing you indications He may be wanting you to consider a change in your life right now? How do you know? Is there a goal of yours that you know is being prepared ahead of you right now?

❑   Do what you can in your immediate situation. Work as though you were in the job you'd love most, and God was your immediate supervisor.

My Personal Growth Journal—

❑ Read *Psalms 37* and *Psalms 62* today and list the ways and reasons David trusted God.

❑ List five things Joseph was faithful over. How did one thing lead to another?

❑ Examine Goethe's prescription for contentment below. In the course of the next nine days, strengthen your ability to accept each one.

> *Health enough to make my work a pleasure.*
> *Wealth enough to support my needs.*
> *Strength enough to battle with difficulties and overcome them.*
> *Grace enough to confess my sins and forsake them.*
> *Patience enough to toil until I accomplish some good.*
> *Charity enough to see some good in my neighbor.*
> *Love enough to move me to be useful and helpful to others.*
> *Faith enough to make the things of God real to me.*
> *Hope enough to remove all anxious fears concerning the future.*
> *—Goethe*

~ Chapter 8 ~

I Am Third: "The Principle of Others First"

When Joseph arrived in the morning, he noticed that they were feeling low. So he asked them, the two officials of Pharaoh who had been thrown into jail with him, "What's wrong? Why the long faces?" (Gen. 40:6-7)

The Joseph story....

Joseph was languishing in an Egyptian prison for a crime that he did not commit. Egyptian prisons were known for their bleakness, and Joseph must have wondered if even his God had forgotten him. But Joseph did not despair. He was made keeper of the prison and again entrusted with a measure of responsibility. With him in the prison were two officers of the Pharaoh's court, the king's wine taster and baker. They too had been accused of crimes and sentenced to punishment. One night, the two men had strange dreams that they were unable to understand. In the morning, they awakened with looks of anguish upon their faces. Joseph noticed. Instead of dwelling upon the unfairness of his own circumstance, Joseph concerned himself with the welfare of his fellow prisoners and the frustration they shared regarding their visions in the night.

Principle Truth: You will accomplish more with others in two weeks trying to meet their needs than you will in two years trying to have them meet yours.

Gayle Sayers was the premier running back for the Chicago Bears several decades ago. He wrote a popular book entitled *I Am Third*, which was made into an even more popular movie *Brian's Song*. The book's title reflected Gayle Sayers' philosophy of priority in life. His God came first. His family and friends came second. He came third.

Someone has said that the priority to which we assign our concerns in life define the meaning of the word "joy": Jesus first, others second, and yourself last. While this may be true, it is easier said than done. Sometimes life becomes heavy, and our own difficulties often weigh us down. Sometimes we wonder how we can go on, and the problems of others do not seem nearly as important as ours. Let's be honest, sometimes the help God wants us to offer others in need seems more of a burden on us than an opportunity for virtue. In sharing the burdens of others however, our burdens are made lighter.

Joseph sat apparently forgotten in the Egyptian prison. Joseph had tried to live righteously. He had tried to do the right thing. Yet, here he was, imprisoned with two of the Pharaoh's servants. Joseph had every reason to pout and complain over his unfair treatment. Instead, he expressed concerned for the problems of others.

While teaching the Joseph story to my Bible class, I made a point one evening to emphasize all the noble characteristics he displayed in his difficult circumstances. As I was finishing, one student voiced a frustration that Joseph seemed almost *too* noble. He personified a standard, the student continued, almost impossible to measure up to.

Even if we may not always show the nobility of Joseph, the examples from his life give us direction we would do well to follow. One example is how Joseph arranged the priorities of his life. Joseph's priority in placing the concern for others ahead of his own concerns opened a great door of opportunity for him later. Because Joseph was concerned for others—even when his circumstances were difficult—God blessed Joseph with blessings beyond his fondest dreams.

God has not promised to bless us with the greatness He bestowed upon Joseph. Nevertheless, genuine concern for others brings with it at the very least, the blessing of personal satisfaction. To practice the principle of "others first" will reward you richly—not just in your own life, but as the lives of others are touched by the care you invest.

How can you invest in the lives of others? God will give you many opportunities to put others first today.

- ❑   *Lift in encouragement*—Living the selfless life sometimes is as simple as speaking an encouraging word at the proper time. Solomon tells us *"A word fitly spoken is like apples of gold in settings of silver" (Proverbs 25:11 NKJV)*. Jonathan was the son of King Saul, and had God not intervened would have been the next king of Israel. David was Jonathan's friend, despite the fact that Saul hated David and tried to kill him several times. God had decreed that David—not Jonathan—would be king. This put Jonathan in a difficult situation. Not only was he at odds with his father, he was also bound by friendship to the man who would replace him as the next king. Despite knowing that his future did not hold the promise that David's future held, Jonathan faithfully encouraged David in his flight from Saul *(I Samuel 23:16-18)*. David never forgot Jonathan's sacrificial encouragement and blessed Jonathan's family after Jonathan died. Could you be such an encourager today? Call someone that may be going through a difficult sickness or situation. Encourage them with words of support. Don't quote scripture to them. Tell them how much they have meant to you. Offer them specific rather than generic support. *"So speak encouraging words to one another. Build up hope so you'll all be together in this, no one left out, and no one left behind. I know you're already doing this; just keep on doing it" (I Thessalonians 5:11)*.

- ❑   *Learn to forgive*—Selflessness does not hold a grudge. Joseph was forgotten in the Egyptian prison by the wine taster who promised to put in a good word to the Pharaoh. Many years would go by before Joseph himself stood before the Pharaoh. In the king's court, Joseph would have seen the wine taster. But we are never told of Joseph reminding the officer of his broken promise. Are you as willing to forgive, as you are to accuse? Joseph knew how to forgive: *"See that no one pays back wrong for wrong, but at all times make it your aim to do good to one another and to all people" (I Thessalonians 5:15 GNT)*. Is there someone who has hurt or forgotten you, or has caused you to hold a grudge? First, forgive them in your heart. You should be willing to forgive that person, for much more has been forgiven you *(Matthew 18:21-35)*. Secondly, do something nice for them as an expression of this forgiveness. *"Instead, do what the Scriptures say: 'If your enemies are hungry, feed them. If they are thirsty, give them something to drink, and they will be ashamed of what they have done to you. Don't let evil get the best of you, but conquer evil by doing good'" (Romans 12:2-21 NLT).* This may not be easy, but it is key to living the selfless life.

❑ *Lift a burden*—Putting others first means that sometimes we need to share the load. Do you remember when someone shared your load when life's burdens became heavy? Is there someone you know that is experiencing an extremely busy time in his or her life right now? Offer to share the load by running an errand, doing a favor, or just letting them vent! Shift your center of gravity from *self* to *service*. Put yourself in another's place right now, and think what you'd appreciate someone doing for you. Let this be a prompt on what you might do for someone else. Lift someone's burden. Share a load. *"Bear ye one another's burdens, and so fulfill the law of Christ" (Galatians 6:2).*

❑ *Lend an ear*—I have learned in many years of dealing with teenagers that sometimes the most selfless type of help I can offer is to simply listen. To do nothing more than to listen can help another to solve their own problems and reach proper conclusions. You do not always have to have those "golden words of wisdom." Often, just lending a shoulder for another to lean on or cry on is important. Sometimes lending an ear is the best help you can offer. Learn how to listen. Do you find it easier to offer advice than listen to an expression? Try lending an ear. Look directly at the person you are listening to. Try to feel what they feel. Fitly spoken words are golden. But sometimes, so is silence: *"Indeed I waited for your words; I listened to your reasoning, while you searched out what to say" (Job 32:11 NKJV).*

Power Points:

➢ Does Joseph seem almost *too* noble? Why? Why not?

➢ How do you think Joseph felt about Potiphar as he sat in jail for committing no crime? How would *you* feel about Potiphar?

Reflection Section:

❏ What is the most distressing circumstance you face right now? Try putting it aside and calling a friend or acquaintance that you know is going through their own trial.

❏ When you say to someone: "How are you?", you *really* mean _____

❏ Sometimes the best thing to say to someone who is distressed is *nothing*. Agree? Disagree? Why?

❏ Do something completely unexpected for someone else today. Pay a compliment when you normally wouldn't.

❏ When was the last time you touched another person's life in a way that made a difference to you *and* them?

❏ Put others first for a week, and give God an opportunity to bless you as he blessed Joseph.

My Personal Growth Journal—

❏ Call someone up right now that you know is in fact hurting. Encourage them as Joseph encouraged.

❏ Send one card to someone who may be grieving right now over a sickness, death, or some other type of loss.

❏ Reflect back upon someone in your life who has benefited you in some way. Is there something you might do for them today that would totally surprise them and make you an answer to prayer?

~ Chapter 9 ~

Using your Gifts: "The Principle of God's Multicolored Garden"

"...I was holding Pharaoh's cup; I took the grapes, squeezed them into Pharaoh's cup, and gave the cup to Pharaoh." Joseph said, "Here's the meaning. The three branches are three days." (Gen. 40:11-12)

The Joseph story....

Dreams were considered important in ancient Egypt, and the men's inability to discern their meanings concerned them greatly. Joseph made their concern his concern. Despite all of the unfair treatment he had endured at the hands of his brothers, Potiphar's wife, and even his master who sentenced him to prison, Joseph put the concerns of others ahead of his own. Now was an opportunity for Joseph to use his gift of dream interpretation, and God revealed to him the meaning of the disturbing visions. Joseph interpreted the dreams of both the wine taster and the baker. While his interpretation concerning the baker was not good news, Joseph faithfully explained the meaning of the dream as God revealed it to him. His interpretations were proved correct by events that soon came to pass. Joseph correctly predicted that the wine taster would be found innocent and released from prison, but that the baker would be found guilty and executed. Because Joseph faithfully exercised his gift of dream interpretation in his prison setting, opportunity would, in time, present him with an audience before another Egyptian disturbed by dreams—the great Pharaoh himself. In interpreting the dreams of his Pharaoh, the two nations of Israel and Egypt would never be the same.

Principle Truth: God has equipped you to serve Him as He has equipped no one else, and you will be responsible for what He has given you.

All Christians have gifts. A gift of the Spirit glorifies God and others and may or may or may not use a talent. A talent generally edifies the user and others and does not depend on a gift. A gift works by love. A talent may not. God gives us individual gifts and talents to use in His service. God wants us to discover our gift and use it. As we offer our talents to God, He is able to perfect them into the spiritual service that brings satisfaction to us and glory to Him.

One day a little boy went with his mother to a concert hall where she warned him not to touch anything while she ran a brief errand. The boy looked on stage and saw the grand piano. Overwhelmed with curiosity, he sat down at the piano and began to play the only song he knew: *Twinkle Twinkle Little Star*. As he continued to play, the Maestro entered. The great man quietly walked up behind the boy and whispered, "No matter what, keep playing what you're playing." The boy obediently continued to play as the Maestro reached around him, adding chords and tune with his right hand, and counter melody with his left. The people listening were amazed at the beauty of what they were hearing. When the performance was complete, they broke into spontaneous applause. Bewildered, the boy whispered to the Maestro: "But it was only a simple piece." "Yes," said an onlooker overhearing the comment, "but in the hands of the Maestro, the humblest effort becomes a masterpiece."

Like that small boy, we must use our gifts and talents to the best of our abilities. It is the accompaniment of the heavenly Maestro that transforms our humble efforts into masterpieces. Our job is to do what we can with what we have. He does the rest.

God gives all His children gifts. He does not give all His children the same gifts. God knows our abilities and desires and equips us accordingly. The variety of God's gifts and their use in His service is much like a beautiful, multi-colored garden of flowers—or a symphony of diverse instruments—through which God accomplishes His will through the body of Christ. Every gift is as unique as it is necessary in the make up of the whole. To waste your gift is to diminish the fellowship of *all* believers. To not use your gift is to be the butterfly—transformed from the lowly worm, yet choosing to fold his wings and crawl again.

> *What you are is God's gift to you; what you do with yourself is your gift to God.*
>
> ❧

As believers utilize their gifts and talents, God is glorified through the teaching of His Word, the administration of His churches, and the comfort of

His children. While all Christians have spiritual gifts, all believers are not given the same gifts. God assigns His gifts according to His own purposes—not merely for the gifts themselves, but also for the one to whom such gifts are given. Sometimes our gifts are revealed to us early in life. Sometimes they're not.

Bezalel had always been a skilled artisan. He could work with wood and metals better than anyone in Israel. Later in his life, Bezalel was called by God to help build the tabernacle. God created a gift for His service through the talent Bezalel had always possessed *(Exodus 31:3)*.

Joseph was given the gift of interpreting dreams. He used his gift faithfully to interpret the dreams of the prisoners, as well as the Pharaoh's. God equipped Joseph with this gift knowing that Joseph would someday faithfully exercise it to save two nations. Joseph knew from his youth what his gift was, but Joseph learned only after many years the ultimate purpose in being given his gift. Like Joseph, we may not know exactly when we may be called upon to use our gifts, but God knows just when and where to put us so that our gifts and talents can be best utilized to His glory. *"A man's gift makes room for him and brings him before great men" (Proverbs 18:16 NASB).*

The main purpose of the gifts and talents given to us is primarily to benefit others, not just ourselves. Despite the many difficulties Joseph experienced in Egypt, God provided the precise opportunity for Joseph to use his skills to serve others. Because he was not afraid to utilize his gift, Joseph—and all those he met—was blessed.

We must trust that God will do the same for us, if only we are willing to utilize our gifts and talents as Joseph did. As we bless others through our gifts and talents, we lend color to the garden of God's work upon the earth.

❑ *Does every Christians have a gift?*—Yes. All God's children are given a gift of the Holy Spirit. Your gift may work through a talent you were born with. On the other hand, it may work apart from talents. Remember—this gift is from God, through the Spirit, to you. *"God has given each of us the ability to do certain things well" (Romans 12:6 NLT).* *"And now, dear brothers and sisters, I will write about the special abilities the Holy Spirit gives to each of us, for I must correct your misunderstandings about them" (I Corinthians 12:1 NLT).*

❑ *Can I choose my gift?*—No. God chooses which gift, to whom it is given, and how many gifts each person receives *(James 1:17)*. Some Christians may have more than one gift. *"It is the one and only Holy*

Spirit who distributes these gifts. He alone decides which gift each person should have" (I Corinthians 12:11 NLT).

❑ *How can I know my gift?*—The gifts are listed in *Romans 12, I Corinthians 12, Ephesians 4, and I Peter 4:10-11.* The gifts include teaching, encouraging, giving, and leadership. In identifying your gift, ask yourself the following questions:

- What do I seem to be able to do naturally, with little effort?
- What have others mentioned to me that I do extremely well?
- What do I find I truly enjoy doing when I get the chance?
- What makes me feel the most satisfied when I do it?

❑ *Why did God give me my gift?*—Your gift is to God's glory and for the benefit of *others,* not yourself. Yes, you may feel especially satisfied when you exercise your gift, and using your gift is helping you become the best you can be. But if your gift isn't bringing benefit to others, it may not be a spiritual gift. Is your gift drawing attention to the gift, or the *Giver?* God's gifts are given through the power of His Spirit, and the Spirit never draws attention to Himself *(John 16:13).* By this, you can know if your gift is from God. *"A spiritual gift is given to each of us as a means of helping the entire church"* (I Corinthians 12:7 NLT; Cp. 12:18).

❑ *How do I use my gift?*—You use your gift through using your gift! Since it is given for the benefit of others, exercise your gifts whenever you are able. *"Do not neglect the spiritual gift that is in you, which was given to you when the prophets spoke and the elders laid their hands on you. Practice these things and devote yourself to them, in order that your progress may be seen by all"* (I Timothy 4:14-15 NLT).

❑ *What should I remember about my gift?*—Your gift is not for your private use. Your gift is not to flaunt. As Joseph understood about his dreams, your gifts are to be exercised in humble service to God. God will open the door for you to use them. Be thankful that God can use you to perform His work. Although God will not take your gift from you *(Romans 11:29),* you are responsible to use it. If you neglect the gift in His service *(I Timothy 4:14),* God can use another means to accomplish the same plan *(Esther 4:14).* God's plans cannot be frustrated *(Daniel 4:35),* but our blessings can be forfeited. Whatever services your gift is geared toward, use your gifts to the best of your ability and leave the rest to God.

❑ *Does God reward faithful use of my gift?*—Yes. But God does not judge the merits of service the same way we might. In the Parable of the Talents *(Matthew 25:14-30; Cp. Luke 19:17)*, we are given some telling insights into how God views the use and rewards of our gifts and talents.

- *First,* all the servants of the master were entrusted with *something.* No servant was left with nothing to invest in his master's service. God has given you at least one gift and expects you to use that gift in His service to the benefit of all His children *(cp. Romans 12:3-6).*

- *Second,* the master was more concerned with the *increase* on investment than with how much he left each servant. Maybe God has given you but one gift. One gift or many, God expects you to put His gift to work and return a "profit" on His investment in you. *"From everyone who has been given much, much will be required; and to whom they entrusted much, of him they will ask all the more" (Luke 12:48 NASB).* God knows your abilities and skills, and assigns your gift accordingly. God will never gift you with something you have no desire or skill to perform. Are you a teacher? Teach! Did he entrust to you the gift of helps? Encourage and support others!

- *Third,* when the master returned, all servants whose investments returned *anything* were praised *equally.* The *amount* of that increase was not the issue. All the servants were also *equally happy* with their reward. The only reprimand from the master was addressed to the servant who buried his talent and showed the master no increase. God will not reward you any less for using your one gift than He will someone with greater capability to work in His service. This is hard for us to understand, but God does not always settle His accounts the way we might. You will be rewarded for *faithfulness* to service, not how much your service *achieved.*

- *Fourth,* the reward for faithful service was not rest, but *more responsibility!* Joseph had been faithful over every small opportunity he was given to serve. Because of his faithfulness, God did not give him rest. God blessed Joseph with charge over all Egypt!

God's rewards far exceed our work that earns them. While we may not understand this aspect of God's reward, we may be sure God is both good and fair in His accounting. He will reward you far beyond what you deserve *(cp. Luke 16:10-11; 19:12-26)*.

Power Points:

➤ How do you think Joseph felt interpreting the two dreams?

➤ Would you have told the baker that he was going to die? Why? Why not?

➤ How do you feel about dream interpreters and fortunetellers *today*?

➤ What is your gift of the Spirit? When was the last time you used it for others?

➤ How can you distinguish your gift from a natural talent?

➤ What do you think is the most unusual aspect of God's reward system?

Reflection Section:

❑ Discover what gifts and talents you have. Ask yourself what things you enjoy doing, and seem to do particularly well. Three things you feel you do *particularly* well are _____

❑ Three things I truly *enjoy* doing are _____

❑ I feel my three greatest gifts are _____

❑ *Why* do you feel this way? _____

❑ My three closest friends feel my three greatest gifts, talents, or abilities would be _____

❑ Find opportunities to use these skills, and having done all, fall upon God's wisdom to bring the remaining opportunities to you.

❑   Finally, as did Joseph, utilize those skills to the best of your ability. Having done your best with the gifts and talents God has given you, move on, and trust God *(Esther 4:16)*. You never know where God may lead you.

My Personal Growth Journal—

❑   Ask ten people who know you what they think are your three strongest areas from the list of the gifts mentioned in this chapter. What are strengths they agree on? Are you surprised?

~ Chapter 10 ~

Carpe Diem: "The Principle of Personal Responsibility"

"Only remember me when things are going well with you again—tell Pharaoh about me and get me out of this place." (Gen. 40:14)

The Joseph story....

Joseph correctly predicted that the wine taster would be released from the Egyptian prison and restored to Pharaoh's court. Joseph had been faithful to his conscience, his God, and those in his prison care. Surely, in gratitude to Joseph, the one man who could now help him would remember Joseph before the Pharaoh. Surely, because of his faithfulness and responsible attitude, Joseph too would soon be released from the prison. Counting on the wine taster's gratitude, Joseph asked the man to put in a good word for him in the king's court. But Joseph would be forced to wait far longer than he'd ever imagined.

Principle Truth: *God's sovereignty controls all His plans— including His sovereign decision requiring you to do everything you can to fulfill those plans.*

Have you ever heard someone say: *"If God wants me to do it, He'll make it happen and I won't need outside help."*? Too often, we forget that, while God can certainly work in spite of us, often He works *through* us and the people and circumstances we encounter. God wants us to have faith. He also wants us to put feet to our faith.

The ancient Greeks assigned everything that happened in the lives of men to fate. Fate worked apart from men, and humans were mere agents of divine will and whim. The Greeks left us the old maxim: *"The dice of the gods are loaded."*

Our God is not the God of fate or accident. God is sovereign and is never surprised nor defeated. While God can and does work apart from us to perform His will, He also works *through* us. The same God who controls all things also requires faithful service from us *(cp. Luke 12:41-48)*. Though God is sovereign, He often chooses to perform His sovereign will through our *personal* responsibility. In doing so, He allows us to experience both consequences and blessings from the choices we make.

Too often, we forget that an all-powerful God is also all-wise. He can do miraculous things beyond our control and efforts. However, God sometimes requires our actions to become a *part* of the things He does. Take prayer, for example. If God does what He desires apart from us, why does He instruct us to pray? Is He not able to act apart from our requests and give us what we need? Yes. But God prefers to act *through* our prayers. Why? So that we can glorify Him not just for providing the request, but also for listening to the prayers of His children.

> *How high I reach, how far I see; how much gets done—depends on me.*
>
> ❧❧

Personal responsibility is that part of God's purpose in the world that keeps us from being puppets which He mechanically operates. Scripture tells us that God's sovereignty *chooses* those whom He would save *(John 15:16,19; I Thessalonians 1:4; Romans 8:29-30,33; Ephesians 1:4; I Peter 1:1-2; Cp. Acts 9:15)*. Yet Scripture also tells us that we have a personal responsibility in this process too—we must *come (II Peter 1:10; Philippians 2:12; Hebrews 4:11; Cp. John 6:37 & 39)*.

While God is sufficient in Himself and does not need us in order to perfect His will, God has given us choices and opportunities in life, that we might be instruments of His design. For example, when Paul was aboard the ship that would take him to Rome, a great storm sprang up on the sea. An angel of God assured Paul that no lives would be lost *(Acts 16:22-24)*. God would spare every man on board. However, Paul insisted on personal responsibility of the sailors to accomplish that end: *"But Paul said to the army officer and soldiers, 'If the sailors don't stay on board, you have no hope of being saved'"* *(Acts 27:31 GNT)*. God used personal responsibility to perfect His will.

Because He has given us personal responsibility and personal choice, we cannot accuse God of leaving the world—and our lives in it—to chance. God works through purpose and design; He does not work through fate. God works through our actions and expects us to do everything within our power to bring to pass that which He will certainly accomplish.

Joseph understood the mysterious tension between God's sovereign control and his own personal responsibility. Although Joseph knew that God could deliver him from the Egyptian prison, Joseph also understood that he himself was responsible to use any proper leverage that might present itself to do the same. Although Joseph knew that God alone could save Egypt from the approaching famine, he also understood that God would work through the Pharaoh, and thus tells him *"Let Pharaoh do this..."* *(Genesis 41:34)*. Joseph would still require the people to do their part and come for the food *(Genesis 41:57)*.

Joseph did not hesitate to utilize his connection with the wine taster in securing an audience with the Pharaoh. Joseph understood what the business world refers to as *networking*. To use whatever advantage or favor we have at our disposal is not to *interfere* with God's plan for us. Sometimes, as Joseph discovered, it helps *fulfill* God's plan. To fully trust God is to realize that God may very well put someone in our path to be what the wine taster was to Joseph—an opportunity for advantage as repayment for favor well done. Joseph counted on the wine taster to mention his gift of dream interpretation; Joseph did not extol his own gifts to the Pharaoh. *"Don't call attention to yourself; let others do that for you"* *(Proverbs 27:2)*. Using honest leverage is an integral part of many employment scenarios today. To trust a good reference, or request a good word be put in for us, in no way diminishes our trust in God.

We cannot fully understand how God's sovereignty works through our free will. Our responsibility however, is to do what we can—the best that we can—and trust God for everything else. Put feet to your faith. Stand on God's sovereignty, but only after you have done all you can first. *"...And having done everything,...stand firm"* *(Ephesians 6:13 NASB)*. As you go through today, you will have many opportunities to exercise personal responsibility in performing God's will. What you do today will also affect others and the future that you and others may share. Take advantage of the opportunities God puts before you today, and don't forget to take advantage of the *advantages* which He may offer you.

❑ *I will trust as if everything depended on God*—Joseph could only hope to be released from prison through the grace of the Pharaoh. As a bound prisoner, Joseph could do nothing but pray for such grace. Even if you feel something is too small for God to care about, trust Him to lead you. Celebrate His sovereignty over His creation today!

❑ *I will work as if everything depended on me*—Joseph did everything within his power to seek release from prison. He trusted God, yes. But he also asked the wine taster to put in a good word for him with the Pharaoh. See today as your opportunity to give 110% to everything that comes your way. See yourself as your greatest resource! Visualize yourself working as if everything that comes your way is in need of your skill. Don't exhaust yourself, but dedicate the events of this day to your opportunities. Celebrate your abilities today! *(Cp. Esther 4:10-17)*

❑ *I will pray because God instructed me to*—As you go through today, pray and thank God that you are an instrument of His sovereignty and will! In doing this, you can then thank Him for answered prayers and trust Him by waiting for answers that must come later *(cp. Philippians 2:13)*.

❑ *I will clearly define my need and set my goal*—Without a goal, you have no target at which to shoot. Joseph's goal was his need was for the Pharaoh's assistance. His goal was for Pharaoh to *"…get me out of this place."* What is your need and what is your goal toward fulfilling it? Be specific! Are you having trouble goal-setting? Could it be that you're too concerned with past goals that did not work out as well as you'd hoped? Put the past behind you. Learn from it, but know that future goals are the key *"…the one thing I do, however, is to forget what is behind me and do my best to reach what is ahead. So I run straight toward the goal…" (Philippians 3:13-14 GNT)*. Finally, be sure your goal is realistic and achievable. Do not set goals which might be impossible for you to attain. This will only lead to frustration.

❑ *I will use my gifts and talents at every opportunity*—Joseph was given the gift of interpreting dreams. In prison, he utilized his gift by interpreting for the wine taster that he would be released from prison, and the baker that he would be executed. In looking towards his goal, Joseph continued to use his gifts. Joseph remained prepared to *act*—not just react. Joseph was what we call today *proactive*. It has been said that luck is opportunity plus preparation. Are you prepared to use your gifts for God when opportunity knocks? Are you proactive in making sure that others realize that you *have* these gifts? Are you practicing and refining your skills as you wait and work towards your goal? Promote your skills in the presence of others. Make yourself *remembered*.

❑ *I will sow the seeds of kindness toward others*—Joseph clearly did not help others in the prison just to curry favor from them. He showed acts of kindness because he knew it was the right thing to do. But Joseph also knew that these actions wouldn't hurt him later, either. King David never forgot the kindness shown to him by his best friend Jonathan. Jonathan risked his own father's anger in befriending David, and, long after Jonathan had died, David sought an occasion to bless his family *(II Samuel 9:1)*. Decide to plant kindness. Wear it all day today, for the whole world to see! *"So then, you must clothe yourselves with compassion, kindness, humility, gentleness, and patience" (Colossians 3:13 GNT)*. Are you going that extra mile for those you are in contact with? Are you taking a proactive approach and sowing little seeds of kind actions that can grow to benefit you someday? Make yourself *remembered as good*.

❑ *I will recognize the importance of timing*—Carpe Diem. Seize the day! Timing is everything. Joseph knew that the wine taster was about to be released from prison, just as Joseph had predicted for him. If he did not ask now, he might never get the chance. Joseph understood the importance of seizing the moment. He was decisive and proactive in making his request. Are you keeping your eyes open for that moment of opportunity? Are you prepared to act wisely, decisively, and proactively when it comes? Make yourself *ready!*

❑ *I will network and utilize connections*—Joseph knew the wine taster would return to the Pharaoh. He trusted God above all, but did not hesitate to ask the wine taster for a favor. Joseph used his connection. He was proactive in his request. He did not sit and ask God to make the wine taster remember that Joseph had once done him a favor. We all choose our own networks. The more diverse your networks, the greater your opportunity for benefit. Networking opens doors for you, but once inside, your abilities must speak for themselves. The Apostle Paul trusted God's protection in his endeavors to spread the gospel to the Gentiles. One day, Paul's preaching started a riot among the Jews and brought in the Roman chief captain who was preparing to punish him. Had Paul simply done nothing, he would most certainly have been beaten on this occasion. But Paul was a Roman citizen—exempt from such torture. He used his advantage and announced his citizenship, thus avoiding unnecessary hardship *(Acts 22:25)*. Sometimes trusting God is to understand that God expects *us* to do all we can first. Utilizing a connection is not wrong. Networking is an active process—you must let people know how they can help you and what you have to offer. Abigail put in a good word to King David for her husband *(I Samuel 25)*. Rahab put in a good word to Joshua for her family *(Joshua 2)*. Even Jonathan, recognizing that his friend David would someday be king, put in a requested favor for his family *(I Samuel 20)*. Use whatever leverage God has given you. This does not show a lack of faith in trusting God, but in reality shows you are following Christ's command to: *"…be shrewd as serpents and innocent as doves"* (Mathew 10:16 NASB). Why would God desire His children to be less wise than the world? *"…the people of this world are much more shrewd in handling their affairs than the people who belong to the light"* (Luke 16:8 GNT). As you pray for God to move in your life, job, or circumstance, try to seek out anyone who might assist your endeavor. Don't be afraid to use any honest leverage you are given, for that very leverage might be a favor from God.

Power Points:

➤ Was Joseph wrong in trusting the wine taster? Why didn't Joseph just trust God *alone*?

➤ Why do you think the wine taster forgot Joseph for so long?

Reflection Section:

❑ Realize that you will never understand the mystery of God's ways. Your job is to understand that He can work in your life when you are able to do nothing, but more often, works through your life as you do what you can. God will direct our arrows, but expects us, whenever we are able, to string our own bow.

❑ God is never surprised or defeated. Do you agree? Disagree? Why?

❑   When people hear your name today, will they think positively of you? Why? What can you do today that will make people think positively of you tomorrow?

❑   What are some goals you have set for your life? Are you working toward them today? In what areas do you need to be more proactive? How can you better *network*?

❑   In completing a task before me today, the first proactive step for me would be to _____

❑   Have you ever considered that you might be an instrument of God in helping someone else? Do you realize this may make you an answer to someone's prayers?

❑   Are you trusting God to perform something in your life that He is expecting you to do yourself? Might it not be better if you became the answer to your own prayer?

My Personal Growth Journal—

❑   Write down your need and what goal you want to accomplish in the most specific words you can use. Then, redefine both in as few words as possible still being specific. Remember—needs may be *wants*—but all wants are not *needs*. Set for yourself a goal.

~ Chapter 11 ~

Survival in the Pit: "The Principle of Sacrificial Praise"

But the head cupbearer never gave Joseph another thought; he forgot all about him. (Gen. 40:23)

The Joseph story....

Joseph had predicted that the wine taster would be released from prison. He had counted on the gratitude of the man and humbly requested that this court officer remember him before the Pharaoh. But year after year passed and Joseph remained in the Egyptian prison. The wine taster had forgotten Joseph, but God had not. Through the years of further discouragement, Joseph continued to offer sacrificial praise to the God he knew still controlled all circumstances. Praise from the pits of life. The hardest praise a human being can offer. Surely, God had a purpose in the delay as He had a purpose in all that had transpired in Joseph's life. Seemingly fruitless years were passing for Joseph, but God was weaving good for the young man who was trusting Him. Back in Canaan, years were also passing for Joseph's father, Jacob, and for the brothers who thought their sins against Joseph were long forgotten.

Principle Truth: Your most valuable praise to God is to glorify Him for His goodness in allowing you to hurt as you have never hurt before.

When my mother was in remission from cancer, I thanked God. The night she died, however, praying at all was difficult. Praising God was all but impossible.

Praising God is easier on sunny days. God is pleased when we fellowship with Him in prayer. But undoubtedly He is most pleased when that prayer is a sacrifice, because there may be no particular blessing for which to thank Him for. In fact, as with Joseph, there may nothing but discouragement and frustration. This is when thanking God becomes sacrificial praise *"...let us continually offer our sacrifice of praise to God by proclaiming the glory of his name" (Hebrews 13:15 GNT)*. Praise is hard when God answers our prayers with *no*, or allows circumstances to overwhelm us. But prayer is never more difficult than when God appears to have abandoned us to the circumstances of our own despair. At such times, praising God becomes a sacrifice—a unique and special thanksgiving to God that may touch His heart as can no other way.

> Faith is deliberate confidence in the character of God whose ways you may not understand at the time.
>
> —Oswald Chambers

In such times, we glorify God in our acknowledgment His *goodness*—who He *is*, rather than His *blessing*—what He *does*. We must remember that God is God. He does what He chooses *(Psalms 115:3)*, and He does everything right. Understanding this, in especially difficult circumstances, we need to hold on to our faith *(I Timothy 1:19)*. Our faith is our armor against discouragement, frustration, and disappointment. Faith a part of an entire suit of protection God has given us for survival in life's pit *(Ephesians 6:10-17)*.

Sometimes God's greatest blessings come to us from the sacrificial praise offered to him from the pits of life. William Cowper composed his finest hymns between fits of insanity. John Milton did his greatest writing after he became blind. John Bunyan sat forgotten in a Bedford jail, but God's strength enabled him to write *Pilgrim's Progress*, one of the best-selling books ever penned. From a prison also, Daniel DeFoe wrote *Robinson Crusoe*. God does not abandon His own in the dark dungeons of life. Often however, it is there that His power is best manifested through our weakness.

Joseph could thank God for delivering him to a fair master such as Potiphar, when his brothers cruelly sold him into Egyptian slavery. Joseph could thank God for delivering him from the death penalty when Potiphar's wife accused him of rape. But now Joseph seemed abandoned in a place from which he had once been assured remembrance. Joseph had predicted that the wine taster would be released from prison. He humbly requested that this court officer remember him before the Pharaoh, and in gratitude, the wine taster agreed. But years passed by, and Joseph remained in the Egyptian prison. The wine taster had forgotten Joseph, but God had not. Joseph surely must have been discouraged, but just as surely praised his God who he knew still controlled all circumstances.

God hears our prayers of request, but He is most glorified when we praise Him for His goodness—from the darkest depths of our disappointment and despair.

- ❑ *Tell God you praise Him today—because He's God*—Praise and thanksgiving are different. Thanksgiving is blessing God for what he *does*. Praise is blessing God for who He *is*. Praise God for His goodness. God would be good and holy even if He never did anything for you. God's works are always good, even if sometimes His will in your life tastes bitter. Sometimes God allows bad things to happen to good people. Joseph understood this from his prison. Although we are not told, Joseph surely praised God for His goodness of character, even when God had, to all outward appearances, left him in another pit. Thank God because you recognize Him as a holy and righteous God, and praise Him for that fact alone.

- ❑ *Tell God you trust Him today—simply because He's in control*—Even though Joseph did not deserve to be in the Egyptian prison, he was sure the wine taster would remember the request to get him out. The wine taster forgot Joseph. Discouraged though he certainly was, Joseph could continue to trust his God because he knew God was in control. Nothing in Joseph's life could take place unless it first passed through God's permission. Joseph was not merely resigned to his fate; he was resting in his God. Someone has said that fear is nothing more than *false evaluation about reality*. Are you concentrating only on your circumstances? God tells you: *"Don't worry about anything; instead, pray about everything. Tell God what you need, and thank him for all he has done" (Philippians 4:6 NLT).* Are you fearing the worst instead trusting a God who can work everything together for good *(Romans 8:28)*? When your world seems out of control, let God know you recognize His sovereign power over your life.

❑ *Tell God you love Him today—simply because He's with you*—The wine taster had been released. The baker had been executed—both events predicted correctly by Joseph. He may now have been alone in the prison. Certainly, being forgotten there, he could have felt alone. Joseph felt this loneliness once before, when his brothers had thrown him into the pit. But Joseph realized that even though the world seemed to have forgotten him, his God was with him *"...for He Himself has said, "I will never desert you or forsake you" (Hebrews 13:5 NASB)*. Joseph understood God in a way that his father Jacob did not. Jacob was also discouraged when he had no choice but to send Benjamin to Egypt while Simeon sat in the Egyptian prison. He thought both the boys might die, when in fact God was in full control and protecting them all *(Genesis 43:14)*. When you feel abandoned, see this as a private time to tell the God who promised never to leave you how much you love Him.

> The greatest test of courage on earth is to bear defeat without losing heart.
>
> —Robert Ingersoll
>
> ৵৸

❑ *Tell God you thank Him today—simply because of what He is going to do*—Joseph never surrendered hope that someday, God would release him from his prison. Joseph looked forward in hope to what he could not actually see, and trusted God to bring it to pass. This is called "faith." *"To have faith is to be sure of the things we hope for, to be certain of the things we cannot see" (Hebrews 11:1 GNT)*. The prayer of faith during difficult times is one of the hardest prayers. That is why it is called "sacrificial praise." In the midst of your difficult time, it is one thing to pray for God to deliver you. That's *trust*. It's another thing to thank God because you know He *will* deliver you. That's *faith!* Thank God right now for the deliverance that will come from this difficulty. Act on your assurance that He is a God who knows your future, has planned it for you, and is preparing you right now for it.

❑ *Tell God just how you feel today—simply because He already knows*—Job learned the sovereignty of God. He also cried out to God how hopeless and frustrated he felt. *"My days pass by without hope, pass faster than a weaver's shuttle" (Job 7:6 GNT)*. So did Jeremiah. *"I do not have much longer to live; my hope in the Lord is gone" (Lamentations 3:18)*. Moreover, God did not get angry with either Job or Jeremiah because they expressed their pain. He let them vent. Are you hurting as you God trust today? Do you worry that telling God just how you feel shows a lack of faith? Faith is an *attitude*. Crying out in frustration is an expression. God understands. He made you out of clay, not gold. It's OK to tell God just how you feel sometimes. He already knows anyway.

❑ *Tell God you worship Him today—simply because He's put you through this trial*—This is the most difficult prayer of sacrificial praise. This is also the most demanding proof of your confidence in God and the most rewarding aspect of praising Him. To worship, praise, and thank God for *putting* you through—not just *getting* you through—this difficulty is evidence of Christian maturity. In thanking God for this trial, you recognize Him as a holy, sovereign God who loves, hears and cares about you. It tells God you accept His plans, even plans you may not understand, and know that they are for your good. Can you tell God right now that you in truth appreciate Him trusting you with this difficulty? You're in good company! You are not supposed to figure out all of God's ways. *"Don't you know? Haven't you heard? The Lord is the everlasting God; he created all the world. He never grows tired or weary. No one understands his thoughts"* (Isaiah 40:28). Are you having trouble trusting when you just can't figure God out? God wants you to fall on your trust—don't lean on your understanding. *"Trust in the Lord with all your heart, and lean not on your own understanding; In all your ways acknowledge Him, And He shall direct your paths"* (Proverbs 3:5-6 NKJV). Rejoice—this is a most special time in your life! Do you realize that the opportunity for this most difficult aspect of sacrificial praise may never come again? When this trial is over, don't you want to be able to thank Him that He knew best how to teach you the lessons you learned? Right now, make a list of lessons you feel God may be teaching you through this difficulty. Thank God for what you're enduring right now, so that, when the trial is over, you can look back and know you offered God the highest worship of all— the worship of *sacrificial* praise! *"He who offers a sacrifice of thanksgiving honors Me..."* (Psalms 50:23 NASB).

Power Points:

➤ Why do you think sacrificial praise means so much to God?

> ➢ What do you think Joseph felt towards the wine taster? How would you feel towards him?

> ➢ How did Joseph feel towards Potiphar at this moment? How did he feel about Potiphar's wife?

> ➢ What is the difference between praise and thanksgiving?

> ➢ Why should we pray when God already knows our heart and what we're going to say?

Reflection section:

❑ Try to praise God just as fervently when hardships come as you thank Him when He blesses.

❑ Think back on a situation in your life when you were discouraged over a situation that *was* your fault. How could you have praised Him— even in that predicament?

❑ Learn more about praise to God. Read *Psalms 107* and *Psalms 147*, and list the different aspects of praise and thanksgiving toward God.

❑ Realize that sacrificial prayers, though difficult, acknowledge to God that we love and trust Him no matter what.

❑ "Diamonds and rainbows are best viewed against dark backgrounds." How does this statement relate to this chapter?

❑ Like Joseph, draw from the deep well of discouragement prayers that reveal to Him you have confidence in His will for your life.

❑ Sometimes it is hard to pray. Sometimes you just don't know the words you want to say to God. When you can't pray as you would, pray as you can.

My Personal Growth Journal—

❑ Write down the most discouraging—seemingly hopeless—situation in your life right now, and describe how you feel about it. Ask God to help that situation, and then spend as much time as you can thanking Him for allowing that situation in your life. This is the ultimate prayer of sacrifice. This will truly test your relationship with God.

~ Chapter 12 ~

Turning Lemons into Lemonade: "The Principle of Unexpected Opportunity"

Pharaoh at once sent for Joseph. They brought him on the run from the jail cell. He cut his hair, put on clean clothes, and came to Pharaoh. "I dreamed a dream," Pharaoh told Joseph. "Nobody can interpret it. But I've heard that just by hearing a dream you can interpret it." (Gen. 41:14-15)

The Joseph story....

The great Pharaoh over all Egypt was plagued by dreams. Seven fat and lean water cows, seven good and withered stalks of grain. What could the dreams mean? Was there no one who could ease the Pharaoh's mind? "There is a man…" replied the wine taster to the Pharaoh. Joseph's reputation for interpreting dreams had at last made its way to the Pharaoh's court. Though it had taken much longer than Joseph had hoped, the Pharaoh was summoning Joseph from the prison into the palace, giving him a chance to exercise his godly gift. With little advance warning, Joseph was brought before the Pharaoh. For many years, Joseph had been waiting for the opportunity to get out of the Egyptian prison. For many years he had been punished for a crime he had not committed. Joseph had been punished for being good. Forgotten by the wine taster he had helped and the family that had estranged him, Joseph had only the hope in his God's sovereignty to sustain him. Would his life, his gifts—his dedication to God and character—ever pay dividends? In a moment he would never forget, Joseph's services were requested by the most powerful man in the world.

Principle Truth: God often wraps His greatest opportunities in the cloak of hardship and presents them to you when you least expect them.

When God gives us lemons, learn to make lemonade. We've all heard the trite sayings offered to explain hardships. Bad things happen to good people. How we deal with life's lemons reveals much about our character. Sometimes bad things happen because we cause them through ill-advised actions. Sometimes bad things happen because we become careless and fail to act in preventing a foreseeable problem. But most of the time, bad things happen simply because we live in a fallen world. When Adam sinned in the Garden of Eden, sin entered into our world. With sin came death, suffering, and pain. God has not removed the effects of sin that cause us so much trouble. God *has* given us opportunities to turn these troubles into good. It's how we prepare for and handle the opportunities bad things present us that determine whether our life is filled with lemons—or lemonade.

> *Chance is always powerful. Let your hook be always cast; in the pool where you least expect it, there will be a fish.*
>
> *—Ovid*

Paul was a missionary. He was ready and willing to follow God's instruction to preach the gospel in Asia, when God mysteriously shut that door *(Acts 16:6)*. The reason God closed this door did not become immediately apparent to Paul, until another opportunity made clear God's plan for the gospel to reach Europe. *"For a wide door for effective service has opened to me, and there are many adversaries" (I Corinthians 16:9 NASB)*. God does open doors of opportunity for us if we prepare for, pray for, and watch for such opportunities.

Egypt was about to experience a terrible famine. There is no indication that the famine was caused by the sinfulness of the people. Neither was Joseph abandoned in the Egyptian prison because of his sinfulness, but for the sin of his brothers. Nevertheless, Joseph kept his eyes open for any opportunity to use the gift of dream interpretation God had given him. The famine, and the misfortune Joseph suffered, were a part of God's plan, however. Through the famine, God provided Joseph an unexpected opportunity.

It has been said that when God closes a door, He often opens a window. When God opens the door of opportunity, He expects us to *move*. Joseph had faithfully used his gifts. When the opportunity arose to exercise them during this sudden and unexpected opportunity to address the Pharaoh, he took advantage of it. Joseph could not help the famine that God would send on

Egypt. The famine happened because famines are a part of nature. Nevertheless, Joseph took this unexpected opportunity to use the wisdom he'd been given. He was prepared and available, and he knew he might never have such an opportunity again.

> *Four things come not back, the spoken word, the sped arrow, the past life and the neglected opportunity.*
>
> ❧

The Rich Young Ruler was also given an opportunity. He had prepared himself for what he thought was the key to his eternal life. He had faithfully obeyed the commandments and approached Jesus wanting the opportunity to inherit eternal life. When reminded that eternal life was more than keeping the commandments, he failed to take advantage of his opportunity, and *"...went away sorrowful" (Matthew 19:22 KJV)*. We must not only prepare, pray, and watch for opportunities, we must take advantage of them. Opportunities not taken become opportunities lost.

Opportunity also creates responsibility. Because Joseph seized the opportunity to gain an audience with the Pharaoh, God would promote Joseph to the high office of Egypt's vizier. As vizier, Joseph became responsible for the lives of not only Egypt, but eventually his family as well. The reward for taking advantage of opportunities is often greater responsibility *(Matthew 25:23)*.

We should look for God to open windows whenever doors seem to close to us. God gives us opportunities—sometimes they are found where we look for them, and they may not always appear in the way we are expecting.

Watch for and consider the opportunities God gives you today. Remember, some opportunities come unexpectedly, and some come in the form of difficulties—lemons, waiting to become lemonade.

❑ *My opportunity may not be from God*—Not every opportunity comes from God—especially when we are out of God's will. Sometimes what may seem to be an opportunity to better ourselves is an opportunity for God to allow the consequences of our actions to remind us of how much God hates sin. God had informed Saul that young David would someday replace him as king of Israel. Saul was

> *Opportunity is missed by most people because it is dressed in overalls and looks like work.*
>
> —Edison
>
> ❧

jealous of God's favoritism toward David, and hunted him day and night. Finally, *"Saul learned that David had gone to Keilah and thought immediately, "Good! God has handed him to me on a platter! He's in a walled city with locked gates, trapped!" (I Samuel 23:7)* Because Saul was out of God's will, the very opportunity he thought was from God became the punishment for his own sins *against* David. Saul did not understand that, while God does provide for us opportunities, He does not tempt us with opportunities to do evil. Examine your opportunities to make sure they are from God. If they are opportunities to do something improper, morally wrong, or against God's teaching, it's not an opportunity from God.

> *A ship in a harbor is safe, but that is not what a ship is for.*
>
> —John Shedd

☐ *My opportunity may come through others*—God can use many avenues to create opportunities. Often, He uses other people—some you least expect. Have you ever heard of Bezalel? Most people haven't, but everyone has heard of Moses. God put Moses in charge of building the tabernacle. But Moses knew of someone else who could build it build it better than he could, so he offered an unexpected opportunity to Bezalel. Bezalel was the architect of the house of God in the wilderness. Bezalel's opportunity came through another person, and he was prepared to take advantage of the offer. Be ready to display your skills so that, if someone gives you the opportunity to use them, you will be ready (*cp. Exodus 38:21-22*).

☐ *My opportunity may require me taking the initiative*—Opportunities may knock, but we are responsible to open the door. We have to make them happen. Ezra was searching his records for workers willing to volunteer service to God. Hard workers were needed to help rebuild God's temple in Jerusalem. Ezra sent out the call. The Levites were the priestly tribe and should have been the first to volunteer, but they did not. In not volunteering, the Levites missed a golden opportunity to work on the great temple and glorify their God. Often, God wants us to *create*—not *wait* for—opportunities. God wants us to take the initiative, not merely sit back and wait for the opportunity to find us. Offer your skills in a way that you might open the door for opportunities instead than waiting for opportunities to open a door for you (*cp. Ezra 8:15*).

☐ *My opportunity may come only one time*—The ancient Greeks used to say that opportunity approaches with flowing locks, but is bald in its passing us by. We must grasp opportunities when they come, for when they pass, they may be impossible to recover. God had promised the

Hebrews the glorious land of Canaan. It was literally theirs for the taking. Caleb was willing to enter and possess the land, but others were afraid: *"Caleb interrupted, called for silence before Moses and said, 'Let's go up and take the land—now. We can do it.' "But the others said, 'We can't attack those people; they're way stronger than we are'"* (Numbers 13:30-31). What happened? Those who were fearful never got a second opportunity to enter the land. Sometimes, we get but one chance to seize an opportunity. One chance. Take particular care that you aren't careless in letting a golden opportunity slip by. Seize your opportunities! To try and still fail is acceptable. To fail to take advantage of opportunities that may only come your way once is not. See every opportunity as if it might only come once. Seize the day!

❑   *My opportunity may require me to be responsible for the consequences—* Every action has a consequence. Risks and consequences occur when we take advantage of our opportunities, and in different ways, even when we don't. We must weigh the risks and consequences against the advantages and responsibilities in considering the opportunities we are given.

Because Joseph took advantage of his opportunities in Egypt, the consequences included being given more responsibility. Joseph had been faithful over Potiphar's house, therefore God entrusted

> *Be ready when opportunity comes. Luck is the time when preparation and opportunity meet.*
>
> —Roy Chapin Jr.
>
> ঌড়

him with faithfulness over all Egypt. Taking proper advantage of opportunities seldom creates rest. It usually creates the reward of further responsibility *(Matthew 25:21-23; Cp. Luke 16:10-12)*. The Hebrews, on the other hand, failed to take advantage of their opportunity to secure the land of Canaan. Nevertheless, they were forced to face the terrible consequences of disobedience to God. *"But as I live and as the Glory of God fills the whole Earth not a single person of those who saw my Glory, saw the miracle signs I did in Egypt and the wilderness, and who have tested me over and over and over again, turning a deaf ear to me—not one of them will set eyes on the land I so solemnly promised to their ancestors. No one who has treated me with such repeated contempt will see it"* (Numbers 14:21-23). Opportunities—taken, as well as ignored—result in consequences. Consider the consequences of opportunities that come your way today.

❑ *My opportunity may go to someone else if I fail to use it*—I always tell my students that God put them in this world to do something better than anyone else can do it. I encourage them to use their gifts and talents to keep their eyes open for opportunities God presents to them. In the discussion in the Parable of the Talents, the master entrusted all his laborers with talents to invest. Upon his return from a far country, the master noticed that one laborer had failed to use the talent entrusted to him. The talent was taken from the servant and given to another *(Matthew 25:28-30)*. Queen Esther was a Hebrew girl who was made queen over all Persia. During her reign, her people—the Jews—were about to be exterminated by Haman, the king's wicked advisor. What could Esther do? As the queen, she alone had the opportunity to request a special audience with the king. There was risk involved, however. By Persian law, approaching the king without permission could have cost Esther her life. Nevertheless, her uncle reminded her that perhaps this was the very reason she had been chosen by God to be queen in the first place. Mordecai encouraged Esther to use her opportunity to beg the king for the lives of her people. He also reminded her if she did not use her opportunity, God would save the Jews through another method. God's plans do not depend on our obedience. However, He does sometimes give us opportunities to help bring His plans to pass. Don't let God's opportunities slip by! *(Esther 4:10-17)*

Power Points:

➤ How would you have felt when the word came that Pharaoh was calling you?

➤ "God *caused* the famine in Egypt for Joseph's benefit." Do you agree or disagree with this statement?

➤ "Joseph's faithfulness over *small* things proved to God that he could handle the more important ones." Do you agree or disagree with this statement?

Reflection section:

- ❏ How do you look at difficulties? Are they burdens to be endured or opportunities to be grasped?

- ❏ What gift or talent do you have ready and waiting for any possible call to service?

- ❏ What door do you recall God closing in your life where He later opened a window?

- ❏ Is there an opportunity that you took—or didn't take—that has never come again? What advice could you give someone else about *opportunities*?

- ❏ "Any opportunity is better than no opportunity at all." Do you *agree* or *disagree* with this statement?

- ❏ "If I miss an opportunity in life, it just wasn't God's will." Do you agree or disagree with this statement?

- ❏ "People have to make their own opportunities!" Do you agree or disagree with this statement?

- ❏ Realize that bad things will happen to good people. It's how we handle these difficulties that is important.

- ❏ Recognize and acknowledge that your particular strengths might be waiting for an opportunity to express themselves for the benefit of others.

- ❏ See difficulties for what they are—opportunities that you may not have again.

My Personal Growth Journal—

- ❏ Think of the gift or gifts that God has given you. Write down the one that you feel would be most beneficial to you if God opened the door for you to do whatever you wanted to do in life. Now list five ways you are keeping that gift fine-tuned for that service.

~ Chapter 13 ~

The World is Watching Me: "The Principle of Glorifying God"

"I dreamed a dream," Pharaoh told Joseph. "Nobody can interpret it. But I've heard that just by hearing a dream you can interpret it." Joseph answered, "Not I, but God. God will set Pharaoh's mind at ease." (Gen. 41:15-16)

The Joseph story....

Because Joseph was skilled in the interpretation of dreams, the Pharaoh called upon him to use this skill in translating his own disturbing messages of the night. While Joseph utilized his gifts in his opportunity to serve his king, using his gifts also brought glory to his God. Joseph was careful to credit God alone with the power to reveal the meaning of dreams and refused to take personal credit for his skills. The interpretation of the Pharaoh's night visions would be up to God alone. Good or bad, Joseph understood that he would bear the consequences. The power of Joseph's God no doubt left a lasting impression on the king's mind when Joseph's interpretations proved correct.

Principle Truth: The world will conclude more about God through observing your life than through any other observation it can make.

The world is watching you. The world is curious to see if you glorify the God in whom you trust when He blesses you. The world is also watching to see if you blame your God when life seems to go against you. Too often, we are tempted to take credit for the good things that happen to us in life and blame God for the rest.

But God is holy. He is righteous and just in everything He does. God is deserving of glory from all His creation. Glory is to God as wetness is to water. But God deserves to be glorified not just for His actions. He deserves glory simply because He is God and is perfect in all His ways.

Every gift and talent we have is from God, and we glorify Him through their use. Too often, however, it becomes easy to respond to the world's praise by taking credit to ourselves. We bring no glory to God when pride gets the best of us, and we accept for ourselves the credit He deserves.

This does not mean that we should be so humble when the world praises our skills that we become a bore. It does mean that we should use every opportunity in the eyes of the world to credit God for the good that happens and glorify Him through the trust we maintain in Him even when His answer to our requests is no.

> *God is most glorified in us when we are most satisfied in Him.*
>
> —Piper

Sometimes, however, glorifying God might not be popular. Certainly many popular performers and athletes would be afraid for their reputations if they too publicly credited God for their achievements.

Life also presents us many opportunities to glorify God—through our failures as well as our successes. After much discouragement, Joseph was finally given the opportunity to glorify God using his gift of interpreting dreams. But Joseph would be proclaiming the greatness of his God over all the hundreds of Egyptian gods. He would be proclaiming his God superior even to the Pharaoh, whom the Egyptians considered a god on earth. Nevertheless, Joseph boldly made it clear that his God alone deserved praise for such a gift. In doing so, he brought more glory to God in Pharaoh's eyes than any preaching he could have done.

The glory we bring to God, through His blessings or withholding of blessing, is easier seen by the world through our conduct than through our words.

Nevertheless, we should strive to glorify God in everything we do. The world is watching us.

You may glorify God in more ways than you could imagine today. Make it a point to glorify God with every part of your life today. Remember, God's camera is always running. So is His microphone.

- ❑ *I will glorify God with my hands*—Because he trusted God in every aspect life, Joseph glorified God through all his actions and abilities. When people watch what you do each day, would they conclude that your actions were dedicated to God's glory? Look at your hands right now. What was the last thing you did with them that brought glory to God? Glorify God today by an action. Pick up the phone and call a hurting friend. Write down notes from a Bible study. Write a letter to someone who would feel their day was blessed if they heard from you. *"Whoever serves is to do so as one who is serving by the strength which God supplies; so that in all things God may be glorified through Jesus Christ, to whom belongs the glory and dominion forever and ever. Amen"* (I Peter 4:11 NASB).

- ❑ *I will glorify God with my mind*—*"In conclusion, my friends, fill your minds with those things that are good and that deserve praise: things that are true, noble, right, pure, lovely, and honorable"* (Philippians 4:8 GNT). How did Joseph glorify God with his mind? Joseph refused to allow impure thoughts to enter his mind. In resisting the sexual advances of Potiphar's wife, Joseph refused to dwell on the immediate satisfaction. Instead, he considered the sin it would be against God. How did Joseph know this temptation was wrong? He thought of his upbringing at home. He listened to his conscience. What do you think about most in times of pondering? Is it how to satisfy yourself? Is it how you can glorify God? Determine to fill your mind with things of God. Study His Word and learn God's measures of right and wrong. Does your conscience need a recharge? It has been said that a man whose conscience never troubles him must have it pretty well trained. Fill your mind with godly things, and the glory your hands bring to God will soon follow!

- ❑ *I will glorify God with my mouth*—Joseph glorified his God in front of the Pharaoh. We never see Joseph telling the Pharaoh his Egyptian gods were stupid. We never see Joseph telling the Pharaoh he was bound for eternal punishment. We see Joseph simply glorifying his God, and letting his words and deeds make the impression. What impression do your words make on others? James tells us that our tongue is extremely small, but capable of much damage *(James 3:6-10)*. Solomon warns us that to watch our tongue is to protect our life *(Proverbs 13:3)*. With your same tongue, however, you can glorify God through praise and thanksgiving *(Psalms 50:23)*. Do you glorify God through prayer? *(Cp. John 14:13)* Do you remember to glorify God in appreciation when He blesses you? *(Cp. Luke 17:11-19)* Estimates are that in the course of a day you will have an average of thirty conversations and speak over 25,000 words. If you were to record every conversation you had with others in the course of a day, would you be ashamed to let God hear it? Do you have a vocabulary that needs changing? Would you mind if your children used the words of your conversations? It has been said that words are cheap because the supply exceeds their demand. Remember, words once spoken take on a life of their own. They are like arrows. Once we release them, we have little control over the damage they can do. Do you need to learn that sometimes it's best to say nothing at all? *(Proverbs 10:19; 17:28; cp. Psalms 39:1)* If it can go without saying, don't insist on repeating it! One especially effective way to avoid trouble is to be careful of what you say: *"Lord, place a guard at my mouth, a sentry at the door of my lips" (Psalms 141:3; Cp. Proverbs 21:23)*. As a teacher, I understand that one improper expletive can ruin a year's worth of character modeling. In addition to improper words, improper attitudes can be destructive. Gossip, criticism, and sarcasm can also hurt others. Your words reveal your inner self. Make a concerted effort today to speak wholesome, helpful words *(I Timothy 6:3)*. Think before you speak today, and give wisdom a chance to grace your conversation *(Proverbs 37:30)*. As someone once said: don't push the *accelatonguerator* until your *brainsmission* is in gear! Ask a friend to gently remind you every time you say something that would be inappropriate if your children said it. Clean up your conversations *"...that you may with one mind and one mouth glorify the God and Father of our Lord Jesus Christ" (Romans 15:6 NKJV)*.

❑   *I will glorify God with my eyes*—Joseph refused to look with lust upon Potiphar's wife. It has been said that our eyes are the windows to our soul. We learn more through what we see than through any other sense. Our eyes are also the avenues to our temptations. It only takes a single look to leave a lifetime of impression upon your mind. Today, make a covenant with your eyes as David did. Keep an eye on what you're keeping an eye on! Determine that you will not allow yourself to look at things that might stir your passions to sin. *"I will set no wicked thing before mine eyes" (Psalms 101:3 KJV).*

❑ **I will glorify God with my feet**—When Potiphar's wife tried to talk Joseph into sin, Joseph ran from her. He never looked back—even when she grabbed his garment. Joseph glorified God by refusing to be in a place that was sinful. *"Flee also youthful lusts" (II Timothy 2:22 KJV).* Do your feet lead you to places your where you would be ashamed to be found? Would you be ashamed if your friends and their children knew every place you visited in the last month? God wants you to let Him guide your feet *(Proverbs 3:5-6)* through trust in Him. Have your feet taken you somewhere you'd be ashamed to be found if Jesus returned to find you there? Joseph was not at fault being in Potiphar's house, but he was right in listening to God and leaving. *"He leads me in the paths of righteousness For His name's sake" (Psalms 23:4 NKJV).* Sometimes sin finds us. God knows that, because of sin, we are not always the best judges of where we should walk *(Jeremiah 23:10; Proverbs 20:24).* But God has promised that, if we trust Him, He will direct our steps *(Proverbs 16:9).* If you follow righteousness, you'll seldom have to worry about fleeing from sin. *"Therefore be careful how you walk, not as unwise men but as wise" (Ephesians 5:15 NASB).* Be careful to walk where God wants you to walk today.

- *I will walk in the light today, and not in the shadows of sinful temptations (I John 1:7).*

- *I will walk in truth today, and not in dishonesty and deceit (III John 3,4).*

- *I will walk by faith today, and not merely in the realm of what I can see and understand (II Corinthians 5:7).*

- *I will walk in love today, and not in anger and impatience with others (Ephesians 5:2.)*

- *I will walk in wisdom today, and not where trouble is waiting for me (Colossians 4:5).*

❑ **I will glorify God with my tears**—Joseph's life is often seen as glorious. He became vizier over Egypt—the second most powerful man in the world. Yet, before becoming this, he suffered many hardships. His life was made hard because he tried to live righteously. Do not expect an easy life just because you are a Christian. Living for God assumes hassle from the world. Can you dedicate your entire life to God—even if He requires you to be persecuted for your beliefs? Is God your Lord only when He blesses you? Give God your tears, and trust that even the troubled times are His sandpaper to make you better. People will suffer in this world, Christian or not. Understanding that, allow your suffering to glorify God. It is not the easy praise that God appreciates most. God especially honors praise offered from pain. Glorify God with your tears as well as your joy. *"Yet if anyone suffers as a Christian, let him not be ashamed, but let him glorify God in this matter"* (I Peter 4:16 NKJV).

❑   *I will glorify God with my influence*—Joseph was being watched. Potiphar glorified God through Joseph's influence. Joseph's servant also made mention of the blessing of Joseph's God. Without once telling the Egyptians the plan of salvation, Joseph's influence spoke for him. Joseph glorified his God in the midst of the many gods of the Egyptians by his conduct alone. You and I are being watched. Our influence is being felt being felt by those we don't even know, and especially by those we do. Are others being made stronger or weaker in their relationship to God by watching you? It has been said that as a Christian, you are the only Bible some people will ever 'read'. Remember your influence. People are watching. *"They will glorify God for your obedience to your confession of the gospel of Christ and for the liberality of your contribution to them and to all"* (I Corinthians 9:13 GNT).

❑   *I will glorify God in everything I do*—Make God's will and plan in your life your top priority today. Trust and praise Him through all your words and actions! God has promised to meet your needs through the glory of His Son *(Philippians 4:19): "Whether therefore, ye eat, or drink, or whatever ye do, do all to the glory of God"* (I Corinthians 10:31).

Power Points:

➤   Do you think Joseph was nervous in glorifying his God before the most powerful man in the world at the time? Would you have been?

> ➢ Why do you think Joseph did not attempt to convert Pharaoh to his religion? Was Joseph still faithful to his God in *not* doing this?

Reflection section:

❑ When was the last time you offered God credit for something good that happened through you?

❑ How would you feel attempting to glorify your God in an *Islamic* culture?

❑ Are you ashamed to praise God in public?

❑ Have you missed an opportunity to bring glory to God by giving Him full credit when you were successful in the use of your gift or talent?

❑ When was the last time you thanked God for the meal in a restaurant? Remember, all gifts are from God. Like Joseph, we must never be ashamed to recognize Him for such. People are watching.

My Personal Growth Journal—

❑ You and your best friend make separate lists of the last ten things each of you has done to glorify God. Write how you feel about that list, and then share the lists.

~ Chapter 14 ~

Telling it Like it is: "The Principle of Integrity"

"It is as I have spoken to Pharaoh: God has shown to Pharaoh what He is about to do. Behold, seven years of great abundance are coming in all the land of Egypt; and after them seven years of famine will come, and all the abundance will be forgotten in the land of Egypt, and the famine will ravage the land." (Gen. 41:28-30)

The Joseph story....

The Pharaoh had been troubled by his dreams. No one in Egypt would help ease their king's mind. After much delay, the wine taster brought to the Pharaoh's attention that Joseph possessed the gift of interpreting dreams. At last, Joseph was called in to the great king's presence. The Pharaoh narrated his dreams to Joseph, and the palace waited in silence for the interpretation. What God would reveal through Joseph was not all good news. Through the dreams, God revealed that Egypt would have seven good harvest years. But afterwards there would come upon the land a time of great famine. For seven years, the great Nile would cease to flood and bring its life-giving soil to lower Egypt. Joseph revealed the interpretations exactly as God had given them to him. There was no way this famine could be avoided. The palace awaited the Pharaoh's response.

Principle Truth: The measure of your personal integrity is determined by how honest you are according to God's standard—not the world's.

Fudging the truth. So easy to do—especially when we are scared. Little white lies to make sure we don't offend. Everybody's doing it, we are told. Better to stretch the truth, we are told, than to hurt someone through adherence to strict honesty.

Partial truth is total falsehood. As a teacher of middle school children, I have watched the honesty and integrity of teenagers decline precipitously over time. Many kids feel that right and wrong actions are determined by whether or not they get away with something. Not to get caught means that the action must be right. This has come to be known as situation ethics. Situation ethics is honesty stemming from circumstance, instead of honesty stemming from integrity.

God does not condone situation ethics or partial truths. God requires complete honesty. Sometimes complete honesty means telling someone something unpopular or something that may be hurtful. None of us want to intentionally offend or hurt the feelings of another. Often we are put into a position where the truth may hurt. How do we handle this?

> *An honest man does not make himself a dog for the sake of a bone.*
>
> *—Danish Proverb*

It is easy to fudge on the truth, but this often brings only short-term comfort. In telling the full truth, we may be more of a help to others than in striving not to offend. Of course, the truth must be offered in tact and kindness. While truthfulness may not always be popular, and we may offer many excuses for fudging on the truth, honesty will generally be appreciated even if the truth might be hurtful.

Joseph was sometimes faced with situations where honesty would not bring good news. For example, God revealed to Joseph that the baker was going to die. Joseph could have withheld the news, but, upon the request from the baker, he revealed to him the truth *(Genesis 40:19)*. Later, Joseph faced the task of revealing to the Pharaoh that a terrible famine was to come upon the land of Egypt. Joseph's life was in the Pharaoh's hands. Should Joseph avoid the revelation from God and curry to the Pharaoh, or tell the king the truth and risk his wrath?

Joseph spoke the truth about the famine. He did not fudge on the truth or soften the reality of the impending disaster. By telling the truth, Joseph built credibility in Egypt, as the Pharaoh—and the Egyptian people—learned they could trust his word. The Pharaoh did not punish Joseph for his honesty. Instead, the Pharaoh realized that this truth would require an honest man to make provision during the famine. Joseph's honesty opened the door to Joseph's opportunity.

Honesty and truthfulness often pay future dividends as well. Joseph's integrity gained him the complete and total trust of the Pharaoh. After Joseph's father died, Joseph requested to leave Egypt in order to bury Jacob in the land of Canaan. Would Joseph forsake Egypt to embrace the home he had not seen in twenty years? Would the Pharaoh have reason to be concerned that Joseph might not return as he promised? *(Genesis 50:5-6)* Pharaoh granted Joseph's request without hesitation. True to his word, Joseph returned to Egypt. Joseph was a model of integrity.

Honest actions stem from integrity, and God requires the same of us.

❑ *God desires for me to be honest in my walk*—Joseph was honest in his warning before the Pharaoh because Joseph was honest in every aspect of his life. God requires that you be honest in everything you do. Are you honest in your place of employment? Do you give an honest day's work for an honest day's wage? Do you come in late and leave early? God expects honesty in your workplace *(II Corinthians 8:21)*. Honesty should lead the way for every step you take today. *"If you are good, you are guided by honesty. People who can't be trusted are destroyed by their own dishonesty" (Proverbs 11:3 GNT).*

❑ *God desires for me to be sincere in my integrity*—Your daily walk is what you do. Your integrity is what you are. Someone has put it this way: We sow an action, reap a habit, mold a character, and seal a destiny. Your actions become your conduct, and your conduct determines much about your future. Your reputation is your most valuable asset. *"If you have to choose between a good reputation and great wealth, choose a good reputation" (Proverbs 22:1).* Joseph could be honest in his conduct because he was sincere in his integrity. Jacob, Joseph's father, was a deceiver. Joseph certainly did not learn integrity from him. While Jacob's integrity was questionable, Nathaniel's integrity was not. Nathaniel was a disciple of Jesus. One day, while Jesus was talking to His other disciples, Jesus noticed Nathaniel walking in their direction: *"When Jesus saw Nathaniel coming to him, he said about him, "Here is a real Israelite; there is nothing false in him!" (John 1:47 GNT).* Jesus peered right into Nathaniel's heart and soul and perceived integrity. If

> Character is lost when a high ideal is sacrificed on the altar of popularity.
>
> ～※～

God were to tell you what He sees when He looks into your heart, your motives, and your thoughts, how would you feel? Would you be embarrassed? You do not have to be a Christian to lead a moral life. Only through the leading of God's Spirit, however, can the integrity of your faith be sincere before a holy God.

❑ *God desires for me to be truthful in my words*—Only by telling the Pharaoh the truth about the coming famine could Joseph allow him to decide how to survive it. Though the interpretation of Pharaoh's dreams brought unpleasant news, the king did not punish Joseph. Instead, he asked Joseph for advice! People respect honesty. Most people appreciate you telling them even unpleasant news so they can address the problem. *"Correct someone, and afterward he will appreciate it more than flattery" (Proverbs 28:23 GNT).*

Power Points:

➢ Do you think God would have punished Joseph if he had been not so honest about the news of the coming famine? Why? Why not?

➢ Why do you think Pharaoh believed Joseph's interpretation?

➢ How did Joseph's reputation make a way for him to reach this point? Do you think Joseph was having any second thoughts about his gift of dream interpretation? Why?

➢ Why do you think Joseph grew up with such integrity, when his brothers and father seemed to possess so little?

Reflection Section:

❑ I think little white lies are _____

❑ The last time I did not tell the truth, I felt _____

❑ If my child or best friend were to describe my integrity in one word, it would be _____

❑ Is your reputation such that people will believe you with no immediate proof? If not, why? How could you make it so?

❑ What is more important to God—not offending, or being completely honest?

❑ How has being completely honest brought blessing to you in the last year?

❑ "I would prefer that God not speak through me at all than to have me tell someone tragic news." Do you agree or disagree with this statement? Why?

❑ When was the last time your conscience truly bothered you?

❑ "I could be a little more honest at work by _____"

❑ The next time you have an opportunity to fudge on the truth, remember that Joseph saved two nations through revealing the truth. His honesty provided an opportunity for Pharaoh to act with full information. Be tactful, but be honest.

My Personal Growth Journal—

❑ Make a list of three things you might tell a *little white lie* about. Then write down your best reasons why you might lie about these things. Now talk to God about them. When you finish, write down how you felt inside as you prayed. Would you still tell these little white lies?

Personal Integrity Recipe (One Serving)

These ingredients have been tested and approved according to the PURE standard (Personal Upstanding Role model Exemplar), and found to be safe for human instruction. This product has been found to cause physical and emotional transformation when ingested over an extended period. Effective only as taken in moderate doses for an extended period. This product should NOT be discontinued if symptoms of situational ethics persist.

Directions for Use:

NOT FOR USE WITH INFANTS. To be used in early childhood. Mix thoroughly with effectual prayer, in an attitude of desire to please God. Continue through teenage years. **DO NOT USE SPARINGLY.**

Active Ingredients:

Internal essence of honestly 22%
Highly pasteurized conscience 19%
Concentrate of pure motive 16%
Carefully selected pure & edifying speech 16%
Doubly refined work ethic 14%
Tincture of tactfulness 5%
Naturally flavored worship 8%
Total 100%

CAUTION:

THIS PRODUCT IS HABIT-FORMING!

~ Chapter 15 ~

Being Too Heavenly-Minded: "The Principle of Practical Living"

Then Pharaoh gave Joseph an Egyptian name, Zaphenath-Paneah (God Speaks and He Lives). He also gave him an Egyptian wife, Asenath, the daughter of Potiphera, the priest of On (Heliopolis). And Joseph took up his duties over the land of Egypt. (Gen. 41:45)

The Joseph story....

Joseph not only interpreted the Pharaoh's dream regarding a great famine that would come upon Egypt, he also suggested a solution. To survive the famine, the Pharaoh would need to set over Egypt a wise and trustworthy governor to store grain during the seven years of plenty. The Pharaoh was impressed by Joseph's plan and elevated Joseph to the position of vizier—a position in which Joseph could carry out the precise solution he had offered. The Pharaoh also honored Joseph with a new Egyptian name and an Egyptian bride. Though Joseph had been Hebrew by birth, and never forgot his Hebrew God, he had spent twenty years of his life in Egypt. For all practical purposes, Joseph the Hebrew had now become Joseph the Egyptian. Joseph accepted the Pharaoh's favors. While not compromising his conscience, he understood that his life was now bound up in the affairs and customs of the Egyptians. The Pharaoh gave Joseph the name *Zaphenath-Paneah*, meaning: *"the living provider and savior, through whom God reveals secret things."* Joseph now had a position and a name that the people of Egypt would respect and honor for years to come. He would also raise two young sons and learn to forget the great hardships he had endured for in the many years he had been away from his home in Canaan.

Principle Truth: You will turn off more people to God by being too holy in irrelevant issues than by just about anything else you can do.

Sometimes we can act just too holy. Yes, we are to live holy and apart from sin. As Christians, we are freed from sin's death grip *(Romans 6:7-22)*. Understanding that, how should we interact with the sinful world?

Have you ever know well-meaning people who were so heavenly-minded they seemed to be of no earthly good? Sometimes Christians project a holier-than-thou attitude without meaning to, and they are just a bore to be around. God wants us to be holy. But by being too holy, we run the risk of alienating others.

I have taught students whose religion requires them to dress a certain way, eat only certain foods, and exclude themselves from participation in many of our classroom activities. While each religion has a right to practice whatever code of conduct it chooses, sometimes those restrictions isolate followers—rob from them the freedom to enjoy many of the things God has given us for pleasure.

God wants you first to live righteously and with your eyes wide open to the temptations of this sinful world *(Titus 2:12)*. Understanding that, there are the things that aren't classified as right or wrong. Sometimes compromising on non-sinful issues can provide a finer testimony to others than mere words. You must live in the world and be its light and salt *(Matthew 5:14)*. But God is concerned with more than just your actions. He's concerned with *why* you do what you do. He's concerned with your motive *(Galatians 2:20)*.

Joseph understood how to live peaceably among the Egyptians without adopting their sinful customs. Joseph did not accept the religion of the Egyptians. Nevertheless, he did graciously accept the Egyptian bride—given him by Pharaoh—who would one day bear him wonderful sons. Out of gratitude to Joseph, the Pharaoh also honored him with an Egyptian name. Joseph graciously accepted both gifts.

Joseph could have made an issue of taking his Egyptian name and wife, but he didn't. Joseph was not yet married, and having only one wife was a legal and highly encouraged custom in both Egypt as well as Israel. Taking a wife was not against Joseph's faith. But Joseph was being given a *foreign* wife. Since God continued to bless Joseph mightily, He obviously did not consider Joseph's actions to be wrong. Far more harm might have been done had Joseph protested that he could not accept this Egyptian honor. For all practical purposes, Joseph was now a citizen of Egypt, and he was gracious in accepting the bride from the people who sought to honor him. Later, Joseph observed the Egyptian custom of eating separately from foreigners, though the 'foreigners' were, in fact, his own brothers *(Genesis 43:32)*.

Sometimes we can cause more harm in seeing as sinful every action not specifically permitted by God. We complicate the freedom we are given through God's grace and make life difficult for others and ourselves around us. God does not want us to suffocate under restrictions that are not, in themselves, wrong. The Apostle Paul instructed the Corinthian church: *"Someone will say, 'I am allowed to do anything'. "Yes; but not everything is good for you. I could say that I am allowed to do anything, but I am not going to let anything make me its slave" (I Corinthians 6:12 GNT)*. Consider the motive of what you do. Is your motive to glorify God? *(Romans 14:7-8)* Is your *motive* to glorify Christ? *(I Thessalonians 5:10)* Motive is the key. With a godly motive, you will seldom stray into actions displeasing to God.

Joseph would not compromise regarding sin, but rather than insult those who respected him, he agreed to conform to certain Egyptian customs. In the same way, concerning matters that do not involve our compromising with doctrinal precepts of the Christian faith, we might remember not to be so heavenly-minded that we become no earthy good.

Practical living in a sinful world requires a road map.

❑ *It's OK to have physical desires, as long as I keep my passions under control*—God made you with physical desires. They are natural. As long as they are used as God intended they are not improper. It has been said that sexual passion is much like vanilla extract. In proper amounts, it is pleasing; in excess, it brings bitterness. It is when improper and unhealthy physical desires are entertained excessively—or apart from God's intention—that problems arise. Joseph understood this well. So did the apostle Paul. *"I discipline my body and make it my slave, so that, after I have preached to others, I myself will not be disqualified" (I Corinthians 9:27 NASB)*.

> *In matters of style, swim with the current; in matters of principle, stand like a rock.*
>
> —Thomas Jefferson

❑ *It's OK to enjoy myself as long as I obey the law*—God did not intend legal authority to terrorize the good citizen *(Romans 13:1-7)*. He did intend the laws of the land to govern us in His place *(I Peter 2:13-15)*. Laws are to protect us and we are bound to observe them. Even paying taxes is encouraged by God *(Matthew 22:18-21)*. "*Be a good citizen. All governments are under God. Insofar as there is peace and order, it's God's order. So live responsibly as a citizen…the government working to your advantage. But if you're breaking the rules right and left, watch out. The police aren't there just to be admired in their uniforms. God also has an interest in keeping order, and he uses them to do it*" *(Romans 13:1,4)*.

❑ *It's OK to utilize the environment as long as I remember to respect it*—"*Good people take care of their animals, but wicked people are cruel to theirs*" *(Proverbs 12:10 GNT)*. Many would tell us that we should never cut a tree, kill an animal, or take from "Mother Earth." But Father God tells us that we are stewards of the earth, not its slaves. God created the beauty of the natural world to reveal His glory *(Psalms 19:1-8)*. The earth is to serve us. The earth is not to be worshipped. "*Be fruitful, and multiply, and replenish the earth, and subdue it: and have dominion over the fish of the sea, and over the fowl of the air, and over every living thing that moves upon the earth*" *(Genesis 1:28 KJV)*. The earth yields its bounty to us. The animal world serves us with labor, companionship and food. We are not to abuse either the earth or its creatures. We are to enjoy and care for both.

❑ *It's OK to have the friends I want as long as I hang with the proper company*—"*Don't envy bad people; don't even want to be around them*" *(Proverbs 24:1)*. We are made social creatures.

Few of us desire to live alone. God understands your desire for companionship through friendship. It has been said that a good friend is someone who can put a finger on your problem without rubbing it in. But God instructs us to choose carefully those with whom we socialize. *"Do not try to work together as equals with unbelievers, for it cannot be done. How can right and wrong be partners? How can light and darkness live together?" (II Corinthians 6:14 GNT)* Be careful which friends you choose.

❑   *It's OK to spend my money as long as I also save prudently*—*"You lazy fool, look at an ant. Watch it closely; let it teach you a thing or two. Nobody has to tell it what to do. All summer it stores up food; at harvest it stockpiles provisions" (Proverbs 6:6-8)*. Money is not the root of all evil. It's the *love* of money *(I Timothy 6:10)*. The money you work hard for is yours. Remember the old truism, though: *"When your outflow exceeds your income, your upkeep becomes your downfall."* You are not to spend your money on things that are sinful or inappropriate. Instead, you are responsible to pay your debts and give to God's service. Other than that, you are free to spend your money as you choose. But God also urges you to save *(Proverbs 10:5)*. Saving keeps you from presuming on the future *(Proverbs 30:25)*.

❑   *It's OK to go where I want as long as I follow the right road*—*"The road of right living bypasses evil; watch your step and save your life" (Proverbs 16:17)*. My grandmother would never be seen near a theater. To her, going to a movie of any kind was wrong. Had she done so, it would have been wrong for her. Although I knew going to some films would obviously be wrong for me as a Christian, I did not share my grandmother's view that all movies were sinful. Where you go or don't go is up to you. Just be sure your road and your reputation won't be compromised. Examine your path carefully, for not every path may lead where it appears. *"What you think is the right road may lead to death" (Proverbs 14:12 GNT)*. Ask God to direct your path. Trust Him for direction and speed, and He will not lead you wrong *(Proverbs 3:5-6; cp. Matthew 6:13)*.

❑ *It's OK to stand up for right and wrong as long as I don't argue over irrelevant things—"Don't let people waste time in endless speculation over myths and spiritual pedigrees. For these things only cause arguments; they don't help people live a life of faith in God" (I Timothy 1:4 NLT)*. God gives you clear instructions in His Word regarding right and wrong. Your responsibility is to know His instructions about these and to teach others God's precepts. What you are not to do is create standards of right and wrong regarding 'neutral' things, and impose these standards on others. The Jews changed custom and tradition into ethical matters of right and wrong. This made life difficult for the people. Live peaceably with others, and God can mysteriously cause others to be at peace with you *(Proverbs 16:7)*. Even Joseph reminded his brothers not to argue on their way back to Canaan *(Genesis 45:24)*. Don't argue over trivial concerns. If God doesn't worry about them, why should you?

❑ *It's OK to do whatever I want as long as I don't offend God, my conscience, or weak Christians! "We are allowed to do anything," so they say. That is true, but not everything is good. "We are allowed to do anything"—but not everything is helpful. None of you should be looking out for your own interests, but for the interests of others. You are free to eat anything sold in the meat market, without asking any questions because of your conscience.*

For, as the scripture says, 'The earth and every-thing in it belong to the Lord'" (I Corinthians 10:23-26 GNT). Here is the key to practical living in a sinful world: we are free to do as we desire in light of God's moral instruction. God created us with a conscience as a pilot light—a "mini monitor"—of His moral will. But our conscience is not foolproof. Neither should it be identified with the Holy Spirit. God's Spirit *directs* us; our conscience *inspects* us. The Spirit is that shadow that pursues us when we run from our actions. It is that still small voice that sometimes makes us feel smaller still. Jesus even taught us that sometimes we need to be a little more 'worldly wise' *(Luke 16:8),* and encouraged us to use the practical wisdom of the world remembering to be careful not to sin. *"Listen! I am sending you out just like sheep to a pack of wolves. You must be as cautious as snakes and as gentle as doves" (Matthew 10:16 GNT).* We are also free *not* to do something that would cause another believer to be offended. If something you feel comfortable in doing might offend a believer not as strong in the faith as you are, just don't do it. People are more important to God than your liberty in Christ *(I Corinthians 8:9; I Peter 2:16).* Remember, not all Christians are as liberated in their Christianity as you are. *"We then, that are strong ought to bear the infirmities of the weak, and not to please ourselves. Let every one of us please his neighbor for his good to edification" (Romans 15:1-2 KJV).* Joseph took an Egyptian wife. He also took an Egyptian name. No doubt he followed Egyptian customs as he ruled this foreign people. But Joseph did not worship Egyptian gods. Like Joseph, follow your conscience, follow your God, do your best not to offend Christians who do not accept the liberty we have in Christ, and try not to be so heavenly-minded that you become no earthly good.

"Stand fast therefore in the liberty wherewith Christ hath made us free…" (Galatians 5:1 KJV).

Power Points:

➤ Was Joseph wrong in taking the Egyptian name and wife?

➤ Why do you think God never refers to Joseph as *Zaphenath-Paneah* after this chapter?

➤ How do you think the wine taster felt when Joseph was exalted?

➤ How do you think Potiphar felt?

➤ How do you think Potiphar's wife felt?

➤ How did Joseph decide it would be OK to take the Egyptian wife he had probably never met?

Reflection Section:

❑ Knowing when it is OK to compromise without sinning assumes that we know God's standards of right and wrong. Do you study your Bible enough to know right from wrong, or do you merely believe what others tell you?

❑ Do you know any believers who are "weak" in the faith? How do you make special considerations for them?

❑ "It's OK to date non-Christians as long as you try to lead them to Christ." Do you agree or disagree with this statement? Why?

❑ "You can never go wrong if you just follow your conscience." Do you agree or disagree with this statement? Why?

❏   "Killing trees and animals is not right. After all, God made them, and they have a right to exist too." Do you agree or disagree with this statement? Why?

❏   What would you have done if the most powerful man in the world presented you with a mate you had never met before?

❏   Understand that loving others and showing them the ways of God is what God put you here for, and that a stuffy, holier-than-thou attitude never brought any soul to Christ.

❏   Live to make others thirsty for God, not frustrated with the minor details of conduct. You must be *insulated* from the world's sinful influence, but not *isolated* from the people in it that you may lead to God.

❏   Is there someone who might secretly think you are *too* holy in your conduct, or perhaps, that you probably aren't a Christian at all? Why might they think this? What can you do?

My Personal Growth Journal—

❏   Make a list right now of the twenty most distinguished characteristics Joseph displayed that make him a role model for youth and adults. When you finish, number from one to seven the ones you feel are his greatest assets. How can you become a better Christian from what you wrote on your list?

~ Chapter 16 ~

Chickens Always Come Home to Roost: "The Principle of Sowing"

His brothers said, "So! You're going to rule us? You're going to boss us around?" And they hated him more than ever because of his dreams and the way he talked. He had another dream and told this one also to his brothers: "I dreamed another dream—the sun and moon and eleven stars bowed down to me!" When he told it to his father and brothers, his father reprimanded him: "What's with all this dreaming? Am I and your mother and your brothers all supposed to bow down to you?" (Genesis 37:8)

Joseph was running the country; he was the one who gave out rations to all the people. When Joseph's brothers arrived, they treated him with honor, bowing to him. (Genesis 42:6)

Do not be deceived, God is not mocked; for whatever a man sows, this he will also reap. (Galatians 6:7 NASV)

The Joseph story....

Joseph, once sold by his jealous brothers into Egyptian slavery, was now the second most powerful man in the world. As vizier over Egypt, Joseph had initiated a course of action that would save the people from the terrible famine God had predicted. Grain was stored in silos during the seven years of good harvest. But, just as God had revealed, the famine followed. All the lands were ravaged. The famine was widespread and eventually reached Joseph's homeland of Canaan. Jacob, Joseph's older brothers—even little Benjamin—were facing certain starvation. But word came of a vast storehouse of grain in Egypt. Sent with payment silver by their father Jacob, Joseph's older brothers were forced to make the long journey in search of food. Upon their arrival, the brothers stood before *Zaphenath-Paneah*—their brother—and the second most powerful man in the world

Principle Truth: You will harvest what you plant. The time factor alone is the variable.

What goes around comes around. Your chickens will always come home to roost. These are modern spins on an old truism—a truism as old as nature itself. What you plant is what grows. The harvest far exceeds that which was planted. The harvest takes time. These principles also work in life, as Joseph's brothers would soon find out to their utter dismay.

Good actions almost certainly harvest good results, and bad ones result in bad. This is divine justice, prescribed by a Divine Accountant. *"He who digs a pit will fall into it, And he who rolls a stone, it will come back on him" (Proverbs 26:27 NASB).* But does it always happen? So often, we see the good seeds planted by good people, which never seem to come to fruition, while evil people seem to get away with everything they do. We reap what we sow. But not always tomorrow.

> The fire you kindle for your enemy often burns you more than him.
>
> —Chinese Proverb
>
> ❧❧

Take Naboth for example. Naboth planted a vineyard and grew some of the finest grapes in Israel. One day, King Ahab decided he would take Naboth's vineyard for his own. The king could have had any vineyard he wanted, but chose the precise one that was not for sale. In despicable cruelty, King Ahab's wicked wife Jezebel promptly had Naboth murdered. But God's principle of sowing and reaping dictated through Elijah the prophet that, by the wall in that same vineyard belonging to Naboth, dogs would someday eat the flesh of the wicked queen. Though Naboth would not see it, God would show the same lack of pity for Jezebel as Jezebel had for Naboth *(cp. I Kings 21:23; II Kings 9:36).*

While God works through the agricultural principle of sowing and reaping, seeds do not grow overnight. Seeds take time to produce their fruit. When it grows, that which is produced far exceeds what was planted. God often mysteriously allows not only payback in like currency, but usually with interest! We see God's principle in His judgment of Israel's sin: *"For they have sown the wind, and they shall reap the whirlwind..." (Hosea 8:7 KJV).*

What we must not forget is that Joseph's brothers hated Joseph because of his dreams. Dreams of grain, foretelling that someday they would bow down to him in servitude. Surely this would never come to pass! Ironically, however, the very crime against Joseph that resulted *from* the dream also resulted in that dream's fulfillment. In selling their brother into Egyptian service, Joseph would become the savior to whom those very brothers would have to bow down begging for grain.

Whether we are always privy to seeing the process of sowing and reaping realized, we must not forget that God is the great Accountant who balances all books and that someday every man's account will be settled. Therefore, be extremely careful what you plant today. Remember that you are planting today for future harvests—good harvest or bad. Consider this principle more specifically in the following thoughts:

❑   *My planted seeds grow the same crop*—You cannot plant tomatoes and hope to grow apples. What you plant is what you grow. *"Don't be misled: No one makes a fool of God. What a person plants, he will harvest. The person who plants selfishness, ignoring the needs of others—ignoring God—harvests a crop of weeds. All he'll have to show for his life is weeds! But the one who plants in response to God, letting God's Spirit do the growth work in him, harvests a crop of real life, eternal life"* (Gal. 6:7-8).

We see this principle in the lives of:

■   *Jacob*—Joseph's father Jacob deceived his own father Isaac with the hide of a goat. He tried to appear as Esau, whose skin was rough and hairy, so that he could steal the family blessing. Later, it was the blood of a goat that Jacob's own sons put on Joseph's coat to deceive *their* father. A goat became the object of deception by, and against, Jacob *(Genesis 27:16; 37:31).*

■   *Joseph's brothers*—not only did they bow to and serve the very one they had thought would never be their master, they reaped the harvest of many other "seeds" they once planted in selling their brother:

As Joseph was forced to travel to Egypt in great hardship, so too were the brothers *(Genesis 37:28; 42:1-5).*

As they accused Joseph of spying, so too were *they* accused of the same *(Genesis 37:2, 18; 42:9).*

As Joseph was tested when first arrived in Egypt, so too were *they* tested *(Genesis 39:7; 42:16).*

As Joseph had been cast into the prison, so too were the brothers cast into the same prison *(Genesis 39:20; 42:17).*

As they had separated Joseph from his family, so too was Simeon separated *(Genesis 37:28; 42:24)*.

As Joseph was bound while imprisoned, so too was Simeon bound *(Psalms 102:18-19; Genesis 42:24)*.

- *Absalom*—David's son was proud of his long hair. Later, in trying to escape Joab, David's captain, Absolam's hair became entangled in a tree, and he was killed. The object of his pride became the object of his fall *(II Samuel 14:25-26; 18:9)*.

- *Haman*—The wicked advisor to the king sought to destroy all the Jews in Persia. He built a hangman's gallows to hang Mordecai. Haman was eventually hanged on the very gallows he built for another *(Esther 7:10)*.

❏ *My planted seeds grow slowly over time*—Seeds you plant today seldom produce fruit tomorrow. It takes time for the process. The same is true with the good and bad seeds of deeds you plant in the lives of others. Have you planted seeds of hate, unkindness, deception, or evil and not seen them grow back against you? Have you planted seeds of good will, generosity, or kindness and not seen them return good to you? Growth takes time. Be patient, the harvest comes.

❏ *My planted seeds grow far more than what I planted*—Joseph's brothers vowed they would never bow to their brother. In truth however, we are told they bowed before him several times! *(Genesis 42:6, 43:26, 28)* When you plant one kernel of corn, do you expect the harvest to be one kernel? Of course not. The harvest is much greater than the seed planted. Jesus taught this principle in the Parable of the Mustard Seed: *"...which indeed is the least of all the seeds: but when it is grown, it is the greatest among herbs..." (Matthew 13:32 KJV)*. As long as God is doing the accounting, you can expect your investment to produce a return with interest. *"Treat her exactly as she has treated you; pay her back double for all she has done. Fill her cup with a drink twice as strong as the drink she prepared for you" (Revelation 18:6 GNT)*.

As we have seen, the principle of sowing and reaping works with seeds of evil that we sow. But let's not forget—the principle also works with good seed.

Good seed—good fruit. What fruit does God expect from you? God has sown the Holy Spirit in your heart, and expects you to produce certain fruits of Christianity. You must understand, your Christianity *produces* these fruits— these fruits do not *make* you a Christian! A dog barks *because* it's a dog—it's not a dog because it *barks*! Also, understand that you may not always produce these fruits every day. Nevertheless, these are fruits you should expect to see growing in your life:

- God says I will produce the fruit of love for other Christians *(I John 2:29; 3:3-5).*

- God says I will produce the fruit of being led by His Holy Spirit *(I John 3:24; 4:13; 5:10).*

- God says I will produce the fruit of righteous living, and not sinning as a habit of life *(I John 1:8; 3:9).*

- God says I will produce the fruit of love and prayer—even for those who don't like me *(Matthew 5:44-45).*

- God says I will produce the fruit of enduring patiently through troubles from this sinful world *(Philippians 1:28; II Timothy 3:12).*

- God says I will produce the fruit of sometimes being disciplined by God *(Hebrews 12:6-8; Revelation 3:19).*

- God says I will produce the fruit of praying and receiving answered prayer *(Galatians 4:6; I John 3:22).*

- God says I will produce the fruit of living by faith and trusting in God *(Hebrews 10:31).*

- God says I will produce the fruit of living a Christian life *(I John 2:3, 19 II John 9; John 8:31).*

Fruitcake Christianus

The ingredients of this product have been carefully selected by the Heavenly Farmer and must be carefully blended in the proper amounts for a properly flavored cake. The cake will not bake properly or develop the traditional *fruitcake Christianus* aroma if all parts of the recipe are not mixed as instructed. Product has been indicated in the symptoms of well-roundedness, and assurance of salvation. CAKE WILL DEVELOP A MORE INTENSE FLAVOR IF BAKED AT LIFE'S HIGHEST HEAT SETTING.

Directions for Use:

Mix equal parts of all ingredients in moderately-sized life bowl. Add one cup daily of spiritual water and bake at moderate to high heat until cake becomes well-rounded and aromatic. **SERVE IMMEDIATELY. DO NOT LET COOL.**

Active Ingredients:

Fruit of living in Christ's teaching .... *I John 2:3;19*
.... *II John 9; John 8:31*
Fruit of living in faith and trust in God.................... *Hebrews 10:31*
Fruit of praying, and answered prayer .... *Galatians 4:6*
.... *I John 3:22*
Fruit of sometimes receiving God's discipline........*Hebrews 12:6-8*
.... *Revelation 3:19*
Fruit of facing trouble from a sinful world ....*Philippians 1:28*
Fruit of love for my enemies .... *Matthew 5:44-45*
Fruit of living a righteous life .... *I John 1:8; 3:9*
Fruit of being led by the Holy Spirit ....*I John 3:24; 4:13; 5:10*
Fruit of love for other Christians .... *I John 2:29; 3:3-5*
Total .... **Filled with the Spirit**

CAUTION:

DO NOT TRUST THE SINCERITY OF THESE INGREDIENTS IF THE SEAL OF THE SPIRIT IS NOT EVIDENT!

Power Points:

➤ Do you think Joseph's brothers had ever explained to Jacob the truth about Joseph?

➤ Why do you think Joseph's brothers did not recognize him?

➤ Why do you think Joseph chose not to reveal himself to them immediately?

➤ Why do you think Joseph did not inquire about the health of their father?

➤ What do you think were the first thoughts of Joseph as he laid eyes on his brothers for the first time in over twenty years? Do you think 'payback' ever crossed is mind?

➤ Do you think Joseph remembered his dream regarding his brothers?

Reflection section:

❏ What seeds are you planting at this point in your life?

❏ How many of the Fruits of the Spirit can you identify in your life?

❏ Had you been Joseph, would you have revealed yourself to your brothers right then and there? Why? Why not?

❏ If you could be sure that what you were investing in your life, your family, your job, and your friends would someday produce a harvest in like kind, would you be happy, or fearful?

❏ Make an effort today to plant kindness in someone's life.

❏ Avoid the temptation to say or do something today that you would not want to grow into a harvest you might someday be forced to reap.

❑ Have you planted good things that have yet to grow? Don't get discouraged. Trust God and remember—*growth takes time*. Be patient.

My Personal Growth Journal—

❑ Pick from *one to five words* that would describe your feelings if you had been Joseph when you first laid eyes on your brothers for the first time in twenty years. Now describe *why* you would feel these emotions. Make a second list describing how you think *Joseph* felt. When you finish, compare *your* list with the one you made for Joseph. How do they differ? How are they similar? What does this tell you?

~ Chapter 17 ~

Continually Trusting God: "The Principle of Daily Bread"

When they had eaten all the food they had brought back from Egypt, their father said, "Go back and get some more food." (Gen. 43:2).

Give us this day our daily bread. (Matthew 6:11 NKJV).

The Joseph story....

The seven-year famine God had predicted continued. All the countries of the area were affected, including Joseph's homeland of Canaan. Under Joseph's wise leadership, Egypt had stored vast quantities of grain in silos. Egypt was not only able to weather the famine, but to help others countries which could not. Joseph's brothers had been forced by the famine to come to Egypt to purchase food. Although Joseph's brothers did not recognize him, he recognized them and offered them an ample supply to meet their needs, and the needs of Benjamin, Jacob, and Jacob's household. What Joseph did not give them was enough provision to last the *entire* seven years of the famine. Joseph offered them only enough grain to ensure they would eventually run out. Little did the brothers know that the provider they were trusting this time was the provider they would be forced to trust again. But Joseph did not fully trust his brothers. He wanted to test them to see if their integrity and love for a brother was now different than it had been when they sold him into Egyptian slavery. In giving his brothers a limited provision of grain, Joseph put the payment silver back into their bags. He also demanded that his brothers leave Simeon in Egypt to make sure they returned.

❧

Principle Truth: Recognizing the provision and opportunity God gives you today reveals more about your trust in God than all your assumptions about what tomorrow may bring.

We want it. We want it all. We want it all *now*. Our culture has developed not only a short attention span, but also an attitude of immediate gratification. Instant coffee, instant oatmeal, instant soup. We don't want to wait anymore. Waiting stresses our patience and raises our blood pressure.

Recently, I watched a woman impatiently drive away from a restaurant's fast food window because her order was taking more than a minute. We are so impatient to have it all now that lottery corporations have initiated a means for winners to have all the money paid in a lump some, rather than over time, a set-up that usually cuts the payout in half. Never mind. We want it now. We want it *all* now. We are a society of "I need it now." We are so impatient.

God wants us to trust. He wants us to trust Him on a daily basis. God loves us and wants to provide for our needs, but God does not provide our needs all at once. In His wisdom, God has created a world of cycles. His sunshine is provided to us on a daily basis. On a daily cycle we eat, we sleep, we work. On a daily basis, we are required to trust God for our health, the produce of His earth loaned to us—even the unfolding of His plan for our life.

In ancient Israel, people used a small clay container filled with olive oil as their lamp. With this lamp as their source of light, they could make their way through the darkness, carefully avoiding danger which might lie along their path. The lamp was an indispensable tool for survival in the night. Olive oil is limited in its brightness, however. The light from the lamp was only bright enough to reveal the next step along the way. The night journey required a slow and watchful awareness—one step at time.

> *Trust the past to God's mercy, the present to God's love and the future to God's providence.*
>
> *—Augustine*

This is how God wants us to trust Him. As He provides for us each day, God also desires our fellowship. That's why He asks us to pray, so that He can provide for us through fellowship. God promised us daily bread that our needs might be met, but promised *only* daily bread that we might not waste and will need to come to Him for more. Last week's food, last week's sleep, and last week's Bible study just won't carry us through today. God wants us to commit to Him every need we have on a *daily* basis. King Solomon understood what many of us in this fast-paced world today do not. If God granted us everything we needed at once we might be tempted to waste and never fellowship with Him in prayer. If He granted us everything we wanted, we might become presumptuous and glory in our own pride. *"I ask you, God, to let me have two things before I die: keep me from lying, and let me be neither rich nor poor. So give me only as much food as I need. If I have more, I might say that I do not need you. But if I am poor, I might steal and bring disgrace on my God" (Proverbs 30:8-9 GNT).*

God showed us the "daily bread" principle with the manna—the heavenly bread with which He fed the Hebrews after they escaped the Pharaoh's wrath in the Exodus from Egypt. God promised it on a daily basis, not a weekly basis. God loved His people and fed them so that there would be no lack, no excess, and no waste *(Exodus 16:4-21).*

God also showed us the 'daily bread' principle with the pillar of fire that led the Hebrews on a daily basis *(Exodus 13:21-22).* God fed and led his people, but these provisions were to encourage trust in Him. These were only a small part of a greater plan God had for them.

In the same manner, Joseph provided for his family. He loved them and wanted them to trust him for their provision. He provided just enough grain for them that they would not starve, but not so much that they might be tempted to waste. He supplied them with enough to meet their needs, but only so much that they would have to return to him and trust him for more. Providing grain was only a small but necessary part of a greater plan Joseph had for his family.

God's daily provision is all He has promised; He wants us to return to Him daily in trust and fellowship. Meeting our daily needs is only a part of God's greater plan for our lives.

❑ *Today, God, help me to trust you for my necessary requirements*—God promised to supply your daily bread, not steaks and caviar for the next month. God wants to hear from you on a daily basis. Ask God to supply you with your needs today. Even though He already knows them, He loves you and wants you to talk with Him in fellowship. God is glorified in answering your prayers. His forgiveness and His compassion are ever renewed, and available to you on a daily basis *(Lamentations 3:22-23; I John 1:7).* Today, you will trust Him to supply you with your needs, not necessarily your wants, to get you to tomorrow *(Matthew 6:8-11; 25-34).*

❑ *Today, God, help me to remember that you have numbered my steps*— God knows and has planned every step of your life, but you are still required to walk them. Not only has He numbered your steps, God also wants to guide and direct them. God knows that for whatever reason, you cannot always choose the proper steps to take *(Jeremiah 10:23).* All

God requires of you is to trust Him *(Proverbs 3:5-6)*. Today, you will trust Him to lead you in the right direction, to meet the right people, to keep you on the right path *(Psalms 37:28; Matthew 6:13)*.

❏ *Today, God, help me to count on you for the words I should speak*—God understands that sometimes you might not know just what to say, or how to say it. Moses was a poor speaker, but God used him mightily because Moses trusted God *(Exodus 4:10)*. If you are trusting Him fully today, He will even give you the right words at the right time. God also knows that today there will be times you should say nothing *(Psalms 39:1)*. Today, you will watch what you say and trust God to help you say the appropriate things to the people He puts in your path *(Matthew 10:19)*.

❏ *Today, God, help me to use my time wisely*—We are all busy. We all feel we will never get everything done. But we all are given only a certain amount of time in life. God knows exactly how long you will live. In fact, He has numbered your days. David understood that our days upon this earth are relatively short *(Psalms 89:47)*. The Apostle Paul's instructs us that, because of this, and because we live in a sinful world, we are to use our time wisely *(Ephesians 5:16; Colossians 4:5)*. God has given us only two times: *today* and *too late!* Once we "kill time," it has no resurrection! Henry David Thoreau once remarked that we cannot kill time without injuring eternity. Are you using your time wisely? Do you need to take time out to rest today to make your work more productive tomorrow? Are you spending quality time with you children— time that can never be made up? Missed opportunities are gone forever. Plan your days so that you can make the most effective use of the limited time God has given you, and don't forget to give time to study of God's Word *(I Timothy 2:15; Psalms 90:12)*.

❏ *Today, God, help me to be patient if You don't answer a prayer immediately*—Patience is not something that comes naturally to most of us. Patience is something God teaches us while He asks us to wait. Joseph's mother was Rachel. Rachel, like Hannah and Sara, other mothers in Scripture, had waited a long time for a child. Day after day passed before God finally answered the prayers of those women. God always answers our prayers. Sometimes He says yes. Sometimes He says no. Most of the time, He requires us to wait. Waiting is hard, but God does not work according to our clock. God is more interested in making you perfect and complete than giving you everything you ask for.

Sometimes He teaches you this through patience *(James 1:3-4)*. This doesn't mean He won't answer your request. It just means He's asking you to wait *(Psalms 3:5)*. Today, you will continue to pray for things God has asked you to wait for. Today, you will learn to trust even more and not be discouraged over unanswered prayers *(Genesis 30:22-24)*.

❑ *Today, God, help me to influence another life for good*—Since God has ordered your steps today, you can be sure others will observe you, even though you don't realize it. Often, your greatest influence on others is by your conduct, not your conversation. Today, you will live so that even *those you never notice will see the good in you.*

❑ *Today, God, help me to forgive others as You have forgiven me*— Though God has ordered your steps today, this does not mean you will be immune from hurt. Someone may do or say something unkind to you. This is just a part of living. Today, you will remember how much God has forgiven you, and forgive others as you would want them to forgive you *(Matthew 6:12)*.

❑ *Today, God, help me to keep things in Your perspective, not mine*— Finally, remember that today is a tiny piece of your life's puzzle. God sees the finished work. You don't. Today, you will remember that even in doing your best, unfinished things will remain. See these in light of God's perspective. He has things under control. He has even numbered the hairs on your head! Don't become frustrated because your day seems to finish uncompleted *(Matthew 10:30)*.

We are all impatient in this hurried world. But God has chosen to bless us only on a daily basis, that we might have to return to Him for tomorrow's needs. Yesterday is gone forever, and tomorrow may never come. Trust God today in all that you do and say.

Power Points:

➢ Why do you think Joseph wanted to test his brothers by forcing them to return to Canaan, and then back to Egypt? Was he wrong in giving them only *limited* provision?

➢ Why did Joseph choose Simeon as the one to keep in Egypt?

> ➤ What do you think Joseph's brothers might have been thinking as they made the journey from Egypt back to Canaan?

> ➤ How would you feel if you were Jacob and the famine forced your sons to have to beg food in Egypt?

Reflection section:

❑ Trust God to meet your needs today, and pray tonight that He will do the same tomorrow.

❑ Which do you think is a better use of time: memorizing scripture verses or studying small Bible passages each day?

❑ Why should we thank God for things that seem certain in our lives?

❑ Why does God 'need' our fellowship?

❑ Do you ever become impatient with God when He seems to pour out His blessings on others, while trickling His blessings down on you?

❑ "God may have numbered my steps, but walking them is up to me!" Do you agree or disagree with this statement? Why?

❑ Remember, daily bread is all He has promised. It just might be that He is refining your trust-factor, so that you will never presume upon His grace.

My Personal Growth Journal—

❑ Decide today to redeem your time wisely by a regular, systematic Bible study. Get a good study Bible and a notebook. Plan to go through the entire Bible in a year. Start today; do not wait till the New Year.

~ Chapter 18 ~

Safe Forever: "The Principle of Salvation's Security"

"I'll take full responsibility for his safety; it's my life on the line for his. If I don't bring him back safe and sound, I'm the guilty one; I'll take all the blame." (Gen. 43:9)

In the morning he took out two silver coins and gave them to the innkeeper, saying, "Take good care of him. If it costs any more, put it on my bill—I'll pay you…" (Luke 10:35)

The Joseph story....

The terrible famine continued. Joseph had provided a supply of food for his family back in Canaan that they might survive during the seven-year famine. But now the food had run out, and his brothers would have to return to Egypt for more. When old Jacob discovered that the payment silver for the first supply of grain was found in the bags of his sons, he was puzzled. But, when he heard the request that in order to purchase more grain he would have to send his beloved Benjamin, he was grieved to his soul. Joseph was lost to him, Simeon sat in an Egyptian prison, and now Benjamin might possibly be taken from him. But what choice did Jacob have? To appease their old father, Reuben guaranteed the safety of Benjamin with the lives of his own two sons. Judah, however, guaranteed Benjamin's security with his *own* life. Jacob's choices were now limited to starvation or the slow extinction of his family.

Principle Truth: An all-knowing God considered every provision necessary to get you home and promised that you would not get lost along the way.

My grandmother prayed for her salvation every day. She never accepted that the grace of God through His son had saved her from all her sins—sins of her past, sins of her present—sins of her future. My grandmother could not understand that she was secure in the Person of an almighty Savior, and that He had promised to deliver her home safely. In the end, He did. Now she understands.

Sometimes it is hard to understand God—to comprehend His power, His majesty, and His love. Sometimes it is hard to understand the things He allows to enter our life, and why He does what He does. One of the hardest things to understand is how God can keep His sometimes-rebellious children eternally secure.

Like my grandmother, many Christians feel they are responsible for maintaining their salvation and assuring their entrance into heaven. God does require obedience from us. But such obedience should be a loving response to a Savior, not a fearful obligation to a cruel master.

God saved us through the death of His Son. God promised to keep us eternally secure through that Son's resurrection life. We have eternal life through Christ alone. In the same manner, Judah promised full responsibility for Benjamin's security. Reuben offered the lives of his own sons if Benjamin was not safely returned to Jacob. Judah's assurance was *personal*. His own life guaranteed the life of the youngest brother in the journey to the far country, when in reality, Benjamin was safe in the protection of one who loved him more than life itself. Nevertheless, had Judah offered his life for Benjamin, his noble gesture would not have brought Benjamin back to Jacob. Jacob would have simply lost both sons. Christ's death, however, keeps us secure, and He ever lives to keep us that way *(Hebrews 7:25)*. Christ's assurance of security to us provides what Judah's assurance for Benjamin could not. Christ keeps us *eternally* secure in our journey to the far country.

If our Savior cannot keep us saved, we do not have eternal security. We have only conditional security. Conditional security is not security at all. Because we are safe in Christ does not give us a license to sin. Our safety in Christ will motivate us *not* to sin. Such is the working of the Holy Spirit in our lives.

God delights in us recognizing that His Son has become the surety—the guarantee of our salvation forever. Understanding this, we can begin to perform the will of God in our lives through the strength of the Spirit and not concern ourselves with losing our salvation.

- *I know I'm safe and secure as God's child because God specially selected me*—Before you came to God through Christ, He selected you to be His child. Don't try to understand how this all works together. Just accept it. You can feel safe and secure in your salvation in knowing that God had a reason to want you enough to choose you to be His long before you were ever born *(John 15:16,19; I Thessalonians 1:4; Romans 8:29-30,33; Ephesians 1:4; I Peter 1:1-2; Cp. Acts 9:15)*.

- *I know I'm safe and secure as God's child because God said He would never leave me*—God can be everywhere, all the time, all at once, forever. He is timeless. God is the Father who never leaves His children. He promised that you would never perish *(John 3:16; 10:27-29)*, that you would never be lost *(John 6:39)*, and that He would be with you always *(Hebrews 13:5)*.

- *I know I'm safe and secure as God's child because God bought me with a price*—You sinned and became sin's servant. God cannot tolerate sin. Sin is a violation against God's holiness. In God's plan, sin had to be paid for with a price equal to His holiness. You could not afford that cost, but God could by sending His Son to die for your sins. You can feel safe and secure in your salvation through knowing that, if God paid the ultimate price to purchase you from the slavery of sin, He will not change His mind, or renege on the redemption. The story is told of a young boy who exercised great care to build himself a toy wooden boat. As he set it adrift on the pond where he lived, the little boat drifted far from his reach and was lost to him. One day, the boy noticed his boat for sale in the window of a toy store. He went inside and bought the little boat with all the money he had to offer. He stared at it and was heard to say, "Now little boat, you are mine twice. First I made you, now I've bought you." This is the story of God's redemption. First, He made you, then He purchased you back from sin's death grip. You are secure as God's child because He redeemed you. You are His purchased possession. You are His *twice! (Ephesians 1:7,14; I Corinthians 6:20; 7:23; I Peter 1:18-19; II Thessalonians 2:13; Galatians 3:13; Titus 2:14)*

- *I know I'm safe and secure as God's child because God adopted me to be His*—It takes a special love to adopt a child. Adoption is an act of deliberate choice, not chance. God deliberately and purposefully adopted you into His family. In the Roman world, adopted sons inherited equally with sons by birth. They were not treated differently. You can feel safe and secure in your salvation knowing that God had a deliberate purpose in making you a permanent family member. Since He's God, He doesn't change His mind *(Romans 8:15; Galatians 4:5; Ephesians 1:5)*.

• *I know I'm safe and secure as God's child because God put His seal on me*—Sealing and stamping our envelope is usually the last thing we do to guarantee safe delivery of a letter. God has sealed you with the guarantee of His Spirit *(II Corinthians 1:22)*. He has promised that you are safe until the day of His delivery. You can feel safe and secure in your salvation through knowing God has guaranteed to deliver you home as His prized package, and He never loses what is His *(Ephesians 1:13; 4:30)*.

• *I know I'm safe and secure as God's child because God's Son is my heavenly attorney*—God wants you to know that Jesus stands before Him to plead your case before any who would challenge your salvation *(Hebrews 7:25; II Timothy 2:13)*. Jesus is your defense counselor, and Satan is the prosecuting attorney. As he accused Job, Satan accuses *you* before the heavenly Judge *(Job 1:6-12)*. But God had a protection around Job to keep him safe. God has promised the same protection for you *(John 17:12; I Peter 4:5; II Thessalonians 3:3)*. You are not only safe *in* Christ, you are as safe *as* Christ, for God has "hidden" you in Himself with His Son *(Colossians 3:3)*.

• *I know I'm safe and secure as God's child because God says that no created thing can separate me from Him*—God wants you to know that no created thing can separate you from Him. No created thing. Can you think of anything then that could rob you of His eternal security? *"In view of all this, what can we say? If God is for us, who can be against us? Certainly not God, who did not even keep back his own Son, but offered him for us all! He gave us his Son—will he not also freely give us all things? Who will accuse God's chosen people? God himself declares them not guilty! Who, then, will condemn them? Not Christ Jesus, who died, or rather, who was raised to life and is at the right side of God, pleading with him for us! Who, then, can separate us from the love of Christ? Can trouble do it, or hardship or persecution or hunger or poverty or danger or death? As the scripture says, 'For your sake we are in danger of death at all times; we are treated like sheep that are going to be slaughtered' "No, in all these things we have complete victory through him who loved us! For I am certain that nothing can separate us from his love: neither death nor life, neither angels nor other heavenly rulers or powers, neither the present nor the future, neither the world above nor the world below—there is nothing in all creation that will ever be able to separate us from the love of God which is ours through Christ Jesus our Lord" (Romans 8:31-39 GNT).*

• ***I know I'm safe and secure as God's child because God says I have Eternal Life***—God says that you have eternal life. Eternal means for-ever. Eternal life not just a *length* of life, but a *quality* of life. The ancient Greeks told of Eos, goddess of the dawn, who fell in love with the mortal Trojan hero, Tithonus. Eos begged Zeus to grant Tithonus an *unending* life. Zeus granted her request. Too late, both Eos and Tithonus realized that an unending life was not the same as *eternal* life. Tithonus continued to age without the possibility of death. His life was indeed without end, but also without *quality*. God's gift of eternal life is both. God has promised you eternal life without end. He has promised you that the Father will never condemn you *(John 5:24; Romans 8:1)*. He has promised you the quality of eternal life that shapes you more and more into Christ's image every day *(Romans 8:29)*. You can feel safe and secure in your salvation by realizing God says you have eternal life in His son, and God cannot lie *(I John 5:13; John 3:16; 5:24; 10:28; 17:2; Cp. Hebrews 5:9; II Timothy 2:13)*.

Power Points:

➤ Was Joseph being unkind to his brothers and his father in his demand that Benjamin be brought to Egypt?

➤ If you had been Jacob, what would you have thought about giving up your last son by Rachel?

➤ If Satan were accusing you before God, what would be his best argument against you?

➤ In light of all the security factors in the list, why do you think some people still feel they can lose their salvation?

Reflection section:

☐   Examine yourself and make sure you understand what being a Christian actually is.

☐   What you would have to do to meet God's standard for perfection?

☐   Realize that only Christ could meet such a standard and that when we are in Christ, we are secure.

☐   "Only past sins—not future sins—are forgiven." Do you agree or disagree with this statement? Why?

☐   How many of your sins were *future* when Jesus died?

☐   "Eternal security would merely make someone feel they could sin until their heart was content. In effect, it's a license to sin!" Do you agree or disagree with this statement? Why?

☐   "If God chose some to salvation and not *everyone*, God would be unfair." Do you agree or disagree with this statement? Why?

☐   Ask yourself how you feel when the temptation to sin overwhelms your ability to resist. Does sin bother you? The more it does, the closer your fellowship with God.

☐   Is there a difference between *eternal* life and *everlasting* life?

☐   Rest in His forgiveness, and trust in His Word. He promised to deliver you safely home.

☐   Do you ever still feel sorrow over sins you know He's forgiven? Go to Him in repentance and sorrow—for *your* benefit, not for His. This is the secret to fellowship. Don't feel that your salvation is an on-again, off-again relationship with God. Eternal life is forever.

My Personal Growth Journal—

❏ Make a list of the five worst things your child might do to disappoint you. When you finish, consider if any of these would be serious enough to make you disown your child. How much more does your heavenly Father love you?

~ Chapter 19 ~

When Delay Can Become Disaster: "The Principle of Procrastination"

"If we had gone ahead in the first place instead of procrastinating like this, we could have been there and back twice over." (Gen. 43:10)

The Joseph story....

The famine worsened, and Jacob's family was facing certain starvation. The supply of grain purchased earlier in Egypt was now gone. Simeon sat hostage in an Egyptian prison. To purchase more food, on their return to Egypt Joseph had required the brothers to bring with them Benjamin—the last son of Jacob's beloved Rachel. Initially, Jacob refused. He could not risk losing another son as he had lost Joseph and Simeon. The brothers argued. Precious time and food began to run out. Jacob and his sons knew they had no choice but to comply. The only alternative would be to starve; yet, a decision could not be made. Their delay of the inevitable was solving nothing. Something must be done quickly, or the race begun by Abraham would perish. At last, the decision was made. Once more, the brothers would make the journey to Egypt. This time with Benjamin, double payment of silver, and the hope that Simeon was still alive and in good health.

Principle Truth: Delay gives trouble an opportunity tomorrow that is closed to a task completed today.

Never put off till tomorrow what you can do today. Is there a more often-quoted truism? Our world has become so complicated we need day planners and organizers to remember what we're supposed to do each hour, not merely each day! The complexity of our modern world makes it nearly impossible to do everything we should *when* we should. We are so busy that weariness wears us down before we can complete our obligations, and guilt stalks us because we didn't do more.

And so we delay. We put off what we know we should do. We procrastinate. How easy it is to delay that which needs to be done. Maybe delay will make the job go away. But delay seldom eliminates, and more often compounds the task. Better we should take care of the small tasks today than be forced to face larger ones tomorrow. Better to start what we finish, than to halt in the process *"Jesus said, 'No procrastination. No backward looks'"* (Luke 9:62; Cp. Luke 14:28-30).

> Even if you are on the right track, you'll get run over if you just sit there.
>
> —Will Rogers
>
> ❧❧

I learned the truth of this lesson the hard way. My car began to squeak around the front wheels first. I knew that the sound was the wear indicator on my brakes. My brakes needed to be replaced. I decided to put the repair off. I would just wait until the back brakes squeaked too, and then fix them all at once. Weeks passed. By the time the rear brakes began to squeak, the front squeaking had nearly stopped. Strange I thought. I had no idea. I later learned that the wear indicator on my front brakes had worn away, and now my calipers were damaged too. What would have been a simple brake replacement had developed into a costly repair. Had I only not put off the small problem, the big problem could have been avoided. "A stitch in time saves nine."

Jonah also learned the difficult lesson taught by delay. God instructed Jonah to take a boat to the great Assyrian capital city of Nineveh. God wanted the prophet to take the offer of salvation to the cruelest culture in the ancient world. Understandably, Jonah was afraid. By the time Jonah quit delaying his mission out of fear, he had been tossed out of the ship and carried the rest of the way by a great fish. Jonah's delay did not end God's mission for him. Jonah's procrastination only made that mission more difficult. God was going to get Jonah to Nineveh either by sail or by whale! *(Jonah 1:1-2:10)*

Judah's words to his father and brothers rang true. Had they not delayed in doing what the Egyptian required of them, they would already have been back in Egypt. Their procrastination was not solving their food problem, but it was increasing the possibility of making the problem worse. Their procrastination was merely stretching out Simeon's tenure in the Egyptian prison and delaying the greater plan for good that Joseph was constructing for his family.

Procrastination seldom improves anything. Sometimes it makes things worse. When there is a job to be done, just do it. Delay is only an immediate solution to a bigger problem and can result in lost opportunity. Often, small problems only escalate when they are put off. While there is nothing wrong with wise and careful planning, sometimes this only serves as an excuse to delay. Remember that small tasks or obvious solutions seldom require complex planning, and time wasted often compounds difficulty.

How can you do your best to avoid the sometimes-disastrous consequences of delay? Think about these suggestions today. Realize that delay seldom makes problems better, but can make them worse—and sometimes quite a bit more costly.

❑ *I should not put things off because delay can be disobedience to God*— God wants you to finish what you start. Some delays are beyond your control, of course. Nevertheless, generally, to begin something and leave it unfinished leaves you with a life full of loose ends. Today, if possible, try to finish what you begin. Today would be a good today to tie up the loose ends of yesterday *(Luke 9:62)*.

❑ *I should not put things off because delay presumes upon God's goodness*—You never know what tomorrow will bring. The Rich Young Ruler presumed on the goodness of God. He trusted in his own self-sufficiency, and delayed considering the fate of his own soul: *"And I will say to my soul, 'Soul, you have many goods laid up for many years to come; take your ease, eat, drink and be merry.' But God said to him, `You fool! This very night your soul is required of you…'" (Luke 12:19-20 NASB)*. Likewise, the five Foolish Virgins put off filling their lamps with oil, and their presumption cost them their spot in the wedding *(Matthew 25:1-11)*. To plan for tomorrow is to presume God is going to give tomorrow to you *(Proverbs 27:1)*. Never presume on the time or gifts God has given you: *"Also keep back Your servant from presumptuous {sins;} Let them not rule over me Then I will be blameless…" (Psalms 19:13 NASB)*. Try to live today as if was your last. Someday it will be. "Never put off till tomorrow what you can do today" is still a good rule *(Luke 12:18-20; 41-48; James 4:13-16)*.

❑ *I should not put things off because delay wastes the present*—All that today brings is enough to fill twenty-four hours. Your life will only be more difficult if you have to deal today with problems put off from yesterday *(Matthew 6:34)*.

❑ *I should not put things off because delay wastes the future*—Judah realized that the procrastination of the brothers had affected their future. Time was important. Food was short. If they had not wasted time arguing, they would already be in Egypt. Jacob, too, was wasting precious time of his future, although he did not realize it. Because the family delayed, Jacob was wasting the time he would spend with his beloved Joseph when the family got to Egypt. The story of the Prodigal Son is another illustration of wasting the future. He asked his father to give him his future inheritance. Upon receiving it, the son spent all his inheritance on sinful pleasures. When he came to his senses, he returned home to his father. Although he was forgiven and welcomed back into the home, he had squandered all his future inheritance, as well as the quality time he could have spent with his family *(Luke 15:11-32)*. Today, we may still waste our future through delay. Medical delays can not only waste—but also steal—our futures. Detected early, for example, some cancers are easily cured. Allowed to continue untreated, they can sometimes prove fatal. The issues you settle today can become the time you have tomorrow.

❑ *I should not put things off because delay can rob me of God's gifts*—God promised the land of Canaan to the Hebrews. Their job was to take it. Because of fear they delayed in possessing a gift God had promised them for hundreds of years. Today, take advantage of the blessings He puts in your path. Don't let opportunity pass you by *(Joshua 18:3-6)*.

❑ *I should not put things off because delay can cause me to miss an opportunity*—The men who delayed to accept God's gift of the land never got a second opportunity. God was unhappy with their delay in accepting His blessing. Today, see your opportunity as though it was offered to you only once. Don't delay in accepting the blessings God offers you today. They may be offered only once *(Numbers 14:40-41)*.

Prescription for Procrastination

Procrastination has been found to be detrimental to health if taken in large doses for extended periods. If symptoms persist, follow the directions carefully as prescribed by the Great Physician.

Known causes of *procrastinatus putitoffus:*

Chronic fear of failure.
Excessive expectation of perfectionism.
Paralysis of frustration.
Excessive emotional dislike of the task.
Acute rebellious syndrome against known responsibility.
Severe deficiency of time.
Uncoordination of planning.

Mix equal parts of all ingredients in daily life. Add two cups of energy, and one cup of enthusiasm. SERVE IMMEDIATELY. If effects begin to wear off with extended use, replace with prayer and a brief withdrawal. Resume as directed.

Instructions for use:

Organize the task to be performed. *Create a plan of action.*
Prioritize the importance of what must be done.
Divide the task in small *taskettes* suitable to aid digestion. *Conqueror by dividing.*
Set a deadline for completion. *Be flexible, yet realistic.*
Gather any and all support to help in getting the task completed. *Find an encourager.*
Anticipate the unexpected, which may delay the completion of the task. *Remember Murphy's Law.*
Begin the task by attacking the hardest part first.
Get into a routine of performing *taskettes* on a daily basis.
Arrange time-outs for doing something fun at various intervals along the way.
Reward yourself when task is completed. *Celebration required.*

CAUTION:

BEGIN WITHOUT DELAY. USE AS DIRECTED!

Power Points:

➢ How do you think Simeon felt being abandoned in the Egyptian prison while the brothers delayed?

➢ How do you think Benjamin felt about all that was taking place?

➢ Do you think Joseph ever entertained thoughts that his brothers might not return to Egypt?

➢ Was Joseph being too hard on his brothers at this point? Was he being too hard on his father?

Reflection section:

❑ What are you putting off right now that you could get out of the way and over with if you acted today?

❑ Finish something today that you planned to finish next week. How would this make you feel?

❑ What distinguishes careful planning from procrastination?

❑ What distinguishes 'waiting upon the Lord' from procrastination?

❑ Is there someone you could do something for today that might benefit him or her more now than if you waited?

❑ Learn to tackle problems as soon as you can. Even if you cannot finish the solution, the work is at least begun. To put things off assumes you will be able to finish the job just as well some other time, and you never know what the future might hold.

❑ Live today as if you might not have next week, and save next week's time for what next week may hold.

My Personal Growth Journal—

❑   Write down five things that you can do ahead of time instead of waiting. Consider finances, work in your home or place of work, or obligations you have made to others.

~ Chapter 20 ~

Weeds in My Garden: "The Principle of the Long Arm of Sin"

So they went up to Joseph's house steward and talked to him in the doorway. "On our way home, the first night out we opened our bags and found our money at the mouth of the bag—the exact amount we'd paid. We've brought it all back and have plenty more to buy more food with. We have no idea who put the money in our bags." (Gen. 43:19-22)

The Joseph story....

The brothers returned to Egypt to buy more grain—this time with a double payment of silver. Surely, they could not explain how payment for the first supply had ended up back in their grain bags. But Joseph knew. As the brothers once again bowed before Joseph, they confessed their innocence in stealing the silver on their previous trip. Despite the many shameful acts they had committed in their past, the brothers in truth weren't responsible for this mysterious circumstance. In proclaiming their innocence, they were telling the truth. But because of their sin committed long ago against Joseph, a process had been set in motion. A process which would result in many ramifications, not the least of which was their present dilemma. Though innocent of stealing the payment silver, the brothers were nevertheless suffering a consequence of a sin in their distant past. But the consequence of that sin was affecting not only the guilty brothers, but also Benjamin, who had no part in the crimes against Joseph. Joseph chose to not yet reveal himself to his brothers. He must test them first. Had they changed in the twenty years since he had seen them? Had their evil character matured from the hate, jealousy, and dishonesty of their youth?

Principle Truth: The costly effects of Adam's disobedience have invaded every realm of the world we live in, and both man and nature are forced to pay the price.

Some things seem impossible to explain. When I was young, I used to wonder why babies had to die. I used to wonder why bad things happened to good people, and why sometimes I was blamed for things I in actual fact didn't do. I even wondered how the worst weeds seemed to choose *my* garden and try to choke out *my* vegetables.

It came as a surprise to learn that one person was responsible for the action that caused many of these problems I sought answers for. The person was Adam. The action was sin. What? Adam's sin so long ago brought every possible trouble into our world from death to babies to weeds in my garden? Yes.

The Garden of Eden was a perfect place to live for Adam and Eve. There was no sickness. There was no suffering. There was no death. There were no weeds in Adam's garden. Then Adam and Eve disobeyed God. Sin entered their world, bringing every conceivable trouble into their world and ours.

Sin's long arm reaches us today. Adam's sin brings us death, pain and suffering, frustration, and every other imaginable difficulty. Sin has ripples. Our world suffers under the curse of what Adam did. We suffer today from the long arm of *indirect* sin.

Because Adam brought sin into the world, we are all sinners. Even though we did not sin when Adam did, he is the head of our race, and sin was passed through his offspring. Thus, even if we could live a perfect life and never be guilty of direct sin, we would still be guilty of indirect sin, since we all sinned "in Adam" *(Genesis 3; Romans 5)*. This is why innocent babies die. They die from indirect sin.

> The effect of sin on God's creation was to reduce to the song of nature to be sung in a minor key.
>
> —J. V. McGee

Courtney was a straight-A student in my seventh grade class who loved to tease and be teased. Near the end of the year, with most of the lessons taught, I let the students have some free time to socialize with their peers. One day, while I was putting books away, someone took some extra credit passes off my desk. When I noticed they were missing, I thought I noticed a guilty look on Courtney's face, but she insisted she had not taken the passes. Finally, I insisted the passes be returned and had all the students check their belongings. Courtney opened her purse, and there were the passes. Courtney glanced up at me in shock. "I promise I didn't take them," Courtney pleaded, and I could tell she was telling the truth. "But," she continued, "because I have them, I guess I'm just as guilty as the person who did, huh?" Courtney was guilty of *indirect* sin.

Joseph's brothers were not guilty of actually stealing the silver. Nevertheless, they were still *indirectly* responsible for the silver since they committed the initial crime which began the whole ordeal—the sin of selling their brother Joseph. The silver was a resulting consequence for which they were indirectly guilty.

In the same way, because all humankind sinned in Adam's sin, all humankind suffers under the indirect effects such sin has introduced to our race—our sinful nature, death to innocent babies, weeds in my garden. Though we did not sin when Adam sinned, we sinned in Adam and are still guilty *by association* for things which may not seem our fault.

We will always feel the effects of Adam's sin in our lives. It has been a curse brought to our world since the beginning and will continue until Christ removes it someday in His kingdom. While there may be things we can do to speed up or slow down the process, these bad things will always eventually happen—even to good people.

As Joseph's brothers were indirectly guilty for a sin they did not actually commit, so the long arm of Adam's sin affects you today. Many troubles we bring on ourselves. Other troubles are just difficult to explain. As you deal with troubles today, deal with the ones you able, and accept the ones beyond your control. Your sins will cause problems enough, but consider the effects of Adam's. Remember that not every difficulty you experience today is your fault.

❑ *Even though it's not my fault, Adam's sin causes death in this world—* Death. Someone has said: of death: humanity's bones of all the ages are its monument; humanity's groans through history's pages are its epitaph. Did you ever wonder where death came from? God did not intend for you to die. Nevertheless, when Adam sinned, sin passed on to all his descendants. Even though it's directly not your fault, you will die. Everybody will. You won't die because your sins, you die because of Adam's. He was the pilot of humanity. We are the passengers on the plane. He made a wrong turn, and we all pay the price. This is why innocent babies die. This is why your pets, as well as the flowers in your garden, will die. Today, understand that death is a fact of life, and the initial cause was not your fault. In the same way, eternal life is through Christ and not by anything you do *(Genesis 3:19; Romans 5:12-18).*

❑ *Even though it's not my fault, Adam's sin causes suffering and pain in life—*Did you know that labor pains in childbirth are a result of Adam's sin? They are. As is every other type of sickness, disease, suffering, and pain. God did not intend for you to suffer. Nevertheless, sin has plunged our whole world into evil. Just as Joseph suffered in Egyptian slavery—not for his own sins—but due to the sins of his brothers, so we too must suffer due to the sin of Adam. As a result, our body hurts, our emotions become easily damaged, and we grow old and tired *(cp. Ecclesiastes 12:1-8)*. Even though it's not your fault, accept the fact that life will not always be a painless process as it takes you to your grave *(Genesis 3:16)*.

❑ *Even though it's not my fault, Adam's sin causes evil people to affect me*—When Adam sinned, he surrendered up his authority over the world given him by God. The serpent (Satan) seized this authority. Now, *he* is the power in the world. You will be affected by the evil Satan has set loose in the world. Satan can work through the evil tendencies of sinful people, and they can hurt you. Don't forget, apart from being led by God's Spirit, you too have the same tendencies toward evil. You have the power to hurt others. Even though it's not your fault that evil rules in this world today, recognize that evil exists. Make sure that you live through God's Spirit, and try to do good, and not evil *(I John 5:19; Matthew 4:8-9; John 12:31; Ephesians 2:2)*.

❑ *Even though it's not my fault, Adam's sin causes me to affect other peo-ple*—Have you ever seen the cartoon where a little devil and a little angel are always trying to convince a character to do a wrong or right action? Just as the devil and the angel represent wrong and right actions, you have two natures that make up how you feel and act toward others. Your earthly nature tempts you to do and think as the world does. Your heavenly nature prompts you to live like Christ. Even though you didn't sin when Adam sinned, because you are descended from Adam, you have this earthly nature which sometimes can make you unkind toward others when you are not feeling especially spiri-tual. People who are not Christians have this nature alone, and there-fore cannot please God. Because you have *two* natures, you will always feel the struggle. Which nature you surrender to, determines your influence on others *(Romans 7:15-24; 8:7)*.

❑ *Even though it's not my fault, Adam's sin causes weeds in my garden*—Did you ever wonder why you have weeds in your garden and why you have to work so hard to keep your garden, as well as your life, in line? Adam did it. We are told his sin brought a curse upon the ground itself, and the need for you to sweat and toil. Even though it is not your fault, you must understand that there are 'ripples' from Adam's sin that affect your world in every way imaginable. You must deal with the results of these ripples the best you can, and understand that this is why bad things happen to good people. Today, look forward to the day Christ Jesus will lift the curse from the earth and return our world to what He intended it to be! (*Genesis 3:17-19; Romans 8:19-22; Revelation 22:3*)

Power Points:

➤ How were Joseph's brothers still not completely innocent regarding the money they did not steal?

➤ Since Benjamin was not guilty of the crime his brothers committed against Joseph, was it fair he should have been affected, too? How does this illustrate that we can still be guilty of sins we did not actually commit?

➤ What things might have been different if Adam had not sinned?

➤ What do you think happens to babies who die since they have committed no sins? Do you think God has made a special provision for them? Where do you get your scriptural basis for your opinion?

Reflection section:

❑ Are you making excuses for sinful actions?

❑ What are you suffering from today due to someone else's sin, or an occurrence that is not directly your fault?

❑ What do you think would have happened to Adam and Eve—and the human race—had they never sinned?

❑ Who is in charge of this world today—God or Satan?

❑ Is there a secret sin you are harboring, convincing yourself that you can't control because you feel you were just born that way? Sinful actions cannot be corrected until they are seen for what they are—*sinful.*

❑   If you believe infants are safe according to God's grace, when do you think children reach the point at which they are responsible for their sins?

❑   So, how *are* infants—who make no personal choice—actually saved?

❑   Stop making excuses for pet sins. While it may not seem fair that you are sinful because Adam sinned, understand that neither is it fair that you can be saved because Christ paid for those sins for you.

❑   Remember, troubles are a part of life. You have no control over some things. Learn from every trouble God allows, but do not dwell on them. Get on with your life.

My Personal Growth Journal—

❑   Read *Ecclesiastes 12*. List the references Solomon makes to the failure of the human body as it ages. Such was the effect of Adam's sin.

❑   Look up the many Old Testament passages that discuss the future Kingdom when the curse brought about by Adam's sin will be removed.

~ Chapter 21 ~

God, Standing in the Shadows: "The Principle of Discerning God's Mysterious Ways"

The steward said, "Everything's in order. Don't worry. Your God and the God of your father must have given you a bonus. I was paid in full." And with that, he presented Simeon to them. (Gen. 43:23)

The Joseph story....

Joseph's brothers had returned to Egypt once again with silver for more grain, as well as silver for the grain they took back with them the first time. How the first payment silver had gotten back into their sacks, they had no idea. But they must pay it again. It was the right thing to do, and, too, Simeon was being kept hostage in the Egyptian prison. But how had the payment silver gotten into their bags? Why was this mysterious Egyptian vizier testing the brothers in such a way? Why was Benjamin of such concern to him, and why was he so willing to provide for them, yet only so much that they would have to return? Acting under Joseph's orders, his steward accepts no payment—or repayment—for any grain, adding deeper mystery to the ever-stranger order of events. Simeon is returned to the brothers in good health, and the confusion among them as to what was taking place began to mount. To their surprise, Joseph then brought his brothers into a great feasting room, asked about their father, and seated them according to their birth. Would there be no end to the strange occurrences brought about by the great lord of Egypt? Unknown to the brothers was the fact that the very circumstances that defied explanation were working towards the ultimate good of their lord's master plan.

Principle Truth: God is never surprised, defeated, or limited in His ability to perform His will, though His ways often defy explanation.

God works in mysterious ways. Sometimes God works through circumstances. Often, He works through prayer. Most of the time, God works through our common sense to perform His will. God can and does use a variety of channels to perform His will.

There are times when we cannot be sure just how God is working. His ways seem mysterious, His will—hidden, His voice—silent. Sometimes it is through His silence that God performs His will *(Revelation 8:1)*, and sometimes it is through His silence that God speaks most clearly.

The silence of God does not mean the absence of God, however. For example, God's name never appears in the book of Esther, but His hand can be seen throughout the events that shape the story. While not mentioned, God quietly stands in the shadow keeping watch over His own.

> God brings men into deep waters not to drown them, but to cleanse them.
>
> —John Aughey

The story is told of Queen Victoria and a mysterious train ride back to London many years ago. As the train's engineer surveyed the tracks ahead in the gathering darkness, he was startled as the train's large headlight revealed the mysterious shadow of a man franticly waving his arms. Without hesitation, the engineer brought the train to an emergency stop. To his startled surprise as he jumped from the engine cabin, the engineer saw no trace of the man who had appeared from nowhere to flag down the train. What he did find, however, was a tiny moth trapped against the train's headlight. In desperately flapping its wings in trying to free itself, the tiny moth had cast a giant shadow, which the engineer had mistaken for a man. Not far up ahead, the engineer noticed something else. Just around the next bend, the tracks were blocked by fallen debris. Had the train rounded the bend, it would have surely met disaster. Upon being informed of the incident, Queen Victoria stated that the mysterious occurrence of the moth in the train's headlight was no coincidence. God surely had mysteriously dictated her protection from certain disaster. God—standing in the shadows, keeping watch over His own.

Whether we recognize the mysterious ways of God or not, we can be sure that since God is good, His ways are always right. God never performs an action that is not right. He may not always act as we would, but God can see the best possible outcome of His every action—actions we often cannot understand. *"For now we see through a glass, darkly…" (I Corinthians 13:12 KJV).*

God performs His will in the universe in many ways. He is not limited by time or space in His dealings with man. God performed His will through the dreams of a Pharaoh to save Egypt and through the voice of donkey to warn a prophet *(Numbers 22:28)*. But God—performing His will through silence—is often His most mysterious working of all.

God does not always explain His actions to us. Thus, His ways sometimes seem strange. But God sees His actions in light of the completion of His plan. We see the action only as one point in time. If God were to tell us every difficulty we would endure, we could not learn the deep trust that comes with trials. If He explained everything that was going to happen to us, it would remove not only the challenge of life—it might discourage us beyond our ability to endure. Our problem is not that we aren't given full information regarding the ways of God. Our problem is that we don't always utilize the information what He *has* given us in His Word.

The most common method God uses to perform His will is through natural circumstance—the day-to-day actions of others and ourselves. God does not need to resort to miracles. There is no such thing as a miracle to God. God can perform His will perfectly through normal events, nature, and people who may or may not realize they are performing His will at all. In such a way, Joseph used his steward to place the money back in the bags the brothers carried. Joseph had his personal reasons in testing the character of his brothers—reasons the steward doubtless did not know. But Joseph's ultimate purpose was to bless his brothers. In opening their bags, the brothers could not explain the appearance of the money. They did not realize the mysterious plan Joseph was performing to ultimately work for the good of his family. God does not always explain His actions, but His actions always work for our ultimate good.

Simeon sat in the Egyptian prison waiting for his brothers to return from Canaan. Simeon surely felt as removed from the safety and security of his family and home as he had ever felt in his life. But, like his brothers, Simeon could not see the workings of the mysterious plan Joseph was performing. Alone, afraid, and confused, Simeon had no clue that being in that prison put him closer to his safety and salvation than he knew. Simeon was close to Joseph—his savior, who stood in the shadows ready to protect him from any harm.

The popular story *Footprints* illustrates well God's mysterious ways. When we sometimes feel ours are the only footprints in the sands of life's hardships, we might be surprised to learn that those footprints are, in fact, not ours at all. They are the footprints of our Savior, who, in allowing us hardships, carries us through them. God's ways are often mysterious, and though we may not understand His divine design in our lives, someday His mysteries will be complete *(Revelation 10:7)*. God does not always explain His purposes to us. Even when He doesn't, we may be sure He is standing in the shadows watching over us, performing a most perfect plan. Though God's ways are often mysterious, they are always right.

As you walk the shores of life today, remember that you do not walk alone. Consider the weaving of God's mysterious ways as multicolored thread which will form the beautiful pattern God has for your life. Today, understand the many ways God works through the circumstances, timing, and people in your life. They are for your good.

❑ *God works His mysterious will through seeming tragedy*—Simeon was put in the same Egyptian prison Joseph had been in. Simeon surely felt alone and discouraged as his brothers departed to their father and land. But what Simeon didn't know was that in this seemingly tragic situation, he was in fact closer to his safety and salvation than he could possibly imagine. Simeon was near Joseph—the one who would save him, and who stood in the background watching over his brother. God is often closest to you when tragedy seems to hold the upper hand. It has been said that the photograph of God's face is often developed in the darkroom of our life. We recognize Him most clearly in the darkest times of our life. When hard times come, remember Simeon. That which he dreaded most was being worked toward his own salvation *(Genesis 42:24).*

❑ *God works His mysterious will through miraculous circumstances*—Esther is the Book in Scripture which does not contain God's name. Yet, God's mysterious design fills the book. Esther was a Jewish girl in the Persian Empire. Through a plan only God could have arranged, Esther became queen of the empire. Through this improbable circumstance, God saved his people from destruction. Miracles do not exist as such from God's viewpoint. Miracles are those things that seem out of the ordinary to us. God can work through extraordinary means to accomplish His will for ordinary people. Don't limit God. Nothing is outside His ability to perform *(Esther 2:17).*

❑ *God works His mysterious will through the natural order*—Mordecai was Esther's uncle and among the many Jews captive in Persia. One day, as Mordecai was performing his daily tasks, he just happened to overhear a man devising a plot to kill the great Persian king. Mordecai decided he must report the plot. As a result, both the king and eventually, all the Hebrews in Persia were spared. One man overhearing the details of an evil plot changed history. What was Mordecai doing when he overheard the plot? He was merely performing his daily duty in the court. God's mysterious plan had Mordecai in just the right place at just the right time. God simply worked through natural order and Mordecai's obedience to a daily task. This is how God works most of the time—through the natural order. As you live today, simply do what you know you're supposed to do. God can make sure you are in the right place at the right time when He performs His mysterious plan through your life *(Esther 2:21-23)*.

❑ *God works His mysterious will through the circumstances of others*— The Persian king was never informed of Mordecai's kind deed. But the Persians recorded everything. One night, through the mysterious plan of God, the king could not sleep. He began to read the royal records and just happened to turn to the page where Mordecai's deed was recorded. The future of both Persian and the Hebrew history was forever changed. God worked through this heathen king's insomnia to save many people. God works as easily through those who are not His as He does through His children. Remember—God can work through others to help you *(Esther 6:1-2)*.

❑ *God works His mysterious will through Divine timing*—The little book of Ruth tells the story of two people who became the ancestors of Jesus. Ruth just *"happened"(KJV)* to be working in the fields of Bethlehem one day, when Boaz just *"happened"(KJV)* to see her. Divine timing brought them together. From their fortuitous meeting came not only Kings David and Solomon, but Jesus, as well. God's timing is never a moment too soon or too late. His mysterious plan is not limited by time as we know it. Are you rushing God to accomplish something in your life? Remember our clock does not always measure His timing, but His time is always correct *(Ruth 2:3-4)*.

❑ *God works His mysterious will and doesn't always tell us everything*— God put Job through many difficult trials and difficulties. Job was never said to have sinned or deserved any of them. God had a purpose in educating and training Job. What that precise purpose was, God never explained. Do you see? God never explained to Job why he was put through his trials. God never explained to me why my godly mother had to die from cancer at such a young age. God informed Jacob that He would make from him a great nation *(Genesis 46:3)*, but did not tell him that process would take four hundred years. God simply does not always tell us everything. Why? Partly for our own good. Would you want to know when and how you were going to die? Would you want to know the heartaches your children are going to suffer? Joseph's brothers were surely confused at the mysterious events that were happening to them in Egypt. But when they met their savior face to face at the end of the story, we can be sure it all made sense. Remember, God is right in everything He does, but He doesn't always explain. Some things are kept from us: *"The secret things belong to the LORD our God, but the things revealed belong to us..." (Deuteronomy 29:29 NASB).* The events God allows in your life—including the explanations that never come with them—are for your own good. At the end of your life's story, everything will make sense *(I Corinthians 13:12; Revelation 10:7).*

Power Points:

➢ What passed through the brothers' minds when the steward refused to take the repayment for the missing silver?

➢ Do you think Simeon ever thought he would see his brothers again? What might he have been thinking in that prison?

➢ If Simeon had not been held hostage, do you think Joseph's brothers would have ever returned?

➢ How do you think *Jacob* was feeling at this point in the story?

Reflection Section:

❑ If you could know the day you were going to die, would you want to? Would you want to know what trials and hardships lay ahead of you— even if you were sure you would survive them?

❑ "To God, there is no such thing as a *miracle*." Do you agree or disagree with this statement? Why?

❑   How do *fate* and God's sovereignty differ? *Do* they differ?

❑   "God only works through the lives of the *willing*." Do you agree or disagree with this statement? Why?

❑   God knows not only what He has planned for our lives, but also how much information about our future we need to know. Trust His wisdom, not the power of fortunetellers and horoscopes. Live today as if you might not have tomorrow, and trust His will, His revelation, and His timing.

❑   God wants you to trust Him in everything—Joseph understood that about trusting God. While it is easier for us to trust God when we have no other choice, God prefers our complete trust on a continual basis. He is a loving father who only desires the best for His children. *"Commit your work to the LORD, and then your plans will succeed"* *(Proverbs 16:3 NLT).* Do you trust God just as much when things are going well in your life? Could you trust God to deliver you from sexual temptation, as Joseph did?

My Personal Growth Journal—

❑   Write down five things you've prayed for that God is still asking you to trust Him for.

❑   Write down the first three questions you want to ask God when you get to heaven.

~ Chapter 22 ~

Vows: "The Principle of Rash Promises"

"If that chalice is found on any of us, he'll die; and the rest of us will be your master's slaves." (Gen. 44:9)

The Joseph story....

The brothers had returned to Joseph with Benjamin, just as they had been ordered. Joseph allowed them provisions as he had promised, but would test them one last time. Were they the same men who had treated him so cruelly? Were they the same men who for twenty years had allowed poor Jacob to believe the lie that Joseph was dead? The test would be to place a valuable Egyptian cup in Benjamin's sack. As the brothers were leaving Egypt with their second supply of grain, Joseph's steward stopped them to inquire about the missing cup. The brothers knew of no cup and made a rash and foolish vow to offer the guilty party to be executed and themselves into permanent slavery if it were found among them. The cup was found in Benjamin's bag of grain. What would the brothers do? Judah had guaranteed Benjamin's safety with his own life. Reuben had promised the same with the lives of his own sons. Now a rash and unnecessary vow had put all the brothers in danger of permanent slavery, and one brother in danger of certain death.

Principle Truth: *A promise without consideration can result in a disaster without a remedy.*

Sudden promises. Easy guarantees. Verbal commitments. It has been said that God created us with two ears, but one mouth, for a reason. Today, we are still encouraged to think before we speak, but sometimes we don't. Promises are so easy to make, and isn't it understood that we shouldn't take them so literally anyway? We promise to tell the truth and nothing but the truth in court, but how seriously do we take that oath? Aren't we more concerned with keeping our stories straight than we are with the seriousness of the vow? How seldom we weigh the consequences of vows we may not be able to keep—even promises we make to ourselves.

> *Those that are most slow in making a promise are the most faithful in the performance of it.*
>
> —Jean Rousseau

The marriage vow, for example, has today has become little more than a formality. Couples make and break the marriage vows so casually they have come to mean little or nothing. "Till death us do part" might as well be "till better comes my way." Courtroom vows are another example. To promise to tell the whole truth is little more than a legal tradition, and few seem to care that such a vow was once considered sacred. When was the last time you ever noticed anyone even think about the question? In the marriage ceremony as well as courtroom testimony, "I do" has become less a promise and more a ritual.

God, however, would prefer you make no vow at all. Instead of making promises you keep only as convenience dictates, God says just do not make them. God looks at promises as serious commitments. God does not look casually on rash vows and easy promises. God wants us to think before we speak. God wants us to remember that there can be serious consequences to the casual statements we so easily make.

Doubtless, Joseph's brothers never considered the seriousness of their proposal when they offered to become permanent slaves in Egypt. They were so confident that the cup would not be found among them that they foolishly swore a vow, never considering the harsh consequences. Not only would they suffer the death of a brother, they would taste the same bitterness of slavery as had Joseph. Little did they know that if the cup was found, and their promise required, only the grace of their brother's love could spare them from the fate of permanent servitude they were calling upon themselves.

We would do well to consider the possible consequences before we make promises which may come back to haunt us. To vow without considering the consequences is to invite trouble. How would you feel if the real consequences of all your broken vows were visited upon you?

Before you make a rash promise today, consider it from God's perspective. Before you promise at all today, consider the consequences. *"For which of you intending to build a tower, sitteth not down first and counteth the cost...? (Luke 14:28 KJV)* With your words today come not only consequences, but also responsibility.

❏ *Before I make a promise, I will remember I may not really need to promise at all*—It should be enough to simply give your word that you will do it. Work on building such an honest reputation among those you deal with that your word alone is enough *(Matthew 5:33-37; James 5:12)*.

❏ *Before I make a promise, I will think of the consequences first*—Rash promises proved exceedingly costly in the Bible. Jephthah lost a daughter *(Judges 11:30-31)*, and King Saul nearly lost his son *(I Samuel 14:24-25)*. In the days of Jesus, Herod Antipas made a foolish promise, and John the Baptist lost his head *(Mark 6:22-23)*. Before you promise something, be sure you count the cost of that promise. Disaster often follows promises made in haste *(Proverbs 20:25; Ecclesiastes 5:2)*.

❏ *Before I make a promise, I will remember how serious my promises are to God*—Promises are made without much thought today. Most promises are not taken as seriously as God takes them. Before you make a promise casually, know that God takes your promise quite seriously *(Deuteronomy 23:21)*.

❏ *Before I make a promise, I will make sure I can keep it, or not make it at all*—If Joseph had not been a loving brother, his brothers could have died for their irrational promise. It would be much better for you to never make a promise than to make one you cannot keep *(Ecclesiastes 5:4-5)*.

Power Points:

➢ What was Joseph's purpose in continuing to test his brothers?

➢ Do you think the steward informed Joseph of the brothers' rash promise?

➢ Why did Joseph's brothers feel the need to make this rash promise at all?

> ➢ Why did Joseph choose to put the cup in Benjamin's bag?

Reflection section:

- ❑ When was the last time you made a promise and actually thought about how God considered that vow?

- ❑ Compared to promises I make to others, promises I make to myself are

  _____

- ❑ Have you ever made a rash promise that you wish you hadn't? What was the result? Has this had any lasting implications? How?

- ❑ How can you stress the importance of this chapter to your children?

- ❑ The last time I made a promise I didn't keep, I felt _____

- ❑ Do your promises mean less to you than they mean to God?

- ❑ Do you think our society actually expects people to keep promises today?

- ❑ Consider how you might feel if those who made promises to you treated those promises as casually as you treat yours.

My Personal Growth Journal—

- ❑ Look up ten promises that God has made us in scripture. Choose the five that mean the most to you personally. Circle the ones you know God has kept in your life. Put a question mark next to the ones of which you are not sure. Do you think God will keep these promises? Why? Why not?

~ Chapter 23 ~

Love That Draws us Near: "The Principle of Fellowship"

"Hurry back to my father. Tell him, 'Your son Joseph says: I'm master of all of Egypt. Come as fast as you can and join me here. I'll give you a place to live in Goshen where you'll be close to me—you, your children, your grandchildren, your flocks, your herds, and anything else you can think of. I'll take care of you there completely. There are still five more years of famine ahead; I'll make sure all your needs are taken care of, you and everyone connected with you—you won't want for a thing." (Gen. 45:9-11; 25-26)

The Joseph story....

The brothers had no place left to turn. They had made a foolish vow and put the life of Benjamin in danger and their own hopes of ever returning home to their poor father Jacob in serious jeopardy. All they could do was bow and beg before the lord vizier of Egypt—their brother Joseph whom they not yet recognized. But Joseph could refrain no longer. He called near to him the brothers who had so cruelly mistreated him over twenty years before. At the moment of their greatest need for mercy came the words they never expected to hear from the lord vizier: *"I am Joseph, your brother."* Grand was the reunion and many were the tears shed in the palace that day. Joseph informed his brothers of the greatness he had achieved in Egypt and instructed them to return home for old Jacob, their father. They were supplied with provisions and many gifts, and sent on their way back to Canaan to tell their Jacob of news that would exceed his grandest expectation. All were to return one final time to Egypt so that Joseph could care for and fellowship with his family once more united. It had been over twenty years. There would be a celebration at this reunion, to be sure.

Principle Truth: The greatest benefit of God's redemption plan is our privilege in sharing our love with Him and with each other.

God is not lonely. God does not need you to keep Him company. God is self-sufficient and isn't made better when you talk to Him. Nevertheless, God wants to have fellowship with you and instructs us to pray and hear Him through His Word. If God doesn't need our company, why does He urge us to fellowship? God requires fellowship so that He might instruct you in His guidance and bless you in His love. God doesn't need us, but God knows we need Him.

Through our fellowship of prayer, we make our requests to God. In answered prayer, He can be glorified through us. As a loving Father, God wants to bless His children, and prayer is God's channel of fellowship with us. Through prayer also, we may confess our sins before our Father. Fellowship involves confession of forgiven sins. Though all our sins were forgiven from the cross when Christ died, through our confession of those forgiven sins God gives us a chance to cleanse our souls. A father may certainly forgive a hurtful action of his child, but is nonetheless appreciative when the child offers confession and apology. The confession is more for the benefit of the child than for the father. So it is with God. While

> *A habit of fellowship with God is the spring of all our life, and the strength of it.*
>
> —H.E. Manning

He has forgiven our sins once and for all, it is to *our* benefit to cleanse our souls through expressing our sorrow over sinful actions He has already forgiven.

But fellowship through prayer is not the only fellowship God calls us to. God wants us to fellowship with other Christians. In this, we bless—and may be blessed by—them. Fellowship is a family privilege. Fellowship is enjoying the presence of the Father and the company of others. Through fellowship with others we can lend support to our other "family" members. This support may take the form of emotional and financial support in difficult circumstances, and spiritual support when the temptations of the world get the better or us.

Joseph could not wait to fellowship with his old father Jacob and the family he had been taken from so many years before. Joseph was the second most powerful man in the world. Yet, Joseph and his Egyptian family no doubt remained one of the few families in Egypt that believed in the one true God. Joseph would welcome the fellowship of godly discussion with his family. He did not need his family, but he loved them and wanted them to be near him and share his glory. Joseph neither mentioned his brothers' sins against him nor required from them a confession, but we can be sure the sorrow felt by the brothers was made known to Joseph the rest of their lives. Joseph's desire for fellowship was not out of need. Joseph's desire for fellowship was out of love. In the same way, God desires fellowship with us.

You will meet many people in the journey of life today. You will have many opportunities to exercise aspects of fellowship that God provides you. Set goals to strengthen for your fellowship today as you fellowship with others and with God.

❑ *To strengthen my fellowship, I will love others as God loves me*—God wants you to genuinely care about others. You must love them expecting nothing in return. You must love them *unconditionally*. That's how God loves you! *(John 15:12,17)*

❑ *To strengthen my fellowship I will confess my sins to God*—You will stumble often as you live each day in a sinful world. God wants you to tell Him about your sins, and seek His forgiveness. This is not for His benefit—He already knows your sins and has forgiven them. He wants you to confess your sins as a personal cleansing process. David's prayer of confession after his sin with Bathsheba is one of the finest examples of confession for sin *(Psalms 51)*. David's sin hurt him because he knew it hurt God. Do your sins make you feel this way? When old Jacob heard Joseph was alive, he undoubtedly thought of how many years his sons had betrayed him with their lie. Though both Jacob and Joseph had forgiven the incident that took place so years before, you can bet that Jacob sought an explanation from his sons. No doubt, they were more than eager to shed the burden of this unconfessed sin which they had carried with them for twenty years! So, God wants you to confess your forgiven sins—not for His benefit, but for yours. God loves your fellowship. He never minds hearing what He already knows *(James 5:16; I John 1:8-9)*.

❑ *To strengthen my fellowship, I will pray for forgiveness toward those who dislike me*—It's easy to pray for those who love you. Praying for those who don't is not so easy. God wants you to pray for those who dislike you because he may want to work in their lives by answering your prayer. In addition, praying for those *you* dislike keeps you from feeling toward them the way they feel toward you *(Matthew 5:44)*. Praying is not always easy, but prayer is required equipment for the Christian in a sinful world *(Ephesians 6:11-18)*. Someone has said, "You cannot know what prayer is for, lest first you know that life is war." Prayer is not an art to be practiced, but a response to God's love. How do you pray?

I must pray in the Person of Christ—We are to always pray "in Jesus' name," or "for Jesus' sake." What do these mean? In the old TV westerns, you heard the sheriff say to the outlaw: "Stop in the name of the law!". "In the name of the law" meant "all that the law represented." To pray in Jesus' name is to pray as He would pray and as if you had the same access to God that Christ does. Do you know enough about God to pray as Christ would pray? Some people talk to God so casually that their requests sound like a wish list to Santa Claus. Praying to God should not be casual, but it should be personal. Praying in the name of Jesus personalizes your request to God. It's makes "in Christ's person" the signature to your prayer. Someone has said well: it's the personal note at the bottom—not the words on the card—that means the most. You are talking to a holy God—the creator of the universe. Remember His awesomeness, but remember too—you do have the right of access to God by Christ (*John 14:13; Ephesians 2:18; 3:12*).

> *Prayer is the slender lever that moves the muscle of omnipotence.*
>
> —Martin Tupper
>
> ✥

I must pray according to God's will—Christ always asked in the Father's will. Someone has said that in a boat on the water, the rower throws a rope across a rock on shore not to pull the rock out, but to pull the boat toward the rock. The rope is our prayer embracing God. Are you trying to pull God in line with your will? Is your desire for your will to be done in heaven, or God's will to be done on earth? Be honest—do you pray seeking *God's* will, or His approval for your *own*? Too often, we pray with the idea of convincing God to do our will. In doing so, we forget that God is perfect, and perfection does not need to be modified. We ask amiss when we do not seek to conform our will to His. Make sure your motive is pure, and that you are not praying for the wrong reasons. Try praying more concerning the things God *has* revealed about His will in Scripture, and be less concerned about the things He hasn't. Ask that His will might be done through you on earth—not that your will be done in heaven *(Matthew 6:10; 26:42; I John 5:14-15; James 4:3; 15)*.

I must pray making specific requests—When you do make requests of God, be specific! "God bless the world" is too general for you to give God specific praise even if He answered it! Don't talk to God as if He were Santa Claus. Make your requests specific so you will have something to thank Him for. Yes, He already knows before you ask, but God loves the fellowship—not to mention the obedience. Think about it like this. If you fail to ask God for something and it *does* come to pass—you have missed an opportunity to glorify God for answered prayer, which God tells us to do *(John 11:41)*. If you do not pray and it doesn't come to pass, you will wonder if failed to happen because you failed to ask *(Matthew 6:8; James 4:2)*. On the other hand, if you *do* make a request of God and what you pray for happens, you can glorify God for answering prayer. If you pray and God says *no*, you can always trust that this *was* an answer not blind chance. When you pray today, make your requests specific.

> Prayer is less about changing the world than it is about changing us.
>
> —David Wolpe
>
> ✑✎

I must pray trusting God to answer—too often, we feel that when God does not answer our prayers either in the way we ask Him to or in our own good time, He has ignored our request. God *does* answer prayer and wants you to remember that "...*When you pray and ask for something, believe that you have received it, and you will be given whatever you ask for*" *(Mark 11:24 GNT)*. God does not work according our pleasure or timing, however. God knows the future and what's best for us at all times. Often God says *yes* to our prayers—sometimes even granting us more than we request *(I Chronicles 1:7-12)*. Sometimes He says *no (II Corinthians 12:8-9; Deuteronomy 3:23-26; Cp. Matthew 26:42)*. But most often, God asks us to wait *(Isaiah 40:31)* and trust *(Matthew 21:22; Ephesians 3:20; James 1:5-7)*.

I must pray continually—God doesn't expect you to pray around the clock. Praying continually doesn't mean dialing God up a hundred times a day. Praying continually means that you never hang up the phone *(cp. Psalms 35:28; 71:6)*. God does want you to be so close to Him that He is always on the line *(Philippians 4:6)*. As youth pastor years ago I used to tell the teenagers *"Stay on the line and you won't need a dime!"* This requires righteous living *(I John 3:22)*, staying close *(John 15:7)*, and trusting completely *(Matthew 21:22)*. Do you have this type relationship with God? *(Luke 11:5-10; 18:1; I Thessalonians 5:17; Matthew 7:1)*

I must pray persistently—Do you think praying with persistence shows a lack of faith? Not at all. God wants you to keep asking, keep seeking, and keep knocking. Jesus expressed the principle of persistent prayer in the story of the friend awakened in his sleep by the knocking at his door. *"I tell you, even though he will not get up and give him anything because he is his friend, yet because of his persistence he will get up and give him as much as he needs. So I say to you, 'Ask, and it will be given to you; seek, and you will find; knock, and it will be opened to you.'"* *(Luke 11:8-9 NASB)* Again, Jesus stressed the importance of persistent prayer in the story of the widow who wearied a judge in an attempt to gain justice against her adversary. *"The judge ignored her for a while, but eventually she wore him out. 'I fear neither God nor man,' he said to himself, 'but this woman is driving me crazy. I'm going to see that she gets justice, because she is wearing me out with her constant requests!' Then the Lord said, 'Learn a lesson from this evil judge'"* *(Luke 18:4-6 NLT)*. How much *more* does God desire to provide for *your* needs? When God says, "wait" as an answer to your prayer, persistent prayer is what pleases Him most *(Matthew 7:7; 18:1-8; James 5:16)*.

I will pray—but consider if I might be the answer to my own prayer—God wants us to pray and loves to answer our prayers. But sometimes, we may pray for God to do or give things we can do ourselves. At such times, we would do better to get off our knees and do it ourselves. Isaiah the prophet was distressed over the sinful condition of his nation. What prophet would God send to proclaim to the people their sinfulness? In his prayer to God, the Lord made Isaiah realize he could be the answer to his own prayer: *"Then I heard the Lord asking, 'Whom should I send as a messenger to my people? Who will go for us?' "And I said, 'Lord, I'll go! Send me'"* *(Isaiah 6:8 NLT)*. In the same way, Jesus urged His disciples to pray for laborers to go out into the world and share the gospel. He then sent them *(Matthew*

9:38; 10:1). Are you praying for that which you can do yourself? Pray for a good garden, and say amen with a hoe!

I must pray about everything—To merely expect something without the asking is presumption. Never presume on God or take His blessings for granted *(Psalms 19:13).* God is glorified when we rely on Him enough to pray even for things that seem certain. That's why He instructs us to pray for even our daily bread *(Matthew 6:11; Cp. Ephesians 6:18).*

❑ *To strengthen my fellowship, I will surround myself with support and encouragement*—God wants you to support and be supported by other Christians. Life is difficult enough without trying to bear life's burdens alone. Jonathan faithfully encouraged David when David most needed a friend *(I Samuel 23:16-18).* As others are blessed in supporting you, so you will be blessed in helping to lift someone else's burdens. Add encouragement, divide the hardships, and multiply the blessings *(Galatians 6:2).*

❑ *To strengthen my fellowship, I will measure my self-worth appropriately*—To care about the concerns of others, you must first care about yourself. God does not want you to have inflated pride. He does want you to realize you are special to Him and are blessed with unique gifts and talents. Accept that. You are not someone else; do not compare yourself with others. The quickest way to inferiority is comparison. Be glad for others and secure in yourself. Recognize that God has given everyone different physical features, talents, and jobs in life. You are important to God. God wants you to measure your self-worth through your obedience in service to Him, not by what others are or do *(Galatians 6:3).*

❑ *To strengthen my fellowship, I will try to live peaceably with everyone*— Evil exists. That's a fact. Some people will desire to trouble you simply because you're a child of God. Others will create difficulty in your life for no particular reason. God wants does not want you to repay evil with evil. He wants you to do everything in you power to live at peace with a sinful world, while not compromising with the lower moral standards it sometimes sets *(Romans 12:18; 14:19; II Corinthians 13:11).*

❏ *To strengthen my fellowship, I will study my Bible, because God tells me to*—God speaks to us today through His Word. Your Bible is the only book ever written where the author is always present when it is being read. In your Bible is everything God has to say to you *(Hebrews 1:1-2).* If God were to speak further, He would merely repeat Himself. He wants to speak to you through daily Bible study and wants you to talk to Him through prayer. Your Bible is God's instruction manual for survival in a sinful world. Someone has expressed this effectively in the acronym for *Bible.* God's Word is *b*asic *i*nstruction *b*efore *l*eaving *e*arth. Remember, Bible study is not a request. It is a command *(II Timothy 2:15; 3:16).* Develop a plan for reading and studying your Bible. It takes 70 hours to read the entire Bible. Only 12 minutes a day will enable you to completely read through your Bible in the course of one year. God's Word should dominate your life and lifestyle. *Know it* in your heart; *stow it* in your mind; *flow it* in your conversation; *grow it* in your lifestyle; *glow it* in your appearance; *show it* in your conduct, and *sow it* in a sinful world. Remember, Bible study is not a request. It's a command! *(II Timothy 2:15; 3:16)*

Power Points:

➢ Had you been old Jacob, how would you have felt hearing the news that your beloved Joseph was alive?

➢ Do you think Jacob had a long discussion with his sons over the twenty-year lie they had been telling about Joseph's death?

➢ What do you think passed through the brothers' minds the instant they heard the words "I am Joseph"?

Reflection section:

❏ If all our sins are forgiven in Christ, does this mean there is never a need to confess sorrow to God when sin overtakes us as Christians? What's the point? Why should we?

☐ Is there someone who would consider your fellowship today as an answer to prayer? What are you waiting for?

☐ What is the hardest part regarding prayer for you?

☐ Why should we pray and tell God things He already knows?

☐ Prayer changes God's mind. Do you agree or disagree with this statement? Why?

☐ If we are to pray with persistence, how can we learn when God has simply said 'no'?

☐ What parts of God's will are you having the most difficulty aligning your will with? Why?

☐ When you close your prayers today in Jesus' name, consider what that truly means. Remember that every good thing you have, are, and ever will be, is in Christ.

☐ "The true measure of your love for God is the degree to which you care about that person in the world you like the least." Do you agree or disagree? Why?

☐ Study some of the great prayers in the Bible, especially *Nehemiah 9, John 17, Daniel 9, Ezra 9 and I Kings 8.*

My Personal Growth Journal—

☐ Write down the names of the three people it is hardest for you to pray for. Make a concerted effort to pray for them in the next week. Ask yourself in one week if you feel any differently about these three people.

☐ List the seven most important things you want to be sure you share with your children before they leave home.

☐ When you speak to God today, try silent prayer. Speak with your mind and heart, and let your lips be silent.

My Prayer Prescription

The ingredients for effective prayer have been carefully tested and proven effective for a variety of ailments. For best results, take several times daily, and continue as necessary.

Directions for Use:

Take daily, BEFORE MEALS, with several glasses of patience. If you miss a dose, you may safely double up. Best taken in kneeling position BEFORE symptoms develop. Most effective with regular use. If you do not see improvement immediately, you may need to supplement with 1-2 tablets of trust supplied without cost from your Great Physician. Unlimited refills. NO EXPIRATION DATE.

Active Ingredients:

Powdered persistence 14%
Thick and sticky faith 27%
Whole nuggets of specific request 5%
Emulsified Gratitude toward God (EGG) 19%
Naturally flavored with the aroma of Christ's will 35%
Sealed in the timed-released capsule of God's sovereignty 100%

CAUTION: WASH LIFE THORUGHLY BEFORE HANDLING!

~ Chapter 24 ~

Delay Is Not Denial: "The Principle of Patient Expectation"

They left Egypt and went back to their father Jacob in Canaan. When they told him, "Joseph is still alive—and he's the ruler over the whole land of Egypt!" he went numb; he couldn't believe his ears. But the more they talked, telling him everything that Joseph had told them and when he saw the wagons that Joseph had sent to carry him back, the blood started to flow again— their father Jacob's spirit revived. Israel said, "I've heard enough—my son Joseph is still alive. I've got to go and see him before I die." (Gen. 45:25-28)

The Joseph story....

Joseph's brothers returned home to their father with word that Joseph— gone from his father for over twenty years—was alive. Jacob could hardly believe his ears. As an old man of nearly 130, Jacob no doubt had kept and pondered over Joseph's bloodstained coat all these years. How many times had he prayed that something good might come from the loss of his son? How many times had he prayed that Joseph had not suffered in his death? How many times had he prayed that God might speed the day of his own death when would see his beloved Joseph once more? Suddenly, with no warning, his sons told him of Joseph—not only alive—but now the second most powerful man in the world. The father who had patiently waited for the God he trusted to finish His master plan was about to behold his beloved son of Rachel face to face.

Principle Truth: God's most difficult lesson is that when He asks you to wait, He is not delaying—He is perfecting!

There is one word not in God's vocabulary. That word is *maybe*. God answers prayer in three ways: yes, no, and wait. There is no maybe with God. Too often, we feel that when God does not answer our prayers—the way we want Him either to, or in our own good time—that He has answered "no" to our request. But God does not work according our pleasure or timing. God knows the future and what's best for us at all times. Sometimes, when God asks us to wait, we become impatient. We get discouraged.

> Only with winter-patience can we bring the deep-desired, long-awaited spring.
>
> —Anne Lindbergh

John the Baptist got discouraged. John had been imprisoned for his teaching that Jesus was the Savior—the promised messiah. While in prison, John began to wonder—to doubt perhaps. Through his followers, John asked Jesus the question for which his heart already knew the answer: *"...are you the one John said was going to come, or should we expect someone else?" (Matthew 11:3 GNT)* John's impatience stemmed from his discouragement. God understands that we sometimes get discouraged. Jesus never chastised John for asking the question.

Sometimes God wants us to wait. But His *delays* are not necessarily His *denials*. Sometimes He has a greater purpose that can be achieved only through delay. Jesus delayed intentionally when Mary and Martha sent word that His friend Lazarus was dying. *"When Jesus heard it, he said, 'The final result of this sickness will not be the death of Lazarus; this has happened in order to bring glory to God, and it will be the means by which the Son of God will receive glory.' Jesus loved Martha and her sister and Lazarus. Yet when he received the news that Lazarus was sick, he stayed where he was for two more days" (John 11:4-6 GNT).*

> The future belongs to him who knows how to wait.
>
> —Russian Proverb

Jesus purposely delayed so that Lazarus would die. Like you and me sometimes, the disciples did not understand why Jesus intentionally delayed going to His friend: *"...but for your sake I am glad that I was not with him, so that you will believe. Let us go to him" (John 11:15 GNT).* Understandably, Mary and Martha were also hurt by this delay. *"When Martha heard that Jesus was coming, she went out to meet him, but Mary stayed in the house. Martha said to Jesus, 'If you had been here, Lord, my brother would not have died!'" (John 11:20-21 GNT)* But Jesus' delay was not His denial. His delay was for a greater purpose. Jesus delayed showing His power over sickness so that He might show His power over death. He delayed his healing so that he might perform a resurrection. What was the result? *"Many of the people who had come to visit Mary saw what Jesus did, and they believed in him" (John 11:45 GNT).* Sometimes God delays—He makes us wait, to bring about a greater good in His Sovereign plan.

Often, God is working at the other end of the desire of our prayers, as He was working through Joseph in Egypt. God teaches us patience through both trial and delay. Waiting is a required course in God's school of maturity! Moses trained in this school forty years in the desert of Midian *(Acts 7:29-30)* before God sent him to face the Pharaoh; Israel then trained in the wilderness forty years until they learned to obey God *(Numbers 14:33).*

Jacob was now only days away from seeing his beloved Joseph. Joseph, his Joseph that for over twenty years he thought was dead. Jacob had probably long since ceased praying for the blessing he would soon receive—the blessing of seeing his son alive and well. Jacob had no doubt thought God had forgotten this desire of his heart, but God had not forgotten. God was working at the other end of Jacob's prayers and in the process teaching Jacob patience. Jacob learned to trust God's *goodness.* He had no idea Joseph was alive. He could only trust that, if Joseph was truly dead, the goodness of a righteous God had permitted it to be so for a greater purpose Jacob could not see.

And what of Joseph's prayers? Had he not surely prayed these twenty-odd years for the health and preservation of his old father? Had he not prayed for the day when God would see fit to bring them together again? Jacob and Joseph both learned patient expectation through waiting. Joseph learned it through trust in God's *timing.* He knew from his brothers that his father was still alive and that he would see him again in God's time.

Do you sometimes feel God has forgotten you? Consider how Joseph must have felt just one hour before Pharaoh exalted him to power. Consider how Jacob must have felt only minutes before his sons returned with news of Joseph. Patiently endure what God permits in His wisdom, and understand that troubles will always be a part of life. Learn to trust God's *timing* in the delays He allows, and that His timing is always perfect. Learn to trust God's *goodness* in God's delays. Be sure He does all things well.

Be patient today. God always answers our prayers. Sometimes He says "yes," sometimes He says "no." Sometimes, however, God asks us to patiently wait, so that He might bring about a greater good or answers our fondest requests—perhaps long after we even stop asking for them.

❑ *God, Help me to plant patience, for I know it will grow character—*
Patience means endurance. Patience tests us. Paul tells us that when we

have endured this testing our character is shaped into what God wants us to be. We will have godly character. Character is what you are—reputation is what the world thinks you are. Someone has said: we sow an action, reap a habit, mold a character, and seal a destiny. Your actions become your conduct, and your conduct determines much about your future. The refining of our character means more to God than what the world thinks of us. Remember, although your patience through this difficulty may not be easy, it will result in a better you when it's all over. Challenge yourself to gain endurance through all that life's challenges bring. The Apostle Paul explained to the Corinthians that life was like a race. But life is more like a marathon than a sprint. God urges us to finish well. The world is full of flashes to ashes, heroes to zeroes. But God has a finer goal for His children. He wants patience to finish its refining work in us. Look at patience or endurance in life as that which you must develop in your life *(I Corinthians 9:27)*.

• *Lord, help me to run hard—there's a prize to win!*

• *Lord, help me to run long—patience, not speed is the goal!*

• *Lord, help me to run life's mountains—to make me strong!*

• *Lord, help me to run life's dark forests—to make me trust in faith!*

• *Lord, help me to run light—that I might lay aside the world's weights! (Heb. 12:1)*

• *Lord, help me to run with confidence—you've already planned my course! (Heb. 12:1; Psalms 37:28)*

❑ *God, Help me to plant patience, for I know it will grow Your approval*—God has not forgotten you in this difficulty. In fact, He has allowed this difficulty for your good. Don't wilt under the pressure you're under right now. When the rope of your life seems to become frayed, tie the knot of faith and hang on. Write these words on your heart: *"I can do all things through Christ which strengtheneth me"* *(Philippians 4:13 KJV)*. God knows how weary you may be right now, but pray for His strength until He finishes with you *(Galatians 6:9; Colossians 1:11)*. Someday God's approval will be worth it all when you hear the words *"well done, good and faithful servant"* (*I Peter 2:20;* *Matthew 25:21*).

❑   *God, Help me to plant patience, for I know it will grow all You have* *promised me*—God has promised wonderful rewards for you if you will patiently endure the troubles that He has allowed to refine you. Someone has said that patient expectation is when we have to put all our eggs in God's basket and count our blessings before they hatch. God wants you to know that the patience He's teaching you is not fruitless. Patience produces hope *(Romans 8:25)*. No doubt, Jacob had given up hope of ever seeing Joseph again. God may have even answered a prayer Jacob had stopped asking. Nevertheless, God's delay was not His denial. God often rewards us with greater blessings than we anticipate. God rewarded Jacob with not only the gift of his son, but full provisions to outlast the famine. Expect God to keep His promises and give you His blessings, but on His schedule, not yours. Moreover, His blessings may exceed your request! *(Psalms 37:5;* *Hebrews 10:36; Ephesians 3:20)*

❑   *God, Help me to plant patience, for I know it will grow into spiritual* *maturity*—You are a work in progress. God is not finished with you yet. Spiritual maturity in understanding is something that doesn't come naturally to our understanding. We have to grow into such knowledge *(I Corinthians 13:11; 14:20; Hebrews 5:11-12)*. Everything you are patiently enduring is God's chisel to create in you His *perfect* work *(James 1:3-4)*. Are you hurting right now? God is working to bring you to His finished work. Don't give up now. Someday, you will see yourself as the spiritually complete person that God desires for you. Despite the weariness you are experiencing right now, you will thank Him that He did it right after all *(Romans 5:3)*.

Power Points:

➤   What distinguishes God's *goodness* from God's *timing*?

➤   Why does God sometimes make us wait so long for answers to our prayers?

Reflection section:

❑   What are you praying for that God has not yet answered?

❑   Can you think of any prayers you are glad God did not answer with a '*yes*'? Why was this best?

❑   What is the difference between *faith* and *hope*?

❑   What is the difference between *patience* and *trust*?

❑   Are you becoming discouraged with God's timing? First, be sure you are in fellowship with God and not harboring secret sins or improper attitudes toward others. Ask God to give you strength to endure while He works out His will for your life.

❑   Remember that when others are involved, God works on their end too. God is never late, but if He answered according to your schedule, He might be too early.

My Personal Growth Journal—

❑   Write down what three prayers you think Joseph prayed most often during his twenty years in Egypt. Now write down the same thing for Jacob, and for the brothers that sold Joseph. How do these prayers compare? List similarities and differences. What did you learn in this assignment?

❑   List five prayers of yours to which God has never answered 'yes'. Circle the two that you are most disappointed He has not answered. Discuss with a friend why you think God has not yet granted your requests.

❑   Using the list in this chapter, write down which part of life's 'race' is the hardest for you.

~ Chapter 25 ~

My Boss Is a Jewish Carpenter: "The Principle of Work Ethic"

The time eventually came when there was no food anywhere. The famine was exceedingly severe. Egypt and Canaan alike were devastated by the famine. Joseph collected all the money that was to be found in Egypt and Canaan to pay for the distribution of food. He banked the money in Pharaoh's palace. (Gen. 46:13-14)

The Joseph story....

There was great rejoicing at the reunion of Joseph and all his family in Egypt. Here they were—brought to Egypt to be cared for by Joseph throughout the famine. As the terrible famine began to take its toll across the lands of Egypt and Canaan, the administrative plan Joseph had suggested to the Pharaoh was called into action. The Pharaoh had entrusted Joseph with the authority to act to save the land and people. Joseph had erected grain silos to store grain during the seven good years of harvest. He was now trusted to collect money from the people to purchase stored grain. Only the self-supporting religious priests did Joseph leave alone. He then banked the collected money to the Pharaoh's account. In every task he performed for the Pharaoh, Joseph kept up an honest, hard-working, dependable appearance at all times. In his heart, Joseph knew he was serving not only the Pharaoh with his wise and honest stewardship, but also a higher Overseer. In serving the Pharaoh, Joseph in truth was working for his God.

Principle Truth: Your faithfulness to God can be measured by your faithfulness to the job which God has entrusted to you, and He is your Supreme Supervisor.

"I hate my job!" Many people have a negative attitude toward their jobs because they feel unappreciated, or treated unfairly. To enjoy the work we do is indeed a blessing from God.

Employment is necessary to survival for most of us. Our employment gives us a paycheck and pays our bills. Our workplace also provides a social environment for us as well as a place for us to utilize our God-given skills.

Enjoying the work we do certainly may enhance our job performance. But enjoying our work is not a requirement for us to do our job with the work ethic God expects of us. Whether we work with children, automobiles, or fast food—whether or not our job rewards us or provides us a pleasant working environment— is irrelevant. God requires us to be faithful and honest in our service simply because it's the right thing to do.

> The only certain means of success is to render more and better service than is expected of you, no matter what your task may be.
>
> —Og Mandino

Most of us want to show a good work ethic. We want to be honest and serve our supervisors to the best of our abilities. But do you show the same work ethic even when your supervisor is out of the building, or when you know your co-workers are not watching? Work ethic is an *attitude*—not merely an action.

Each year, I speak to new teachers at national teaching conferences around the country. Most new teachers have been schooled in theories of teaching, but have little practical knowledge of proper work ethic. For example, I encourage these teachers to come to school a little early each morning and as a rule not to be the first one to leave in the afternoon. They question as to what difference this makes. To them, how they perform in the classroom is the major concern. I explain to them that in the workplace, how they *appear* sometimes means almost as much as what they do. I remind them that while students *are* the primary concern, students come and go. The faculty they must work with will be watching them for years to come. They need to show a good work ethic.

Joseph was made vizier over all Egypt. His service was to the Pharaoh. Joseph had been a faithful employee in every position he occupied. He had faithfully cared for Potiphar's house. He had faithfully supervised and managed the Egyptian jail. Joseph was faithful in these positions even though he endured difficulty and discouragement in each. Potiphar's wife had accused

Joseph of rape in the home, and the wine taster had forgotten Joseph in the prison. Despite the embarrassment Joseph experienced in his workplace, he remained faithful to his work. As vizier, there would be no reason to think his work ethic would be any different.

> *Laziness grows. It begins in the cobwebs and ends in chains.*
>
> *—Sir M. Hale*

Joseph's work ethic did not change. Joseph was faithful in governing Egypt's food supply during the famine. His organization skills brought admiration from the people whose lives he saved. Joseph received honor through honoring every position he was given with total faithfulness.

God expects you to honor your job as Joseph did, with faithfulness, diligence, and dedication. A poor work ethic steals not only finances, but also time from your employer. As you work today, commit yourself to the principle of a good work ethic. As you consider these suggestions, remember—whether your supervisor is watching you or not is irrelevant. Your real boss is a Jewish Carpenter, and God is always watching.

- ❑ *In my job today, God wants me to do my job assignment without excuses*—God sent Gideon to defeat the Midianites. Gideon was a humble man, but also a bit of an excuse maker. Although he obeyed God in this task, at first, he hesitated, telling God his family was poor, and he was not qualified *(Judges 6:11-14)*. Even Moses offered God excuses that he couldn't speak well *(Exodus 4:10)*. In your job, make a sincere effort to do what you are asked without offering excuses. Consider these suggestions for completing your job assignments today:

  - *Be on time.* Better still, to avoid having to make excuses for coming in late—be a little *early.* Tackle the most difficult task first. This will make the rest of your tasks seem much simpler.

  - *Plan, don't react.* To fail to plan is to plan to fail.

  - *Welcome responsibility.* You will stand out among the majority of employees who seek to do less than what they are required.

- ❑ *In my job today, God wants me to put the need of the job ahead of my satisfaction*—Abraham's servant was sent to find a bride for Abraham's son, Isaac. Until the job was done, the servant concerned himself only with that task—even when it meant doing without a few personal needs. In your job today, consider the success of the place you work as more important than the personal wants you may have. Do a little something extra. Volunteer for something instead of waiting to be asked *(Genesis 24:33)*.

❑ *In my job today, God wants me to pray for those who supervise me*—In his task to serve Abraham, the servant not only obeyed his master, he also prayed for him. In your job today, instead of complaining about your boss or supervisor, pray that he or she will conduct their duties the best way they know how *(Genesis 24:12,27,48)*.

❑ *In my job today, God wants me to be faithful over all my responsibilities*—The Roman writer Pliny once said: *"To not mind your work is to plow a crooked row."* God requires of you faithful service in your job responsibility. Jesus spoke about the requirement for faithful service. Faithfulness in responsibilities does not vary, whether your job is small or great. God wants you be diligent in every aspect of your job *(Proverbs 22:29; Ephesians 6:5-8; Romans 12:11)*.

> *The highest reward of a person's toil is not what they get for it, but what they become by it.*
>
> —John Ruskin

In your job today, remember that God put you where you are right now. You are to perform your job as a faithful servant by doing what is expected of you, and not with the attitude of reward *(Luke 17:9-10; 19:12-26)*. God is even ultimately responsible for whether or not you are promoted in your job *(Psalms 75:6-7)*. If you are not happy in your job, of course you are free to leave. Leaving a job is not a divorce. But as long as you serve in your present position, earn your pay. Perform your job description—God requires you to do what you were hired to do—and be satisfied with the salary you agreed to accept *(Luke 16:10-12; I Corinthians 4:2; Cp. Matthew 20:1-15)*.

❑ *In my job today, God wants me to be completely honest in everything I do*—"They won't miss it—after all, everybody does it" Have you ever used this excuse to steal from your employer? God says this is wrong. Period. The Pharaoh trusted Joseph's word alone that he would return to Egypt after visiting his homeland to bury Jacob. Joseph took with him a huge retinue from Egypt and could have simply stayed when he got to Canaan. After all—Israel—not Egypt, was his true home. Nevertheless, the Pharaoh sent Joseph—only needing to hear the words: *"I will return" (Genesis 50:5-6)*. That's honesty and integrity! In your job today, don't try to justify dishonesty. Let everyone in your workplace catch you being honest. *"Our purpose is to do what is right, not only in the sight of the Lord, but also in the sight of others" (II Corinthians 8:21 GNT)*. Earn such trust in your workplace that your word alone is sufficient. God is watching you and calls dishonesty what it is—sinful *(Titus 2:10; Cp. Romans 13:7; II Corinthians 13:7)*.

❑ *In my job today, God wants me to work as if God were my supervisor*—If your supervisor is a good one, you are blessed. Nevertheless, God expects you to honor the *position* of your supervisor, not merely the *person*. God does not require you to *like* your boss. Personality conflicts exist in life, and the workplace is certainly not exempt. But faithful service to a higher authority is a part of God's work expectation for you. In your job today, respect your boss whether he or she deserves it or not. Serve and work for them as you would God if He were your boss—for in reality—He is *(Ephesians 6:5-8; Colossians 3:23; Cp. I Peter 2:18)*.

❑ *In my job today, God wants me to do all I can to make my supervisor look good*—In following God's instructions for the workplace, you will ultimately make your supervisor look good. In your job today follow the expectations of God and make it your goal to honor your boss *above* yourself. This may not be easy, but it is required of a good worker, and for this, God will greatly reward you *(Proverbs 27:18; 25:13; 13:4; Cp. I Timothy 6:1)*.

Power Points:

➤ Jacob's gift to Joseph of the many-colored coat, meant that Joseph was favored. He probably had to do less work than his brothers as they were growing up. Where would Joseph have learned such a good work ethic?

Reflection Section:

❑ What part of your job do you dislike most? Go to work today and see your job as your service to God instead of mere service to your superior. Perform as if God were watching. He will be.

❏   What can you do for your supervisor today to honor him as you would honor God? Perform your activities today with all the skills and effort you can, and know that your earthly boss is only a shadow of the greater Supervisor you are working for in heaven.

❏   How can you be more honest in your job today?

❏   "Respect the position even if you don't respect the person filling it." Explain this statement. Do you agree or disagree? Why?

❏   Rank the following five statements in order of priority:

   ▪   The job must get done.
   ▪   I did my best.
   ▪   My supervisor is pleased.
   ▪   Everyone is happy.
   ▪   I did more than my share.

❏   Remember that your financial reward for service today will pale in comparison to the eternal reward you will receive for the same service.

❏   Remember, your present job may be the training ground for something better someday! Learn from it!

My Personal Growth Journal—

❏   Make a list of seven things you would modify in services performed in your job today if Jesus was your boss. Think about *why* you would perform these things differently.

❏   Write down the five most important things your job has taught you. When you finish, discuss with a friend how these will benefit you in life or in a future job.

~ Chapter 26 ~

Preparation, Anticipation and Tact: "The Principle of Critical Persuasion"

"When Pharaoh calls you in and asks what kind of work you do, tell him, 'Your servants have always kept livestock for as long as we can remember—we and our parents also.' That way he'll let you stay apart in the area of Goshen—for Egyptians look down on anyone who is a shepherd." He had taken five of his brothers with him and introduced them to Pharaoh. Pharaoh asked them, "What kind of work do you do?" They said: "We have come to this country to find a new place to live. There is no pasture for our flocks in Canaan. The famine has been very bad there. Please, would you let your servants settle in the region of Goshen?" (Gen. 46:33-47:4)

The Joseph story....

Joseph had been reconciled to his family, yet the famine still ravaged the land. During the seven years of good harvest, Joseph had wisely stored up much grain in Egyptian silos. Because of this, the Egyptians—as well as his own family—would survive. Nevertheless, Joseph desired to place his family in Goshen, the most fertile area in all Egypt. To achieve this, however, they would have to persuade the Pharaoh. Joseph knew the Pharaoh and had confidence that Pharaoh would allow his family to settle in Goshen. Nevertheless, Joseph would not presume upon the king. He could help his brothers anticipate the king's response, but they would have to ask for themselves. Joseph also knew the Egyptians were not fond of shepherds and would actually prefer the Hebrews to locate in a more isolated area of Egypt. Nevertheless, how they should present such a request would still be critical in anticipating the king's response.

Principle Truth: The manner in which you choose your words, and the timing with which you use them, are the greatest tools God has given you to shape what the world offers in the mold of your need.

The boy's father had never been a great athlete, but took pride in hoping his son would become what he could not. The son wanted desperately to please his father, and, although not a gifted athlete either, he joined the school track team.

On the first day of practice, the son was paired against a teammate who just happened to be the fastest sprinter in the county. His father's work prevented him from attending the practice, and this time would prevent him from watching the resounding defeat his son would most certainly experience. The boy lost, and wondered how he would explain his defeat to his proud father. The boy loved his dad and could not bear to see the disappointment in his eyes. The preparation for the meeting with dad would be critical. The boy knew he must be truthful with his father—as he had always been—yet carefully choose his words.

When the father arrived home later that evening, he anxiously inquired as to the first practice and how the boy had done. In the honest tact of carefully prepared words, the boy replied: "Dad I raced along with the fastest runner in the county today. He finished next-to-last, and I finished second!" The father beamed with pride. Sometimes it's all in how we put it.

How you speak says much about you. This is one lesson I attempt to teach my students, through debate and other proper speaking skills. But it's not just what comes from your mouth; it's how you put those words. Tact and critical persuasion can bring great reward.

> *In business, you don't get what you deserve, you get what you negotiate.*
>
> *—Chester L. Karrass*

Critical persuasion skills can shape our entire future. Learning how to effectively persuade can determine job advancements, how well we defend our rights and beliefs, and how effectively we instruct and lead others.

The world of business and law understands well the value of critical persuasion. Critical persuasion requires knowing one's audience, as well as their needs and concerns of the same. Critical persuasion often hinges on how well one phrases the question, anticipates objections and formulates a point for emphasis.

Joseph understood the importance of critical persuasion too. He knew the request his brothers would have to make in relocating in Egypt. He also knew the Pharaoh. Joseph understood that the audience with the Pharaoh would determine the future of his entire family, and thus prepared them for what to say and how to say it. In their audience with the Pharaoh, Joseph's brothers did not lie. What they did was carefully and selectively choose their words as Joseph had instructed them. They were tactful, yet truthful. Joseph had instructed his brothers in the importance of critical persuasion.

The more we refine the art of critical persuasion concerning people we will meet, jobs we will interview for, and employers we must face, the better will be our chances for success. Critical persuasion requires practice and tact, but rewards richly. Try to practice critical persuasion today. In your workplace, make an *impression* through your *expression*.

❑ *When I practice the art of critical persuasion today, I will make sure I am the best person to do the asking*—Joseph approached the Pharaoh with only five of his brothers, not *all* of them. Certainly these five were the ones Joseph thought would make the best impression—perhaps because they were better speakers. Ask yourself if you are the best person to be asking this question. Is someone else more qualified? Will someone else make a better impression?

❑ *When I practice the art of critical persuasion today, I will have a specific goal I want to be met*—Joseph and his brothers had a clear and specific goal. They did not just want to live in Egypt, they wanted to move to Egypt and live in Goshen—the best part of Egypt. Ask yourself before you make the request what your specific goal is. *"The one thing I do, however, is to forget what is behind me and do my best to reach what is ahead. So I run straight toward the goal"* (Galatians 3:13-14 GNT). What is your intended outcome in making this request? Your goal must be identifiable and achievable. If your goal is not specific, your request may not be clear.

❑ *When I practice the art of critical persuasion today, I will organize my thoughts, and anticipate the response*—Joseph helped his brothers organize their thoughts before they approached the Pharaoh. Joseph knew the Pharaoh well, which enabled him to help his brothers anticipate the king's response to their request. In fact, Joseph predicted correctly what the Pharaoh would say. Anticipation and preparation are traits that usually pay positive dividends *(Matthew 25:4)*. Ask yourself if you have organized your thoughts and chosen your words carefully before you make this request, and if you have anticipated at least three responses you might receive *(Proverbs 11:9; 15:28)*.

❑ *When I practice the art of critical persuasion today, I will present myself in humility*—Joseph's brothers introduced themselves as *servants*. They did not present themselves as relatives of the Vizier. Do not adopt a superior attitude when making a request. Arrogance and excessive pride leave us less pliable—less susceptible to God's shaping that conforms us into the image of His Son *(Romans 8:29)*. The clay used daily by the ancient Israelites was breakable only when it became hard. Present yourself in humility. To become hardened through excessive pride could lead to your downfall. *"Pride goes before destruction, and haughtiness before a fall" (Proverb 16:18 GNT; Cp. Luke 14:11; Cp. Ephesians 4:1-2; Colossians 3:12).*

❑ *When I practice the art of critical persuasion today, I will first de-emphasize any negative situation*—The Egyptians hated shepherds. Sheep carried lice, which the Egyptians made every effort to avoid. Joseph's brothers wanted to bring their sheep to Egypt, but they knew better than to mention sheep to the Pharaoh. Joseph suggested they tactfully use the term "livestock" instead. In doing this, the brothers de-emphasized the negative idea of bringing sheep to Egypt. Ask yourself how, in making your request, you might tactfully choose your words *(cp. Proverbs 25:15).*

❑ *When I practice the art of critical persuasion today, I will begin on complimentary footing*—After the Pharaoh asked the precise question Joseph had predicted, the brothers began by extolling Egypt as the land above all others in which they wanted to begin a new life. Pharaoh would surely take this implication as compliment to his kingdom. Even the Hebrew captives, friends of Daniel, realized the importance of a well-timed compliment as they came before Nebuchadnezzar, the great king of Babylon. *"They said to King Nebuchadnezzar, 'May Your Majesty live forever'" (Daniel 3:9 GNT).* Ask yourself how you may frame your request in the context of a compliment. This will create a positive setting into which you may introduce your further conversation *(II Corinthians 7:4).*

❑ *When I practice the art of critical persuasion today, I will present the situation clearly*—Joseph's brother clearly stated the rationale against which they could present their request: *"There is no pasture for our flocks in Canaan,"* and *"The famine has been very bad there."* Dancing around the issue would have wasted the Pharaoh's time. When you prepare to make your request, present the situation as clearly and honestly as possible *(II Corinthians 11:22-27)*.

❑ ***When I practice the art of critical persuasion today, I will politely make my specific request***—At last, Joseph's brothers made their request. *"Please, would you let your servants settle in the region of Goshen?"* Your request made politely and in few words will stand a better chance of acceptance. Sometimes, it's all in how you present it *(Proverbs 16:24; Cp. Mark 6:24)*.

Power Points:

➤ Was Joseph acting improperly in preparing his brothers regarding what to say to the Pharaoh?

➤ Why didn't Joseph just speak *for* them? How can you relate this point to your children?

➤ Was Joseph acting selfishly in seeking to have his brothers settle in the finest area of Egypt?

➤ Is it ever wrong to selectively leave out information? Do you think Joseph's brothers were dishonest because they were vague in their information to Pharaoh?

➤ Why do you think Joseph selected only five of his twelve brothers to approach the Pharaoh?

Reflection section:

❑ Anticipate questions that may be asked you today.

❑ What do you think is the difference between extreme *tactfulness* and a *"little white lie"*?

❑ In considering effective persuasion, what is the difference between *debate* and *argument*?

❑   Did you prepare for this day with prayer?

❑   Think before you speak today. Is there a way to re-phrase a request you want to make?

❑   "It is better to compliment someone falsely than to miss an opportunity and say nothing." Do you agree or disagree with this statement? Why?

❑   Like Joseph prepared his brothers, prepare yourself to say things in a more appropriate way today. How you speak and how you look make the greatest of impressions.

❑   Anticipate objections to questions you want to ask today.

My Personal Growth Journal—

❑   Write down ten phrases you often say. Rewrite them attempting to put the words in a more pleasing way. Learn to speak them in such a manner.

❑   Write down the ten most persuasive words that someone could use with you. Use them with others.

~ Chapter 27 ~

Provisions of God: "The Principle of Recognizing God's Blessings"

"We have come to this country to find a new place to live. There is no pasture for our flocks in Canaan. The famine has been very bad there. Please, would you let your servants settle in the region of Goshen?" Pharaoh looked at Joseph. "So, your father and brothers have arrived—a reunion! Egypt welcomes them. Settle your father and brothers on the choicest land—yes, give them Goshen. And if you know any among them that are especially good at their work, put them in charge of my own livestock." Next Joseph brought his father Jacob in and introduced him to Pharaoh. Jacob blessed Pharaoh. Pharaoh asked Jacob, "How old are you?" Jacob answered Pharaoh, "The years of my sojourning are 130—a short and hard life and not nearly as long as my ancestors were given" Then Jacob blessed Pharaoh and left. Joseph settled his father and brothers in Egypt, made them proud owners of choice land—it was the region of Rameses (that is, Goshen)—just as Pharaoh had ordered. Joseph took good care of them—his father and brothers and all his father's family, right down to the smallest baby. He made sure they had plenty of everything. (Gen. 47:4-12)

The Joseph story....

Joseph presented his family to Pharaoh—king of Egypt. The Pharaoh had probably heard many stories from Joseph about this family. But now, due to the famine, he would finally meet them. Before the Pharaoh, Joseph had never spoken ill of the brothers regarding the terrible treatment they had given him. The Pharaoh was pleased to meet Jacob and his family, and, through Joseph, saw to it they were well cared for through the duration of the famine and beyond. The Pharaoh even blessed them in a way they had not requested. He offered to let them use their work skills to enhance his kingdom. Through Joseph—and only because of Joseph—Jacob's family was blessed, protected, and cared for from that moment on.

Principle Truth: Though God owes you nothing, through Christ, He has poured out His blessings upon you in ways you may not even realize.

Every blessing we have is from God. Without His favor, we would not only be without food and shelter, we would be without life itself. We sometimes forget how much God provides for us. In wishing we were rich and famous, we forget the daily provisions He gives us. Provisions we do not necessarily deserve, but which are ours through Christ Jesus.

God's blessings do not consist merely of health and wealth. His blessings also include friends and other people who share our experiences. His blessings also include loving us enough to answer our prayers. God's greatest blessing to us, however, is the blessing we deserve least—the gift of His Son.

Through Christ alone we are blessed, and through no merit of our own. The only contribution we could offer was our sinful guilt, which brought the grace of forgiveness. Only as God exalted His Son, could we come to receive forgiveness of our sins. Only through Christ's suffering and exaltation could God provide for us on a daily basis for as long as we live. God even prepared a heavenly home in a far country for His children that we may someday share His glory. Everything we have, we owe to the love God bestowed through His Son.

Through Joseph alone, Jacob and his family were blessed. Through no merit of their own, they were saved. The only contribution the brothers could offer was their sinful guilt, which brought the grace of forgiveness. Only as Pharaoh exalted Joseph could the brothers come to a position of forgiveness for their sins. Only through Joseph's suffering and exaltation could Pharaoh provide for Jacob and the brothers on a daily basis for as long as they lived. Through Pharaoh, Joseph prepared Goshen—the finest land in Egypt—as a glorious home in a distant land for his family, so that they might share His glory. Everything Jacob and his family had, they owed to the honor Pharaoh bestowed upon Joseph.

But Joseph wanted his father Jacob to also bless the Pharaoh. Since Egyptian lifespan was less than the lifespan in Canaan, Pharaoh had probably never seen a 130 year-old man in his life. He would have considered Jacob to have been a wise and honorable man. In blessing Jacob's family through Joseph, the Pharaoh was in turn also blessed.

Our blessings from God are remarkably shadowed in the blessings Jacob's family received in Egypt. Both involve blessing graciously bestowed upon those who were most unworthy. Like Christ, Joseph had suffered much before his exaltation. Joseph was elevated to the office of vizier, and Christ to the right hand of the Father *(Hebrews 1:3)*. Joseph was responsible not only for his family dwelling in the finest part of the land, but also for them being alive at all. Everything they had for the rest of their lives was because of Joseph. So, too, our blessings in Christ. We also bless God through our praise and thanksgiving for His blessings toward us.

Joseph became to his family what Christ has become to you and me. We could never attempt to repay God for all He has done, is doing, and continues to do for us. All these blessings are through our Savior. We would do much better thanking God for all we have than complaining about what we don't.

Today, there will be many blessings for you to receive and share. Some blessings you may not recognize as such. Recognize and thank God for His blessings to you today. In reality, every provision you will have for the rest of your life is through no merit on your part. Your blessings are through Christ alone.

❑   *I will remember that God's blessings do not always include prosperity or health*—Although God sometimes permits them, He never promises you riches, wealth, popularity, fame, or that you will never get sick. God alone gives you the power to make wealth *(I Chronicles 29:11-12).* The disciples of Jesus were poor in possessions, but so too was Mother Theresa. Despite what many claim, all of us will get sick and die. I remember several faith healers urging me to 'claim God's healing' when my mother was sick with cancer. The same ones chastised me for "not having enough faith" when she died. Of course, you should pray for your own health and make every effort to pray for those you know are sick. Sometimes God does heal terminal diseases. Sometimes people do strike it rich. While these are surely blessings, they are not *promised* blessings, merely *permitted* ones. Most often, God's blessings are spiritual rather than physical *(Matthew 19:21; Ephesians 1:3).* Can you trust God to bless you apart from health and wealth? Thank God that He has allowed you to see another day. Thank Him for the food on your table and clothes on your back *(Matthew 6:26-33).* Thank him that His greatest blessings for you are reserved in Heaven *(Matthew 6; 20; I Timothy 6:19; I Corinthians 9:25).* Do you watch the sinful world and long for the prosperity others seem to have? *Don't! (Psalms 37:7)* Today, practice thanking God for your daily needs instead of trying to persuade Him to permit your daily wants.

❑   *I will remember that God's blessings are not finished when I die*—Do you think that your rewards come in this life alone? God also promised heavenly blessings for faithful service to Him on earth *(Hebrews 10:36).* Some of that service is invested in the lives of others that you influence for God. As those lives continue to glorify God, *you* share in those rewards—even after you die! Your works follow you! Live today for heavenly blessings, and invest in the lives of others who may outlive you. Your blessings are not finished when you die *(Revelation 14:13; Cp. John 4:37-38).*

❑ *I will remember that God's blessings are meant to be shared*—Sometimes God blesses us so that we can share the blessings with others. God blessed Joseph with great blessings in Egypt. But in the end, Joseph could share his blessings *with* Egypt, and his family. Sometimes, God blesses you through others. Is it possible God is preparing someone right now to bless you at a later time? Today, ask God to bless you in a way that you can share with someone else. Tonight, write down three specific blessings God shared with you today. Tomorrow, think how you can share these with others.

❑ *I will remember that God's blessings are usually much greater than I could imagine, or deserve*—Joseph's brothers certainly did not deserve the blessings they received from Joseph, yet Joseph blessed them. When asked for a place to settle in Egypt until the famine was over, the Pharaoh not only granted them the finest land, he also offered them jobs! Remember today that God's reward system may not seem logical to us. God rewards on a heavenly standard, which we cannot fully understand. When God hands out his rewards someday, you and I might be surprised! *"But as it is written, Eye hath not seen, nor ear heard, neither have entered into the heart of man, the things which God hath prepared for them that love him"* (I Corinthians 2:9 KJV). (Cp. Matthew 19:30; Cp. Ephesians 3:20; Matthew 13:12; 20:1-16; Cp. Luke 16:10-13)

❑ *I will remember that God's blessings may not always take the form I prefer*—When God instructed Jacob and his family to relocate in Egypt, Jacob probably had mixed feelings. He would be thrilled to see Joseph whom, for twenty years, he thought to be dead. On the other hand, Jacob would surely have preferred to have Joseph come home. Instead, God was relocating the old man to a foreign country with strange customs and foreign gods. Jacob may not have seen this as a blessing! After all, Jacob was well over a hundred years old, and he knew that he would most certainly never return to Canaan. Sometimes God's blessings may not take the form we might prefer, but God knows best. God sees the future, and knows the best way to bring good for us. Sometimes God says *"no"* to our prayers, but it's not because He doesn't love us. Sometimes he brings death—yes, even death—because He *does* love us, and knows what the future may hold *(Revelation 14:13)*. Trust God even when a child is lost, or a loved one is taken. Remember that in God's plan, even death can be a loving and merciful blessing from He who knows best. *"The righteous pass away; the godly often die before their time. And no one seems to care or wonder why. No one seems to understand that God is protecting them from the evil to come. For the godly who die will rest in peace"* (Isaiah 57:1-2 NLT). Can you trust God today, that all His blessings are *valuable*? Can you trust the God of all the earth to do right by you? *(Genesis 18:25)*

❑   *I will remember that God's blessings are not bestowed according to my understanding*—God's systems of blessing through rewarding faithful service may sound strange to you. God is not concerned with the *amount* of service you give, but with the *faithfulness* you show to what He gives you. Let's face it—some Christians are put in a far more influential position than others. Some simply have more opportunity than others do. For example, if you and I were to be rewarded according the service opportunity of Billy Graham or Mother Theresa, we would probably receive exceedingly little. You and I have simply not been given such an opportunity. But God's reward system is based on *obedience (cp. I Samuel 15:22)*. In the Parable of the Talents, for example, the servants are given different measures of responsibility. When they are rewarded, the master rewards them according to their obedient investment of what they were *given*, not how much they *gained*. In fact, the reward was the same for *every* servant except the one who did nothing with his talent! A similar reward system is represented in the Parable of the Laborers *(Matthew 20:1-16; 25:14-30; Cp. Luke 16:1-12; 19:12-26)*. Serve God with the understanding that God's reward system is not like ours. In fact, His system is much more fair. Your rewards will be based upon your *obedience* and *faithfulness* over what He's given you to do. God will not be concerned with the *amount* of what that service produced.

❑   *I will remember that God's blessings should always be appreciated in praise*—Luke tells the story of Jesus healing ten lepers of this terrible disease. Only one returned to thank Him. Make it a point to thank God today—even for blessing you might consider small *(Ephesians 5:20; Colossians 4:2; Philippians 4:6)*.

Power Points:

> ➤ Do you think Joseph ever mentioned to the Pharaoh how his brothers had once treated him? If so, why do you think the Pharaoh did not mention this to them?

> ➤ Why did Pharaoh appear so pleased to meet Joseph's family?

> ➤ What can we learn about God's feeling towards us because of Christ?

Reflection section:

- ❑ What misunderstandings have you experienced about the 'health and wealth' prosperity gospel?

- ❑ Why does God still allow us to sometimes get sick, and eventually—to die?

- ❑ If you could bless others through suffering, would you? How would you choose those who would be blessed?

- ❑ What blessings of reward are you storing up in heaven today through your work on earth? What can you do today to increase these?

- ❑ Why is prosperity not always a blessing from God?

- ❑ "God sure must love the poor—He certainly made a lot of them." Do you agree or disagree with this statement? Why?

- ❑ What blessings are you investing in others at this point in your life, which will follow you long after you're gone?

- ❑ What are some blessings you have from God that you have not thanked Him for?

❑   When did God bless you by *not* answering a prayer the way you wanted Him to?

My Personal Growth Journal—

❑   Make a list of twenty things you have that you've never thanked God for. When you pray today, remember these before Him.

~ Chapter 28 ~

Planning for the Future: "The Principle of Wise Use of Money"

Joseph then announced to the people: "Here's how things stand: I've bought you and your land for Pharaoh. In exchange I'm giving you seed so you can plant the ground. When the crops are harvested, you must give a fifth to Pharaoh and keep four-fifths for yourselves, for seed for yourselves and your families—you're going to be able to feed your children!" (Gen. 47:23-24)

The Joseph story....

As the terrible famine ran its course, Joseph, Pharaoh's wise administrator, instructed the people to purchase seed in order to survive. But they were not to eat *all* of that provision. Some seed was to be planted in order to produce more seed. Other seed was to serve as a twenty percent tax to be paid to the Pharaoh. The remaining seed would serve as food and be eaten. In his wisdom, Joseph instructed all Egypt carefully on how they should invest their seed. They must live not only for today's needs, but plan for tomorrow's.

Principle Truth: It is not important how much money God has entrusted to you, but what your attitude toward it is, and how faithfully you put to work the money you have.

A penny saved is a penny earned. This is one of the wisest investment principles ever penned. Save for the future, and let your savings multiply. They will take care of you someday. More wise advice. Put in a different way, when your outflow exceeds your income, your upkeep will become your downfall.

Wisdom dictates that reinvestment provides for tomorrow what blessing has given us today. To spend all we have brings only temporary satisfaction and long-term difficulty.

But what else does God say about our money? Do we save it all for the proverbial "rainy day"? Are we supposed to pay our taxes? And what does God have to say? Isn't money supposed to the root of all evil?

God never said to us that money was the root of all evil. We just think He did. God said to us that the *love* of money is the root of all kinds of evil *(I Timothy 6:10)*. Money is no different from anything else we have. But the desire for money can be like tasting salty water—

> *Money is an article which may be used as a universal passport to everywhere except heaven, and a universal provider of everything except happiness.*
>
> ❧❧

the more you drink, the thirstier you get. Money makes a great servant, but a poor master *(cp. Luke 16:13)*. The right and wrong of money is in how we use it. J.D. Rockefeller was once asked how much money he would like to have. Already one of the wealthiest men in the world, he answered: *"Just a little more."* The love for money is addictive.

Jesus made a fascinating statement regarding money: *"And I say to you, make friends for yourselves by means of the wealth of unrighteousness, so that when it fails, they will receive you into the eternal dwellings" (Luke 16:9 NASB).* Jesus did not teach that money was evil. In fact, He was teaching that we should use money wisely to help win souls. Money is not evil in itself. Scripture makes that perfectly clear. It's the *use* of money that can lead to evil. In this same teaching, Jesus instructed us that money would eventually fail. God wants you to understand that your relationship to money should be that when your money fails—you *won't*.

It has been said that money cannot buy happiness, but it can finance the illusion. The truth is, even if we had as much money as we wanted, we would not be satisfied. Solomon was the richest king Judah and Israel ever had. Solomon had more gold than even his father, King David. There was nothing

Solomon could not buy. But Solomon was not happy with his riches. *"If you love money, you will never be satisfied; if you long to be rich, you will never get all you want. It is useless. The richer you are, the more mouths you have to feed. All you gain is the knowledge that you are rich"* (Ecclesiastes 5:10-11 GNT). Solomon understood that while wealth might solve some financial problems; in reality, it simply created another set of worries.

Jesus explained the same truth in the story of the rich man who was blessed greatly like Solomon. Was he satisfied? No. His wealth only created another set of worries. *"He began to think to himself, 'I don't have a place to keep all my crops. What can I do?'"* (Luke 12:17 GNT) The love of money is the source of all kinds of evil—it is also the source of all kinds of worry.

God has left us instructions on the use of our finances. Some of our income of course, is to be spent on necessities, as well as on things we enjoy. But investing our finances in order to provide for our future is one of the clearest principles in all scripture, and one that Joseph instituted for the Egyptians to survive the famine. Investing for the future is one of many financial principles that God has given us. These principles are universal in their appropriateness. They worked under Joseph in Egypt. They will work for you today.

"Ten Commandments Regarding Your Money"

I.   *Thou shalt work for thy money*—Joseph understood the dangers of a welfare state. Instead of giving away free grain, Joseph required the people to exchange many of their present possessions. All the way back in Genesis God instituted the principle of working for what you earn *(Genesis 3:17-19).*

II.   *Thou shalt diversify and spread thy surpluses across many realms*—Joseph did not want the people to simply hide the grain given them. Though it might be safe hidden under your bed, God does not want you to simply put all your money away where it cannot produce some measure of return. Joseph instructed the people not to hide all their grain. The grain was too precious to not be of wise use to the Egyptians. Instead, Joseph had the people put their seed to three uses. They were to *eat* some of it, *plant* some of it, and *use* some of it to meet their *daily requirements*. God wants you to *diversify*. *"Be sure to stay busy and plant a variety of crops, for you never know which will grow—perhaps they all will"* (Ecclesiastes 11:6 NLT). Let your money work for—not against—you *(Matthew 25:18; 24-30)*. Use it for today's needs, and also tomorrow's.

III. ***Thou shalt give unto those in need generously***—God wants you to act wisely with your money. Sometimes this will require you to do with it what might seem strange. To be prudent with your money requires you to give some of it away! God wants you to invest your money not only in savings, but also in other people. Give to the work of God through your place of worship *(I Corinthians 16:1-2)*. Understand God's perspective on giving for the benefit of His kingdom. God is more interested in *why* you give and what you *keep* than He is with what is of no sacrifice to you. Your attitude and sacrifice are more important than how much you give *(Mark 12:41-44)*. Give to those less fortunate than you are through charitable organizations. It has been said that when it comes to generous giving—some people stop at nothing. Give *willingly*; give *generously*—not grudgingly *(II Corinthians 9:7; Cp. Exodus 25:2; I Chronicles 29:14)*. Part of your money is best invested by giving it away! *(Proverbs 11:24-25; 22:9; II Corinthians 9:7)*

IV. ***Thou shalt invest a part of thy surpluses for thy future***—Joseph wanted the people to plant some of the seed, as well as eat some to keep them alive. Grain was precious. Planting some of it might have seemed like throwing it away. What if it did not grow? Joseph understood the power of planning for the future. Sometimes such planning involves risk—the risk of investment. It also involves trusting God for the increase. God wants you to invest some of your money so that it can multiply, and secure your future. Investing in the present to grow future returns is God's investment principle *(cp. Mark 4:20)*. Choose your investments wisely. All investment involves some degree of risk. Generally, the greater the risk, the greater the reward *(Proverbs 30:25; Matthew 25:14-22)*.

V. ***Thou shalt pay thy taxes***—Joseph required the people not only to use their seed wisely for themselves, but also to pay as a tax to the Pharaoh. While no one enjoys paying taxes, God wants you to do this to support the government system He has created. Yes, God even created the system of human government, and in God's eyes, even an evil government is better than no government at all *(Matthew 17:27; 22:19-21; Romans 13:6-7; Cp. Matthew 17:24-27; Cp. Genesis 9:6)*.

VI. ***Thou shalt borrow carefully if thou must borrow***—God is not against borrowing money. However, He would have you remember that, when you borrow, you create a debt that must be repaid. Debt has been called an empty purse full of other men's money. Borrow carefully, and always, *always*—pay down existing debt whenever possible! *"When she told the man of God what had happened, he said to her, 'Now sell the olive oil and pay your debts, and there will be enough money left over to support you and your sons'"* (II Kings 4:7 NLT).

VII. **Thou shalt not sign for another's debt without great thought**—The most dangerous financial undertaking is to bear the debt of someone else. Before you cosign for someone else, or take responsibility for someone else's debt, be certain you can repay it if they default (*Proverbs 6:1-5; 11:15; 17:18; 22:26-27*).

VIII. **Thou shalt remember that thy credit is the key to thy future**—Your good credit is second only to your good reputation in this life. Be careful how you use the credit cards that are entrusted to you. They are called *drastic plastic* for a reason! Use them sparingly and wisely. Make sure your debts are paid, and paid on time. Good credit will be the key to every major purchase you will ever make. Therefore, establish it early and guard it carefully.

IX. **Thou shalt understand the power of compounding interest**—Allow the principle of compounding interest to work *for* you, not against you. Whether a savings, or a debt you owe, compounding interest will increase a sum rapidly over time. Remember the '*Rule of 72*'. Whenever the number *72* is divided by the interest rate you earn, or the interest rate you must pay, the result is how long it will take sum to *double*. Compounding interest can be friend or foe. Spend carefully; save all you are able.

X. **Thou shalt keep the desire for money in a proper perspective**—Keep the *desire* for money and the *need* for money in a godly balance. What you think will make you happy is but a short-term illusion. Money makes a wonderful slave, but a ruthless master.

Power Points:

➤ Was Joseph unfair in his 20% tax on the people? Why? Why not?

➤ Why do you think it is only Joseph who is never mentioned in the discussion of "who gets what" during the famine?

➤ Do you feel Joseph had the right to tell the people what to do with their own allotment of food? Why? Why not?

Reflection Section:

❑ Do you agree or disagree with the statement that even a bad government is better than no government at all? Why? Why not?

❑ Do you need to diversify your investments? Do you have too many eggs in one basket?

❑ Can you trust God enough to believe that even if He blessed you with great riches, they would *not* make you happy?

❑ "To save money is to not trust God for your daily bread." Do you agree or disagree with this statement? Why?

❑ Do you need to begin—or increase—your giving to others in need, or to God? Remember, to give to those in need *is* to give to God.

❑ "The welfare system is an unnecessary drain on our economy." Do you agree or disagree with this statement? Why?

❑ None of us like to pay taxes, or store our money away when we would prefer to buy that new entertainment center, that new car, or new house. But try to remember that God has instituted certain investment principles that secure not only our future, but also the future of the government that protects us.

❑ Earn what you can.

❑ Buy what you need.

❑ Spend what you must.

❑   Save what's left.

My Personal Growth Journal—

❑   Go over your finances this week. Consolidate your debts. See how you can reduce your debt by paying off higher interest debts first.

~ Chapter 29 ~

Earned Respect and Honor: "The Principle of Effective Leadership"

Joseph said to the people, "You see, I have now bought you and your lands for the king. Here is seed for you to sow in your fields. At the time of harvest you must give one-fifth to the king. You can use the rest for seed and for food for yourselves and your families." They answered, "You have saved our lives; you have been good to us, sir, and we will be the king's slaves." (Gen. 47:23-25)

The Joseph story....

At last, the terrible famine was ending. As the Pharaoh's administrator, Joseph had instituted a plan for survival that included taxation, sacrifice, and the giving up of many personal freedoms. All this was to insure the survival of a nation. Would the people resent such sacrifice? Would they feel as though their hardships resulted only in profit to line the pockets of the Pharaoh, Joseph, and the royal court? Not only did the people not resent Joseph's reforms, they praised both him and the Pharaoh. Both had proved to be honest and effective leaders in saving Egypt from the terrible famine. Joseph's leadership skills had brought honor to himself, his Pharaoh and his God. Those same skills also saved Egypt, as well as the Hebrew race begun by Abraham. A race that would one day produce the Messiah.

Principle Truth: Leadership is a position of responsibility to be evaluated by a Higher Authority in light of how the shepherd cared for his sheep.

"I hate my boss!" Have you ever felt this way? Do you know someone who has?

Many people have a negative attitude toward their jobs because they feel their boss either under-appreciates them or treats them unfairly. The way administrators and leaders conduct their duties and handle those under them often determines whether their workers are happy or not in their workplace. Or perhaps—whether those workers might prefer to be somewhere else.

But what makes a good administrator? What characteristics do they exhibit in the workplace? What is the most important administrative skill a leader can possess?

The finest administrators are leaders who *motivate*. An effective leader understands that those in their employ are better led than driven and are led best when they are motivated.

Mr. Stewart was one of the first principals I worked for. He was in charge of a small rural school and was not trained in the most advanced theories of personnel management. But Mr. Stewart knew his faculty. He cared for us as individuals, not just as a collective teaching staff. Mr. Stewart motivated us to perform our duties to the best of our abilities—not through technique—but through personal concern. He made us *want* to be better teachers.

Mr. Stewart loved his job. Every morning, Mr. Stewart's would be the first car in the parking lot. On many mornings, I would find an encouraging note in my mailbox. He could sense when our teaching duties were becoming especially heavy, and would put aside his own work to lend a shoulder whenever we simply needed to vent. Mr. Stewart earned our respect in everything he did, and I still look back at him when I remember what an effective leader should be.

Joseph was an effective and respected leader. Entrusted with Egypt's survival during the famine, Joseph required the people to pay for Egypt's stored grain. He refused to initiate a welfare state. Joseph brought honor to his Pharaoh and diversity to his workplace through permitting the Egyptian priests to function according to their own ways. Even in taxing the people, Joseph earned the respect of all Egypt. He remains a model of leadership so successful that even when he required great sacrifice from the people, not once did he drop in Egyptian opinion polls.

But what exactly does an effective leader do? Effective leaders are careful in their speech and prudent in their conduct. Effective leaders realize that they should model the work ethic they expect of those in their charge, and seek the satisfaction of their employees above accolade to themselves.

If you will be leading others today, consider what makes up effective leadership:

- ❑ *An effective leader is committed to God and to his or her job*—Joseph loved his God and the people he served. His success in was evident in his dedication to both *(Proverbs 16:3)*.

- ❑ *An effective leader is confident and instructive*—Joseph had already promised his family the land of Goshen—the finest land in all Egypt *(Genesis 45:10)*. The Pharaoh respected Joseph, and Joseph was confident and certain the Pharaoh would grant this favor to his family. But Joseph would not presume on the Pharaoh. He required his brothers to be accountable and make a respectful request for the land *(Genesis 47:4)*. Like an effective leader, Joseph gave his brothers a reason to get along with their superior, while helping them keep their self-worth in perspective. Joseph was a confident leader who never promised more than he could deliver *(Genesis 46:33-34; 47:1)*.

- ❑ *An effective leader takes advantage of opportunities*—Joseph took advantage of his relationship with the Pharaoh to request safe dwelling for his family in Egypt. Notice, however, that Joseph took advantage of the Pharaoh's *position* as the final authority in Egypt. He did not take advantage of the Pharaoh *personally* simply because the Pharaoh trusted him. An effective leader utilizes his or her advantage—but never unfairly *(Genesis 46:31)*.

- ❑ *An effective leader is tactful*—Joseph instructed his brothers to request the land of Goshen to *dwell* in, not to live in *indefinitely*. They were to do this after approaching the Pharaoh as his "servants." An effective leader is careful in his or her selection of words and their proper use *(Genesis 46:34; 47:2,4)*.

- ❑ *An effective leader sets high but realistic expectations for others*—With God's help, Joseph set a goal of seven years for the storage of grain in Egypt. Joseph knew that beyond that would be the famine, when no crops would grow *(Genesis 41:34-36)*. Joseph set a goal for the taxation—*one-fifth*, not an unreasonable rate, or a burden upon the people *(Genesis 47:24)*. Joseph set a goal for his brothers when they made their request before the Pharaoh. Their goal was the finest land of Egypt in which to dwell *(Genesis 46:33-34)*. It has been said that a goal is a dream with a deadline. An effective leader looks ahead, sets a goal, and knows how to steer others toward that goal *(cp. Colossians 3:13-14).*

❑ *An effective leader works hard at what he or she does*—Joseph was faithful over Potiphar's house, the Egyptian jail, and the Pharaoh's kingdom. He excelled at every job given him. A good leader works *diligently*, uses *time wisely*, and utilizes *talents fully*. Joseph excelled in all three of these characteristics. He required the same hard work from others and refused to initiate a welfare system *(II Thessalonians 3:10; Proverbs 12:24).*

❑ *An effective leader understands the needs of those who serve*—Joseph never left a doubt in the minds of the people of Egypt that their needs were his prime concern. A good leader takes a *genuine* personal interest in those who serve. A good leader understands that those who serve have three personal needs: *respect, appreciation,* and *recognition*. Such leaders learn how to meet these needs *individually* and *successfully*, and recognize that thirty seconds of sincere compliment for a job well done is worth ten minutes of general praise. An effective leader is as sincere in the compliments he or she gives as in the criticisms they must make *(Romans 16:18).*

❑ *An effective leader is a good listener and receptive to those under his or her care*—Joseph listened carefully to the *instructions* of his father and the *dreams* of the wine taster, baker, and Pharaoh. Joseph also listened to the people of Egypt *(Proverbs 18:13,15)*. Joseph required many sacrifices from the people, but, each time he *demanded* something from them, he *gave* something in return *(Genesis 47:14-23).*

❑ *An effective leader brings honor to his or her superiors*—Joseph balanced the requirements he demanded of the people with the benefits he sought for the Pharaoh. Joseph's wisdom made not only himself and his God look good, it also made the Pharaoh appear extremely wise in the eyes of his people for selecting Joseph! *(Genesis 47:18-20)*

❑ *An effective leader is objective in his or her decision-making*—An effective leader is receptive and decisive. Joseph listened to all the information in the dreams of the wine taster, the baker, and the Pharaoh. Only then did Joseph interpret and recommend, and that without hesitation. Joseph was a good listener. He understood the importance of evaluating all the information before addressing the issue (*Proverbs 18:17*).

❏ *An effective leader is a proactive problem-solver and plans ahead*— Joseph made plans for the survival of the people throughout the seven-year famine. He did not wait until the famine came before he acted (*Luke 14:28; Proverbs 24:27*). He also prepared the Pharaoh for both the famine and survival of the famine. Finally, Joseph prepared his brothers on what to say to the Pharaoh. Leaders do not merely steer the ship. Leaders chart the course. Joseph was *proactive*—not reactive!

❏ *An effective leader delegates responsibility*—Joseph understood the importance of delegated responsibility. He himself had been given responsibility by the Pharaoh over all the grain of Egypt. Joseph also established granaries throughout the land of Egypt—a feat he could not have accomplished without delegating responsibility (*Deuteronomy 1:9-13; Exodus 38:21-24*). Average leaders lead through *authority*. Good leaders lead through *accomplishments*. Great leaders lead through *empowerment.*
A good leader understands the importance of transferring authority—allowing others to succeed. Joseph also evaluated all the factors, selected his five most qualified brothers to speak to the Pharaoh, and prepared them to stand on their own merit (*Genesis 47:2*).

❏ *An effective leader accepts responsibility*—Joseph was given the charge to save all of Egypt from the famine. He did not hesitate to accept the job, plan the process, and arrange the financing. The success of the process was due to Joseph. Sometimes, however, an effective leader must accept the responsibility for actions that bring tragedy. When King David sinned with Bathsheba, he took full responsibility before God and man (*cp. I Chronicles 21:8*).

> Successful people are successful because they form the habits of doing those things that failures don't like to do.
>
> —Albert Gray

❏ *An effective leader is sensitive to diversity*—Despite the wisdom of Joseph's plan to save Egypt from the famine, Joseph knew that the Egyptian priests were self-supporting and would not be affected.

Joseph certainly did not worship their gods, but he did respect this religious diversity *(Genesis 47:22)*.

❑ *An effective leader strives to turn negatives into a positives*—Joseph knew that the Egyptians were not fond of shepherds. Sheep carried lice. In requesting the land of Goshen—the finest land in Egypt—the way Joseph had the brothers make the request, the Egyptians would have considered the motive to be separation of shepherds for the benefit of *Egypt*. The request would also show that the brothers were self-supporting, and could contribute to Egypt's welfare. In the end, the request that voiced such concern for the welfare of the Egyptians was a request that enabled the family to settle in Egypt's paradise! Joseph knew how to turn a negative into a positive *(Genesis 47:3-6)*.

❑ *An effective leader is honest*—All the money in Egypt was entrusted to Joseph, and Joseph's reputation was such that his loyalty and account-ability were never questioned. Though he was not Egyptian by birth and did not worship Egyptian gods, even in difficult times Joseph's moral character and integrity were never questioned by the people for whom he cared *(Genesis 47:13-15)*.

❑ *An effective leader is fair and just to those who serve*—Joseph cared for both rich and poor during the famine in Egypt. He cared for Egyptians and non-Egyptians. Joseph never demanded more from the Egyptians than they could give—even during the famine—and Joseph never blamed his brothers for their treatment of him. Joseph was just and equal in his care for *all* the people under his care and was no respecter of persons or rank *(Colossians 4:1; Ephesians 6:9)*.

❑ *An effective leader maintains composure under stress*—Joseph never lost his composure—either in his humiliation, or his exaltation. Joseph kept a steady head in every situation, from fleeing sin during temptation to running a nation during a famine. Someone has said: *"Composure is the noblest aspect of power."*

❑ *An effective leader is respected by those who serve him or her*—Joseph saved Egypt from the famine by virtually reducing the people to servi-tude and then taxing them. In this, the people loved him. Joseph was respected by his actions and his example. He was a model of skill as well as sincerity. The people knew Joseph had their concern at heart, and he never dipped in the people's approval ratings! *(Genesis 47:25-26)*

❏ *An effective leader knows the secret to success!*—Joseph understood—and all effective leaders understand—that success is achieved through one basic formula: $S = P \times D (A + Pr + Hw + P)$, with S being *success*, P being *passion*, D being *dedication*, A being *ability*, Pr being *preparation*, Hw being *hard work* and P being *persistence!* Only as a leader inspires a love and commitment to an endeavor, can preparation utilize the persistence and hard work of the skilled clientele who serve that leader. This is the essence of effective leadership, of which Joseph was a model *par excellence!*

Power Points:

➢ Do you think the people resented being 'bought' by Joseph for the Pharaoh during the famine? Why? Why not?

➢ Where do you think Joseph learned such leadership skills?

➢ Was Joseph wrong in not trying to convert the Egyptian priests?

➢ How had Joseph shown his good wisdom in previous actions while in Egypt, that might make the people respect his decisions during the famine?

Reflection section:

❏ Think of someone who made you work hard when you were younger. Do you respect them? Why?

❏ Have you informed someone how much you appreciate what he or she once did for you?

❏ Are you earning respect from someone right now in your daily living?

❏ Invest wise decisions today that might benefit you later!

❑   Are you trying to earn respect through satisfying the *wants*—as opposed to the *needs*—of those you influence?

❑   Even if you are not a leader, what are seven habits you can develop from this chapter?

My Personal Growth Journal—

❑   Make a list of Joseph's seven *finest* characteristics of leadership. Decide how you might be able to utilize these in your home and workplace.

~ Chapter 30 ~

'What If...?': "The Principle of Unfounded Worry"

After Joseph had buried his father, he returned to Egypt with his brothers and all who had gone with him for the funeral. After the death of their father, Joseph's brothers said, "What if Joseph still hates us and plans to pay us back for all the harm we did to him?" So they sent a message to Joseph: "Before our father died, he told us to ask you, 'Please forgive the crime your brothers committed when they wronged you.' Now please forgive us the wrong that we, the servants of your father's God, have done." Joseph cried when he received this message. (Gen. 50:14-17)

The Joseph story....

Many years had now passed since the end of the terrible famine. Joseph and his family had shared fellowship together and prospered in Goshen—the finest land in all Egypt. But Jacob grew weak in his advancing years, and after a long and full life, the old man died. In the minds of his sons who had so mistreated Joseph, Jacob had served as a buffer against their brother's revenge which they were certain would return against them for their past sins. It was an unfounded concern. Joseph's forgiveness of his brothers for their sin against him so many years before was not only complete, it was also beyond the ability of his brothers to comprehend. They could not imagine a forgiveness that would not seek revenge. So now, with their father Jacob dead, the brothers lived in constant fear that Joseph would repay them for their crimes—only having deferred to this point because of Jacob.

Principle Truth: The degree to which you worry is directly proportional to the measure with which you distrust the God holding your future.

"How are you doing?" the optimist asked the pessimist. "Oh, fine, I guess, under the circumstances," was the pessimist's reply. The optimist responded: "What in the world are you doing under there?" Too often, we worry about things that will never come to pass.

Our world has become so complex. We worry about our job. We worry about our income. We worry about our children. Worry is an accepted part of life. We even have medications to help us deal with our worry. Sometimes when things seem to be going too good for us, we worry about what must surely be just around the corner. We worry about not worrying! "*Worry is an old man, with a bearded head. He carries a load of feathers, and turns them into lead.*"

> The pessimist sees difficulty in every opportunity. The optimist sees opportunity in every difficulty.
>
> —Churchill
>
> ≈ৡ৯

My grandmother worried about a 'secret something' which she never revealed to me. She worried that whatever this secret something was, it might be the one thing God had not forgiven her for. Because she could not forgive herself, my grandmother could not accept the fact that she was forgiven. I recall many conversations with her about God's total forgiveness of sins. I also recall that no matter what I explained to her about God's forgiveness, she could not forget that secret something she had done in her past. I never knew what that secret something was that so worried my grandmother. But I do know she is in heaven, and her worry over God's forgiveness was unfounded.

> Worry does not empty tomorrow of its sorrow; it empties today of its strength.
>
> —Corrie Ten Boom
>
> ≈ৡ৯

So many times, we worry about things that never come to pass. We waste our time and effort in the fear of what may not even exist. Someone has said that fear is nothing more than a false expectation appearing real. Because we often fail to understand that God controls our future as well as our present. We forget the big picture in which He views our life. We concentrate upon the real or perceived difficulties of today and forget that, as the forgiven beloved of God, He will use even these difficulties for the good of our future.

Joseph had long ago forgiven his brothers for their crimes against him. Now—looking down upon them as their savior—Joseph never rehearsed the details of what they had done against him. But the brothers could not comprehend a forgiveness that would not return evil for evil. Because they could not grasp such grace, the brothers feared a punishment that would never come. They feared a retaliation that was never in the heart of this one who wanted only to bless them, and loved them more than they knew.

Joseph was hurt to think that his brothers so misunderstood the forgiveness he so willingly offered them. Does God weep over your underestimating His forgiveness? As you go through this day, do not worry away the precious time God has given you. Realize that worry not only affects you. Worry affects your future, others, and even your understanding of a forgiving God. Before you let worry take hold today, consider that, if the truth were to be known, you might be surprised just how unfounded most of your worry would be.

❑   *God, help me to realize that worry steals from my future*—Worry turns the *possible* problems of tomorrow into the *realistic* problem of today. God wants you to know that we should live for today and understand that tomorrow brings its own problems. Jesus instructed us that worry would not add one milepost to the future of your life. Worry will not transform your future, but it may shorten it. Today, live to the best of your ability and don't borrow problems from tomorrow. You do not know what tomorrow will bring. Don't allow worry to demand the interest on trouble that may never happen *(Matthew 6:26, 34; Luke 12:22-30)*.

❑   *God, help me to realize that worry solves nothing of importance*— Worry cannot create a reality, it can only reflect a fear. God wants you to spend today living constructively. Make this a day of productivity. Create something. Add something positive to the next twenty-four hours! *(Matthew 6:27)*

❑   *God, help me to realize that worry steals from my present*—Worry keeps you from seeking to glorify God and His kingdom. Worry does not empty tomorrow of its sorrow. It only robs today of its strength. Remember, yesterday is history, tomorrow is a mystery, but *today* is a gift. Concentrate on promoting the eternal things of God today rather than concerning yourself with worry over the temporary things of this world *(Matthew 6:33)*.

❏ *God, help me to realize that worry stunts my spiritual growth in Christ*—Your maturity in Christ is based upon your understanding of His growth plan for your life. As weeds can choke a good garden, so worry about the cares of this world can choke your spiritual progress. Today, bury worry in the trash-heap of nonproductivity. Consider it as a destructive weed and fertilize your walk in Christ with "faith fertilizer" instead *(Matthew 13:7,22; II Timothy 2:4)*.

❏ *God, help me to realize that worry insults your sovereignty*—Worry steals from your trust that God works all things together for good. Today, remember that God is timeless, and sees your future as already lived. Concentrate on God's sovereign control that even turned the death of His Son into your benefit. Like God, try to be neither surprised nor defeated by worry *(Romans 8:28)*.

❏ *God, help me to realize that prayer and trust are the remedies for worry*—Instead of worrying, try praying! Replace fearing the future with thanking God for the present. God wants you to know that through prayer, He will give you the peace to deal with today. Peace does not mean an absence of struggle. Peace means an absence of fear. Pray and trust God in all things, and do not let worry replace valuable time *(Psalms 37:1-5; Philippians 4:6-7)*. As you go through this day: *trust* in God's provision *(Romans 3:25)*, *delight* in God's will *(Psalms 40:8)*, *walk* in God's light *(I John 1:7)*, *live* in God's love *(I John 4:18)*, *rest* on God's care *(I Peter 5:7)*, and *act* in God's will *(Philippians 2:5)*.

Power Points:

➢ Why did the brothers still worry about Joseph's forgiveness?

➢ Do you think Jacob actually instructed the brothers to beg Joseph for the forgiveness which had already been given them?

➢ Why did Joseph weep at the request of his brothers?

➢ What reason did Pharaoh have to believe Joseph would return to Egypt as he had promised?

Reflection section:

- ❑ What worries you most right now? Is it possible your worry is unfounded? Is your worry grounded in fact? Are you doing all you can to address the object of your worry?

- ❑ Would you have returned to Egypt as Joseph did, or stayed in the homeland God promised your people?

- ❑ "The brothers were wrong in requesting Joseph's forgiveness." Do you agree or disagree with this statement? Why?

- ❑ Do you worry about your salvation, or doubt God is able to keep you saved?

- ❑ What's the difference between unfounded *worry* and genuine *concern*?

- ❑ Remember that most of the things we worry about will never come to pass. As Joseph's brothers should have done, remember the big picture that God has for your life and endure what difficulties He allows.

- ❑ Understand that even the worries that come to fruition must pass through *God's permission.*

My Personal Growth Journal—

- ❑ Make a list of ten things that worry you most. Sit down with a good friend and talk over these worries with them. See how many of these worries might be unfounded, or dealt with to improve your life.

- ❑ List three ways Joseph's forgiveness toward his brothers is similar to Christ's forgiveness toward you.

~ Chapter 31 ~

Forgiving Others: "The Principle of Unconditional Forgiveness"

"Tell Joseph, 'Forgive your brothers' sin—all that wrongdoing. They did treat you very badly.' Will you do it? Will you forgive the sins of the servants of your father's God?'" When Joseph received their message, he wept. (Gen. 50:17)

The Joseph story....

Old Jacob was dead. With the permission of the Pharaoh, Joseph and his brothers had returned to Canaan to bury their father. Had Jacob been the only buffer between the brothers and the vengeance Joseph might now plot against them for what they had once done to him? Did the same hatred stir in the heart of Joseph, which had brought his brothers to the verge of murder? Joseph's brothers understood the seriousness of their crime against Joseph. They had sold their own flesh and blood into foreign slavery. They had even convinced Jacob before his death that Joseph would return their evil against them. What they did not understand was the grace of his forgiveness—a forgiveness that not only pardoned them of their sins—but in truth saved their lives and would bless them till the day they died.

Principle Truth: Forgiveness opens for others, doors through which you too must someday pass.

The ancient Greeks loved to tell the story of Menthe. Menthe loved Hades, lord of the underworld. But Hades could not return this affection. Hades loved Persephone, daughter of Demeter, goddess of grain. Eventually, Persephone began to resent the affection Menthe showed Hades and vowed to destroy her. Persephone trampled Menthe under her feet. In dying, Menthe forgave Persephone and released before her a most beautiful fragrance. Appreciating such forgiveness, Hades transformed Menthe into an herb—mint, which releases its enticing aroma in presence of those who crush it.

Such is the nature of forgiveness. Forgiveness is that sweet fragrance like none other, reserved only for those who have hurt us.

> Forgiveness is the fragrance the violet sheds upon the foot that crushes it.
>
> —Mark Twain

Sometimes, though, our forgiveness is not complete. Though we forgive the wrongs done to us, we find it hard to forgive the person who committed those wrongs. We say we will forgive but we will not forget, and payback too often crouches within our thoughts, awaiting only an opportunity to spring. However, complete forgiveness forgives _completely_. Complete forgiveness forgives the action _and_ the offender and never seeks revenge. Unforgiveness is a heavy weight that burdens a life unnecessarily.

Joseph understood complete and total forgiveness. Joseph wept because his unconditional forgiveness was accepted, but not understood. Such a sweet fragrance as unconditional forgiveness was beyond Joseph's brothers' ability to appreciate. Perhaps it was because they had never forgiven in such a manner. They could not comprehend that Joseph had not only forgiven their _sin_—he had also unconditionally forgiven _them_. To the dismay of the brothers, such forgiveness could never entertain the thought of retaliation in revenge. _"Love does not keep a record of wrongs; love is not happy with evil, but is happy with the truth (I Corinthians 13:5-6 GNT)._

Because of such forgiveness, the brothers lived a life of gratitude to Joseph. He became their provider and sustainer until the day they died. Through an even greater forgiveness, which God has shown us, could we possibly owe Him less?

Like Joseph's brothers, it may be difficult for us to comprehend the forgiveness of God through Christ. He has not just forgiven our sins; He has forgiven us—unconditionally. God is not vengeful towards us for what we were or what we did before He saved us. Neither does God watch our future, ready to revoke

His forgiveness whenever we sin. After all, how many of your sins were future when He died for you?

God's forgiveness is total and unconditional. He will never again bring up your sins. Is there someone you need to forgive unconditionally today? Is partial forgiveness keeping you from growing in grace toward others?

> Forgiveness is an odd thing. It warms the heart and cools the sting.
>
> —Ward
>
> ☙❧

You may never know what a sweet fragrance your forgiveness may shed on someone who has wronged you. Today, forgive as Joseph forgave his brothers. Forgive as Menthe forgave Persephone. Forgive as God has forgiven you.

❑ *Today, I will forgive because I have been forgiven*—As God has forgiven you, so you are required to forgive others. Do not seek revenge. God will take care of unsettled accounts with those who have hurt you *(Luke 18:7)*. Forgive to the degree to which you have been forgiven—totally! *(Ephesians 4:32; Isaiah 43:25; Colossians 1:14; Cp. Mark 14:24)*

❑ *Today, I will forgive without a limit*—Joseph did not forgive partially. Joseph forgave completely. Joseph's brothers could not comprehend this godly forgiveness. When you forgive someone today, erase that which you hold against him or her completely, as God has forgiven you *(Matthew 18:21-22; Luke 17:3-4; Jeremiah 31:34)*.

❑ *Today, I will forgive to demonstrate my strength, not weakness*—Forgiveness evidences strength of character. Adonijah had plotted against Solomon. Solomon became King of Israel, and, though he had every right to kill Adonijah, in his strength—not weakness—Solomon forgave him *(I Kings 1:52-53)*. Shimei had cursed David when the king left Jerusalem during a time of personal turmoil. When David returned, he had every right to kill Shimei, yet in strength—not weakness—David forgave him *(II Samuel 19:18-23)*. Joseph forgave his brothers in his strength, not his weakness. Today, realize that forgiveness is not the obligation of weakness but the grace of power!

> Nothing in this lost and ruined world bears the meek impress of the Son of God so surely as forgiveness.
>
> —Alice Cary
>
> ☙❧

❑   *Today, I will forgive to disarm the one forgiven*—The quickest way to disarm someone who has hurt you is to let him or her know you forgive them. Today, practice peaceful living with those who have hurt you. Go to them and forgive. Don't wait for someday. Someday never comes *(II Corinthians 2:7-10)*.

❑   *Today, I will forgive completely and move on*—Joseph's forgiveness was unlimited and complete. Afterward, he moved on to the concerns of fellowship and care for his family. Joseph never brought the subject up again and never reminded his brothers how much such forgiveness obligated them. When you forgive, move on to the *benefits* of the forgiveness—don't simply dwell on the nobility of the act. The Prodigal Son demanded his inheritance and squandered it on wine, women, and song. Eventually, he came to himself and returned to his father. The father welcomed his wayward son with open arms and a great feast. Though the boy had embarrassed both himself and his family, the father never brought this up upon the boy's return home. The father forgave completely *(Luke 15:17-24)*. Is there someone today that you have forgiven—but only partially? How secure would you feel if God had forgiven you to the degree which you have forgiven this one?

❑   *Today, I will forgive and bring healing*—Joseph's forgiveness brought healing to a family. To his brothers, yes—but Joseph's attitude of forgiveness also purged Joseph's soul of any improper thoughts he may have harbored against his brothers for their sin against him. Forgiveness is a cleansing process. It brings healing not only to the one forgiven, but also to the one forgiving *(Psalms 32:1; 51:12)*. Is there someone today who can be restored to spiritual health through the healing process of your forgiveness? *(II Corinthians 2:5-7)* Today, benefit yourself through forgiveness of those who have hurt you *(James 5:15-16)*.

Power Points:

➤   Was there anything that you feel Jacob needed to forgive before he died?

➤   Do you think Joseph also forgave Potiphar and Potiphar's wife?

Reflection section:

- ❑ Is there someone who has hurt you that you cannot fully forgive?

- ❑ The thing which keeps me from forgiving them is_____

- ❑ The first thing I can do to forgive them completely is _____

- ❑ "Grace is not just." Do you agree or disagree with this statement? Why?

- ❑ Do you believe that God has forgiven all your sins, or only past sins?

- ❑ "I will forgive, but I won't forget." What do you think of this statement?

- ❑ Whenever I forgive, I feel _____

- ❑ Is there someone whom you have forgiven, but not *unconditionally*? Forgive as though the offence against you had never even occurred. This is *godly* forgiveness.

- ❑ The thing I cannot forgive *myself* for is _____

- ❑ The first thing I can do to forgive myself is _____

My Personal Growth Journal—

- ❑ Is there someone you have not *fully* forgiven for something done to you? Go to them and show an act of kindness.

~ Chapter 32 ~

Life in the Rearview Mirror: "The Principle of God's Overruling Sovereignty"

Joseph replied, "Don't be afraid. Do I act for God? Don't you see, you planned evil against me but God used those same plans for my good, as you see all around you right now—life for many people." (Gen. 50:19-20)

And we know that God causes everything to work together for the good of those who love God and are called according to his purpose for them. (Romans 8:28 NLT)

The Joseph story....

*T*he brothers who had mistreated Joseph so many years ago appeared bowing and trembling before their lord and savior. They pleaded for a forgiveness that had already been theirs, and for mercy they had never required. With the tenderness of only one who could now finally understand the overruling design of God's ultimate plan, Joseph comforted them. What they had meant for evil, God had meant for good. One more time Joseph promised to care for his brothers and their families. The brothers accepted Joseph's reassurance with an uneasy confidence. At the end of his days, Joseph would die and be mummified in his adopted home of Egypt. In another four hundred years, his body would be returned to the land of his forefathers, Abraham, Isaac, and Jacob. Carried out of Egypt at the Exodus under Moses, Joseph would rest once more in the land of Canaan.

Principle Truth: When all accounts are settled, you will look back and see that God was the Master Craftsman of your life, able to weave every triumph and tragedy into your ultimate good.

The Rest of the Story. Paul Harvey has spent many years in holding our attention with his skillful storytelling, which tells us something we might not have known about someone. In retrospect, we see this person in a different light now knowing the previously unrevealed information.

Someday, the life that lies before us will become the rest of the story. When the whole of our life is reflected back upon from a heavenly perspective, we will appreciate the overruling sovereignty of God and understand that He even worked the evils against us for our own good.

In June, 1815, the Duke of Wellington challenged the army of the great Napoleon. In the ensuing battle, 40,000 men would die in a seven-hour struggle. As the news of the battle's outcome was relayed back to Britain, it appeared that all was lost, and Napoleon was truly invincible. Slowly came the news: "*Wellington...defeated.*" But the tragic news was not the final news. At last came the rest of the story: "*Wellington...defeated...Napoleon.*" The very things that today seem to be so disappointing will someday appear much differently. Someday—when we understand the rest of the story.

God is sovereign. He is proactive. God never has to react. God works all things according to the council of His own will. He is neither surprised nor defeated by our actions. God is complete in Himself, and everything about God and His actions is good, right, and just. This is sovereignty! This is the soft pillow for our tired heads when our world seems out of control.

> *What the caterpillar calls the end of the world, the Master calls a butterfly.*
>
> *—Richard Bach*

In 1776, fifty-six men listened to Ben Franklin say that God was the sovereign Creator of the universe and a nation could not rise or fall without Him. The men proceeded to pray, and the Constitution of the United States was formed.

The truth that God's sovereignty overrules even the evils of this world in no way negates our personal responsibility, however. Man has a free will. He is responsible for his actions. How God's total sovereignty and our free will work together *in* God's divine design, we do not know. Yet, both are true. God's sovereignty and our free will are like two railroad tracks existing side by side—never touching, but both necessary for the train of our life to function

Like those tracks, the separate rails of God's sovereignty and our free will only merge into singularity in the distance of a future ahead of us. We cannot understand such sovereignty. God is absolutely sovereign in everything and anything He does. He is neither surprised nor defeated. He does not need our help in running this universe.

> *Faith is believing in advance, that which can only be explained in reverse.*
>
> *—Yancy*
>
> ෴

The evil worked against us, and even the mistakes we make, will work together for good. God does not expect us to either understand or deny this truth. While human truths must be understood to be loved—heavenly truths must be loved to be understood. God expects us to accept this truth, however, and not deny it merely because it is beyond our understanding.

Joseph's brothers, as well as their father, suffered because of the sin against Joseph. Yet, God mysteriously overruled the sin for ultimate good. In the same way, God overruled even the wickedness of His Son's crucifixion to the ultimate good that many might come to salvation. Such sovereignty, however, did not negate the human responsibility involved.

Joseph's brothers clearly did not understand this synergy of circumstances, or how God could work their evil against Joseph toward the salvation of many. In the end however, they did come to realize that this is precisely what happened.

God is sovereign in all His actions, and over every creation of His hand:

❑ *God controls the rulers of this world (Psalms 75:6-7).*
❑ *God controls the kingdoms of this world (Daniel 2:21; 4:17).*
❑ *God controls the politics and economy of this world (I Chronicles 29:11-12).*
❑ *God controls circumstances He sometimes chooses not to explain (Deuteronomy 29:29).*
❑ *God controls things we cannot understand in our limited knowledge (Isaiah 40:28).*
❑ *God controls the ultimate destiny of all things (Psalms 115:3).*
❑ *God controls all things in perfect righteousness (Psalms 119:75).*
❑ *God controls even the smallest things about you (Matthew 10:29-30).*

Since God is sovereign, He can work all things together for good *(Romans 8:28)*. How He is able to do this, we are not told. Someone has said that life is best seen in a rearview mirror, but God requires us to keep our eyes on the road. Life is best seen backward; yet, life runs forward. While following the path in life God has put before you, see your path as *God* sees it—finished.

Move ahead and know that when you look back upon your life someday, you will see that God acted for your ultimate *good*. Do not let the bumps along the way concern you. God never promised you smooth sailing—He did promise He would get you safely home. As you contemplate seeing your life in the rearview mirror:

o *Praise Him*—for His sovereign *divine design* in your life. If it weren't the best possible plan for your life, God would not be all-powerful. Remember, if you are His child, nothing in your life is accidental, or out of God's control. Praise Him, that your life is a part of His plan, and that He can even work the hardships *for your good*.

o *Thank Him*—for though you may not fully understand His plan now, someday you will see that God knew what He was doing. God's mysterious ways are not always explained to us, but they are always *right*. If God did *not* work things in a righteous manner, God would not be holy. Remember, thank God for who He *is*, not just what He *does*. God is *holy*.

o *Trust Him*—that everything that happens is *for your good*—even the troubles! Troubles are God's refining tool—not your enemy. Glorify God and trust Him—even when you are discouraged. Remember, God is shaping you through the sometimes-painful tool of the troubles He allows. Trust His wisdom.

o *Wait on Him*—for God is not on your schedule! God has already seen tomorrow. He knows how to perfectly time the events of your life within His plan. Remember, God is working on the other end of your circumstances too. Be patient. God does not measure time as you do, and He is never too early or too late.

o *Grow in Him*—that you might be conformed to the image of Christ! Study His Word. Grow in His grace. Fellowship with others, and support others as God supports you. Remember, you will have to answer for your time someday. Redeem it wisely.

o *Pray through Him*—that you may have a *part* in His sovereignty and become a means to His end! God can just as easily work around you as through you, but how much better to be a part of—rather than an obstacle to—His plan! Pray so that you can give Him glory when He answers, and be an instrument of His will! Remember, He is sovereign in *all* His actions; sometimes He chooses to perform His sovereignty *through* our prayers. Pray because He instructed you.

o *Rest in Him*—for *all things* are working towards an ultimate purpose. Today, we see the tangled threads on the underside of the weaving. Someday—from the heavenly perspective—it will all make sense. Every thread of the events which made up our lives—events both pleasant and unpleasant—will be seen stitched into the final design which makes up your life. In the end, you will understand that He sewed everything together perfectly. Remember that now, and trust Him. He is working only for your good—in *all things*.

Joseph became a role model of success. He achieved greatness in a foreign land, and earned the respect of people whose gods he never worshipped, and whose king he never viewed as divine. From Joseph's life, we have learned that *true* success can be measured through these godly principles illustrated from Joseph's life.

Success

❖ Trust and honor the God who created you.

❖ Love your neighbor as you want God to love you.

❖ Be responsible in all your endeavors.

❖ Display character and moral integrity without apology.

❖ Forgive completely even those most unforgivable.

❖ Work diligently and use your time and talents wisely.

❖ Be intolerant of evil without compromise.

❖ Have courage enough to take a risk.

❖ Be proactive and plan ahead.

❖ Learn to accept criticism and turn it into strength.

Final Considerations

❑ Realize that your life is a great and complex puzzle which today, only God sees as a finished work. When some of the pieces seem lost or out of place, remember that someday you will look back and see the rest of the story, and how it all worked together for good.

❑ Thank God that He can work even evil for your good.

❑ Live as though everything you did was the ultimate standard by which your life was measured. Trust God as if you could do nothing.

❑ Treat every difficulty as a shadow within the beautiful painting which you will look back on as your life someday. Never forget that shadows are only backgrounds for those things important in the scene, and never forget that shadows, too, are working for God's glory in your life.

Mizraim: Land of My Testing

A Psalm of Praise to his God by Zaphenath-Paneah (Joseph the Vizier) in a distant land

O God—my protection and fortress in a distant land:
Great are thy mercies! I am humbled at the turning of thy mighty hand!
Thou art perfect in all thy ways! O Lord, thou alone knowest goodness
and holiness, and the path thou hast set for thy servant's feet! Be
praised, O Lord my God, for the delight that thou hast taken in forming
me into the vessel of thine own use. For, though thou hast made me a
stranger in mine own house, thou hast exalted me in the house of
strangers. Thou alone, O Lord, hast broken me in pieces at the hands of
mine own familiar friends, and raised me upon high in a far kingdom!
Great is thy name, O Lord, in the land of Mizraim!

Thou art exalted in the words of my mouth, O Lord:
In the words of my lips have I praised thee before a people that knewest
thee not! Be praised for thy forgiveness, O my God! For thou hast
turned mine heart in mercy to those who hated me. Thou hast spared me
from the snare of the temptress. Thou hast delivered me from the pit, and
my feet from the fetters of the prison. Thou hast taught me wisdom in the
land of secrets. Thou hast divided me a portion of thy boundless mercy,
that I might be merciful! In my mercy, I have delivered the souls of mine
accusers for thy name's sake.
In thy mercy thou hast saved me from all mine enemies in the land of Mizraim!

Let all the earth sing praises to thee, O God!
Thou hast given us bread when there was no bread, and the storehouses
of thy kindnesses do overflow! Thy cup of righteousness thou hast hidden in our secret places, O Lord, that we may sing praises unto thee
alone! Thou hast prepared for us Goshen in a dry land, O God, and the
rivers of thy mercies have flowed down to us from high places! Thou hast
weighed mine heart in a distant land, O Lord, and thou hast opened my
mouth in righteousness. Thou hast touched the scale of Truth, O God,
and my heart is lifted up! Be exalted, O Lord, for giving us life, and delivering us from the devourer! Great are thy mercies, O my God—Lord of all

227

the earth! Thou hast seen the end of my days from the beginning, and made them good in my sight.
Thou hast exalted thy servant in the land of Mizraim!

Into thy presence, O God, I shall enter with praise for all thou hast done! Thou hast lifted me above mine enemies. Thou hast made them who knew not thy servant, to fear him in thy wisdom. Thou hast made those who would crush me to bow at my feet. Thou hast caused those who have forgotten me to remember thy servant and lift me up before the lords of the earth! Thou hast turned my testing into glory, my sorrow into greatness. Thou hast woven the threads of my dread into my garment of many colors, and my dreams thou hast called forth in thy time.
Thou hast raised my name in Mizraim!

O God, let the pillars of stone in this distant land crumble to dust before I forget the multitude of thy mercies! Praise to thee, O God, above all the gods of Mizraim, above all the glories of Egypt! Thou hast made my name to resound in all the earth and prepared before me my table in the presence of those who hated me! Lord, grant that I might be buried in the land of my fathers, and that thy holy name be remembered forever in Mizraim, land of my testing.
Amen.

About the author

Dr. Parks earned his B.S., M.A., and Ed.S degrees in education from Eastern Kentucky University, and Th.D in Biblical Theology from Trinity Theological Seminary in Newburgh, IN.

Jerry is a Nationally Board Certified Teacher, and currently Department Chairman, and teacher of ancient civilizations to seventh graders at Georgetown Middle School in Georgetown, KY. He has traveled in Middle Eastern cultures, and has earned numerous *"Teacher of the Year"* honors at the local, state, and national level. He was recently named to the *USA Today 2003 Outstanding Teachers in America* team.

For many years, he has been a speaker at *National Middle School Association* conferences, as well as the conference for *National Council for the Social Studies*. He currently mentors *NBPTS* teacher candidates, and teaches the *GodStudy* Adult Bible Fellowship class at Southland Christian Church, Lexington, KY.

0-595-29651-3

Printed in the United States
31658LVS00003B/128

9 780595 296514